ISLINGTON

Please return this item on or before the last date stamped b
be liable to overdue charges. To renew an item call the num
access the online catalogue at www.islington.gov.uk/librarie
your library membership number and PIN number.

D0512503

Islington Libraries

020 7527 6900   **www.islington.gov.uk/libraries**

Published by
Whittles Publishing Ltd.,
Dunbeath,
Caithness, KW6 6EG,
Scotland, UK
www.whittlespublishing.com

© 2017 Huw Kingston

ISBN 978-184995-274-3

With thanks to Tony Cole, Marco Costa, Jose Ramon
Diaz, Vili Gosnak, Georg Kaltis, Dimitris Kokkoris, Rick
Marchant, Marin Medak, Sacha Myers, Jordi Roch and
Dan Stoneham for kindly providing photos.

Printed by

Gomer Press Ltd.

MEDITERRANEAN

A year around a charmed and troubled sea

Huw Kingston

Whittles Publishing

FOR WENDY FOR EVERYTHING

They are ill discoverers that think there is no land when they can see nothing but sea.

Francis Bacon

IN MEMORY OF JENNY CALDWELL

www.HUWKINGSTON.com

Contents

The moon has risen. Firstly it gently illuminates the surface of the waters, then mounts higher and writes upon the supple water. At last, at its zenith it lights up a whole corridor of sea, a rich river of milk.

Albert Camus, *The Sea Close By*

THE THANKS

After a journey of such length and one that so often depended on the kindness of friends and strangers, my publisher has not been able to give me the luxury of endless pages to list my thanks. Reading this book, you would understand how many pages would be required. But many of those who played roles – extensive, tiny, but all important – are already mentioned in the pages of this book. In summary, my huge thanks again to every one of you.

My journey around the Mediterranean would not have been possible without the backing of some great sponsors. In particular I would like to acknowledge Paddy Pallin, World Expeditions, Osprey Packs, the Australian Geographic Society, ELES, Reno Design, Princeton Tec, Nikon, Certton, Lake Crackenback Resort and Spa, Tiderace Kayaks, MAProgress and Tabacco Maps.

Thanks to Keith and all the staff at Whittles Publishing for believing I could get down in words the feel and experiences of at least some of my wonderful journey. Thanks also to my editor, Caroline Petherick, whose exclamation of 'handsome', a Cornish compliment, on first reading my manuscript gave encouragement and whose tidying up added much to my words.

Save the Children was a wonderful organisation to partner with, and in Fiona McAdam I could not have asked for a finer and friendlier contact. My massive thanks to each and every person who contributed to the fundraising for the children affected by the desperate conflict in Syria. Whether you put in a handful of pounds, dollars or euros, or thousands of them, you can be certain that great work was done.

There are of course many people who were involved in my journey from long before the start to well after the finish. Massive hugs go to Marco Costa and Elena Massarenti in Italy, who got me to that start line and provided so much more support by ensuring my equipment found itself at the right place at the right time. To Erica Galea who worked tirelessly to promote my journey to media in Australia and along my route, and who pushed and prodded me into the world of social media.

To my parents, Jackie and Bernard. Whilst you may not have directly given me the taste for travel and adventure you have given me your love and endless support for over half a century.

Thanks to Kate, Ant, Anna and Anders – stepdaughter, husband and two of my grandkids. Your messages, hidden cards, surprise calls all meant so much so often.

My journey was possible and my life is possible only because of one person. Only you, Wendy, can know what you mean to me.

LIST OF MAPS

AUTHOR BIOGRAPHY

Originally from the UK, where he was born in 1963, Huw is now based in Australia where he lives with his wife Wendy in the small New South Wales town of Bundanoon. He has two stepdaughters and five grandchildren.

With a passion for the great outdoors Huw has spent over 30 years journeying by human powered means in wild places across the world. Before his Mediterranean journey he travelled 25,000km around Australia by kayak, foot, ski and bike and had a longstanding love affair with ski touring in the Indian Himalaya.

As someone blessed to have seen some beautiful parts of this fragile little planet Huw also recognises the huge threats to it. His work in the environmental area, particularly the campaign against bottled water and plastic waste, saw him named by Time Magazine as one of their *25 Worldwide Responsibility Pioneers* and he was a recipient of *the Peter Rawlinson Award* from the Australian Conservation Foundation and the *Sharing Citizen Prize* from the Council of Europe.

The Australian Geographic Society presented Huw with their *Spirit of Adventure Award*, he is a *Fellow of the Royal Geographical Society* and an Ambassador for Save the Children Australia.

Huw is a regular contributor to a range of publications on adventure and travel topics.

For the past 25 years Huw has run Wild Horizons which includes the organisation of some of Australia's best known and most popular MTB events as well as running a range of tours in Australia and overseas.

THE BACK STORY

I quietly sobbed into the pillow in a hotel room at Çanakkale. Twenty-four hours earlier, along with thousands of others, I'd watched the sun set over the Mediterranean in readiness for the dawn service at Anzac Cove on Turkey's Gallipoli peninsula. I looked out across a sea that was to be the focus of my life for the coming year.

I tried not to let Elena see my tears as her thumbs worked deep into my back. I was in substantial pain and had been for a few months now. But the following morning, after years of planning, thinking, dreaming, I was due to kayak away from Gallipoli on a voyage that I hoped would bring me back there 12 months later. A 15,000 km circumnavigation of the Mediterranean by human power. A journey through some 20 countries in Europe, north Africa and the Middle East.

I knew this feeling well enough. A back injury as a teenager 35 years earlier, the result of falling through a skylight 10 metres to a pedestrian subway below, would toy with me before expeditions and journeys. Almost without exception, a month or so before departure my back would 'go' and I'd be incapacitated for a week, a fortnight or more. Then my head would be all over the place wondering, as The Clash had sung, 'Should I stay or should I go?' Most people would, I'm sure, stay – but I'd learned to challenge my back, hobble my way to the start line and begin. It had all started in 1991. I was to lead a ski traverse in the Indian Himalaya. But weeks before departure my back collapsed. For two years I had been planning that particular journey and I had made my way with Carol, Megan and Jamie on a painful journey from Sydney to India and thence up to Kashmir. Once there I lay horizontal on a houseboat on Dal Lake for two weeks watching life on the lake slip past and my expedition with it. The others waited, went on acclimatisation ski trips, waited. In the end I decided I'd get to the start line, begin the journey with them then, after the first day, turn back. My reasoning was that once they'd started they would likely continue without me.

Bent double under heavy packs we set off from Lehinwan and soon found ourselves in very heavy snowfall in a dangerously avalanche-prone valley. With dry throats we scuttled down the valley, as much as you can scuttle on skis, avoiding avalanches by luck as much as judgement. We camped that night behind a rock offering some protection but kept our avalanche beacons on as we slept. I was not going back through that valley alone. Thirty-five days and 600 km later we appeared in the Kullu Valley and a first shower at the end of an unbelievable winter's journey. My back had troubled me no further; there had been too much else to focus on.

A few days later we were back in Sydney – and for the next month I was flat on my back.

My Melbourne2Sydney journey in 1997 (the first of seven City2City journeys around Australia) was the same, as was Perth2Darwin in 2003. Melbourne2Hobart, the final journey in 2004, starting with kayaking across Bass Strait, followed the pattern. As did a ski expedition to India in 2008. Is it psychosomatic? Is it now just a part of my expeditions that I have to deal with? Is it stress related?

On 17 January 2014, two months before I left Australia for Europe and three months before Anzac Day, I smashed my back whilst kayaking through a wave on a glorious day on the NSW South Coast. Here we go, I thought.

It was probably around 2006 when the idea of a Mediterranean circumnavigation had first hit me; when the tell-tale manila folder was opened with a few sheets of scrawled notes. I'm still not sure why. Perhaps after circumnavigating Australia, a continent of one country, I thought a sea of 20 should be next. Originally I had contemplated sea kayaking the whole way, a journey that might take 15 months or more. But each time I thought about it I couldn't get excited about sitting on my rear for that long. So I then considered climbing the highest mountain in each country en route as a means of stretching the legs. With this the journey was stretching out to more than two years and my wife Wendy was none too keen. Again and again the manila folder was opened then closed again to gather dust.

In the spring of 2012 I became aware of the forthcoming Anzac Centenary; it would soon be 100 years since that military disaster, the Anzac landings, had commenced. At dawn on 25 April 1915 thousands of troops from Australia, New Zealand, Britain and France landed on the Gallipoli peninsula in Turkey in an attempt to take control of the Dardanelles, a key strategic shipping route. For Australian and New Zealand troops, the Anzacs, it was the first time they had gone to war as independent countries. The Turks, led by a young colonel, Kemal Atatürk, who would go on to become the first president of modern-day Turkey, were waiting.

In the six months that followed some 130,000 men died, including nearly 10,000 Australians and Kiwis. But the Turks, despite losing over 80,000 men, held firm. In Australia, Anzac Day is commemorated, on 25 April, the biggest commemoration day of the year. The 2015 centenary was going to be a huge event with special services and events across Australia, and over 10,000 people attending the dawn service at Gallipoli on 25 April.

The Anzac Centenary gave my plans the fillip they needed, gave my journey a very Australian connection: an opportunity to honour the memory of those young men from so many nations who had lost their lives on the beaches, cliffs and plateaux of Gallipoli.

Miss Grape feels the water for the first time at Gallipoli

On a grey day, 26 November 2012, I was riding from Jervis Bay on the south coast of New South Wales up to my home in the Southern Highlands, when it came together. I didn't have to kayak all the way around; I could also walk, ride, perhaps tour by ski to mix it up. Could I start at Gallipoli on 26 April 2014 and finish my journey in time for the Anzac Centenary? One year in the Mediterranean.

I was excited by the whole idea and pedalled harder in the rain to get home to the manila folder. Spreadsheets were opened, maps too. Emails sent, questions asked. Over the following months an outline route emerged that might allow me to complete the journey in the 12 months.

In June 2013 I celebrated my 50th birthday by circumnavigating the 600 km coastline of the Mediterranean island of Corsica by sea kayak, stopping for my birthday week to enjoy the company of my wife and friends in a rented villa. The spectacular and rugged coastline of Corsica gave an opportunity to sniff the Mediterranean air and experience some of her moods.

What to call this journey? I planned to call it 'An Anzac Odyssey'. It paid homage to the Anzac diggers, and to my start and finish point. The journey itself was an odyssey and followed the instigator of that word, Homer's Odysseus, and his mythical perambulations in the Mediterranean. However, the use of the word Anzac is protected by Act of Parliament in Australia and, aside from baking Anzac biscuits, application must be made to use it. My application for Anzac Odyssey was rejected by the Department of Veteran Affairs. With the centenary approaching they were being swamped with applications and understandably were being very cautious as to who or what could use the name.

I didn't have much time; there was a website to construct, sponsor proposals to send out. I lighted upon *mediterr année*. Taking the French word for the Mediterranean, splitting it in two to isolate *année*, the French word for year: m*editerr année* – one year in the Mediterranean. Like my middle name, Mostyn, I liked it and hated it. Try spelling www.mediterrannee.com.au in a radio interview.

Back home in Australia, planning continued. I wanted to sea kayak the first three months out of Turkey, through Greece and the Balkans. I wanted to traverse on foot the full arc of the European Alps, one of the most magnificent mountain ranges on earth – a three-month journey in itself. As luck would have it, it became apparent that travelling anticlockwise from Turkey in late April was actually the perfect place and time to start. Indeed even without the Gallipoli connection, the seasons and winds would have suggested a start somewhere in Turkey, somewhere around April. My first three months in the sea kayak following the coasts of Greece, Albania, Montenegro and Croatia would be running into the warmth of summer. My desire to trek 2,000 km along the length of the European Alps could only be accomplished before the winter snows arrived around November. Finally my run back east along north Africa and through the Middle East would be in the cool of winter, not the unbearable heat of a Saharan summer. But there was other heat in north Africa that would impact upon my journey.

When I began the planning I sensed political situations were falling in my favour. The Arab Spring, that had begun in Tunisia in 2011, gave hope that a certain democracy could spread over the region and that my wish to travel freely across Libya might even be realised. But of course within months this hope was in tatters. In August 2013, eight months before my departure, there were riots in Tunisia, a coup in Egypt, chemical weapons attacks by Assad against his own people in Syria – and Libya was descending into civil war after the overthrow of Gaddafi. I'd signed up to the Australian Government Smart Traveller alerts for the countries I planned to pass through and all manner of travel warnings popped into my inbox – Syria, Turkey, Egypt, Algeria, Lebanon, Israel, Libya. Jeez, even the UK and Spain were having a go at each other again over Gibraltar. Over a third of the 20 countries I wanted to traverse had warnings of some severity.

All this conflict had reaffirmed my desire to do something for those who were the collateral damage of war; the innocent victims. And, more specifically, for children, the most innocent victims of all. My journey around the Mediterranean, which had germinated from a commemoration of war, offered more than just an opportunity for a bloody good adventure. I sought out charities that worked with children in conflict zones and lit upon two: War Child and Save the Children. War Child, unknown to me until then, was a charity primarily based in UK that worked solely with children affected by war and conflict. I was impressed by their work and the people I spoke with. Save the Children I knew as a large international charity working across all aspects of child welfare. I engaged with Save the Children Australia and more specifically with the lovely Fiona McAdam, their fundraising manager. In the end it was almost impossible to decide, but I went with Save the Children due to their large presence in Australia, where most of the fundraising and profile raising would take place. We agreed that my fundraising would go towards children affected by the Syrian crisis. We had no inkling then of the scale and quite how desperate that crisis was to become.

All these aspects of my preparation were nothing compared to leaving Wendy behind. My beautiful wife had supported me over many long journeys of three to four months – but this, a whole year, would be so much harder. Paradoxically, and perhaps in a selfish way, the love we have gives me the strength to complete such journeys. I often ponder how much more difficult it might be for me not having someone at home, not having a person I love to go home to. I was leaving behind five gorgeous grandkids too, all under 10: Anna, Anders, Toby, Will and Jack. I love doing stuff with them; going cycling, walking, camping, drinking milkshakes or just threatening with sloppy kisses. It would be hard to not see them for over a year. The realisation that this journey was my choice, my dream, not something forced upon families split by closed borders, conflicts or refugee tragedies, made it a little easier. A little.

In October 2013, six months before I left Australia, we began massive renovations to our house. As half the place was demolished and the roof torn off, we moved into an ever smaller number of rooms. Dealing with builders, preparing for a year away from my business, and planning the journey made for interesting times. The dust hardly had time to settle.

On the evening of 9 January I went for a quick mountain bike ride. I felt fine, and after an hour or so came upon a friend of mine doing some work on the trail. I felt strangely out of breath as I stopped to talk. I said cheerio and rode on, soon to a short but steep climb up a farm track. I felt buggered, my heart racing, my breath short and sharp. I got off halfway up the hill, stopped for a few minutes then pushed the bike the rest of the way. I thought to head home from there but told myself not to be so stupid; it was nothing, could be nothing. I rode on but at the next hill it was the same. I rang home, told Wendy and took the quickest route back. Once home I wondered what to do. On the one hand all those things you read 'If you have the following signs … call 000' versus 'Don't be stupid, it's nothing.' We had dinner and afterwards Wendy drove me the 25 km to hospital. It was the first time I'd been in A&E since my subway fall in 1979. All the tests were done, ECGs and the like. Nothing showed up. I went home after midnight. A false alarm I was very happy with.

Then, a week later, on 17 January in that south coast surf, my back went. At least the time I might have spent getting fit was no longer needed, due to my buggered back. I was moving around gingerly, all the time thinking, as I'd thought often before 'What the bloody hell was I doing with this massive, physically demanding journey just weeks away?' contrasted with the 'You'll be right. Remember; just get to the start line.' At least the enforced rest gave me more time to read about my planned route. Lots of things were happening; sponsors coming on board, equipment to be sorted and trying to understand the wild world of social media. Paddy Pallin, Australia's leading chain of outdoor adventure stores, came on board as major sponsor with instructions to me to go into the Sydney flagship store and select whatever I needed. Talk about being a kid in a candy store. The fundraising for Save the Children was gaining momentum.

Legend

- Kayak
- Bike
- Row
- Walk
- Ferry required to cross closed border
- Transport section due to weather delay

Split

BOSNIA & HERZEGOVINA

MONTENEGRO

BLACK SEA

Durrës

ALBANIA

GREECE

AEGEAN SEA

Gallipoli — Start/Finish

TURKEY

Athens

IONIAN SEA

Finikounda

Marmaris

MEDITERRANEAN SEA

SYRIA

CYPRUS

LEBANON

ISRAEL

EGYPT

As part of it, I was 'selling' each of the 20 countries I planned to traverse for between AU$1,000 and AU$10,000, and in one week seven countries were taken over by new owners. Various media stories put my journey out there. And all the while my head was being messed with by my back. How could I be doing all this when my movement is so restricted? Get to the start line …

At Sydney airport on 16 March, I checked in nearly 100kg of luggage – bike, skis and all manner of outdoor paraphernalia – pushing and shoving to rebuff an attempted AU$3,200 in excess baggage charges. There were too many tears as Wendy, my stepdaughter Kate, Ant, her husband and their kids, two of my grandkids, had a farewell drink. It was too much for me when the kids handed me a little filigree silver bead to wear on my wrist. 'It shows the leaves of the forest, Papa,' said Anna, my eight-year-old granddaughter, and burst into tears. 'You must spin it around and think of us every time you need some strength' took up six-year-old Anders before throwing his arms around me. My heart was aching and my back in agony when I went through customs.

In the past weeks many people had been asking me – and I'd been asking myself – how do you prepare for 12 months of keeping on keeping on? The simple answer is you can't. Sure, I had the knowledge that I'd completed remote human-powered journeys for close to four months, and *mediterr année* was only three times as long. The main thing was to have an eye to the schedule that would get me back to Gallipoli in time, but also to know that many things would affect that schedule: weather, health, political situations. I needed to remain flexible and not become too distracted or disappointed when the inevitable changes occurred.

I'd pored over trekking guides, marine pilots and maps, checking route options. Some of the route planning was rather simple (when paddling, keep the coast on my right …) others, such as the trek across the Alps, needed somewhat more detail. That said there was no point trying to plan every stage in detail, given it would be perhaps a year before I reached some of them.

An amazing array of people had been in contact offering help along the way; nowadays the tentacles of the internet and social media are likely to bring contacts your way. A Croatian, Dorijan, was in touch to say that not only was he the spokesman for the UN Refugee Agency in Croatia but was also the head of the Croatian Mountain Guides Association. He noted that I planned to sea kayak the Croatian coast but said it was his duty to ensure I also saw the Croatian mountains. Bulent, who ran marine businesses in Turkey, had done everything from contacting ministers in the Turkish government regarding my journey, to organizing emergency smoke flares for my kayak. Matilda, an Englishwoman based in Israel, had put me in touch with an incredible list of contacts across the Middle East and north Africa, all eager to help. The list went on as the jigsaw pieces found places to fit.

TO THE START LINE

I landed in Milan to be met by Marco Costa. This fine young man had become a great friend in recent years. Together we were running mountain biking tours through Umbria, Tuscany and the Alps; the following week we had a small group of Australians booked for a ride across Sicily. Marco and his wife Elena lived in a tiny house in Val Maggiore, a tiny village in the Alps north of Milan. Marco and I hit the trails, surrounded by snow-capped mountains, a perfect antidote to jetlag. But it hurt not only my back, but also, this being the first real ride I'd had in a couple of months, a few other parts of my body as well. We returned home to find a truck offloading a six-metre-long cardboard box. Inside was the sea kayak I would use for five months of my journey.

★   ★   ★

'Sicily is part of Italy, but it is not Italy. It is richly hospitable and generous. It is poor and dysfunctional. It is beautiful and filthy. Sicily will surprise you on many levels.' Nadia, a good friend back in Australia but originally from Sicily, had told me.

As we rode toward the refuge, Bruce exclaimed, 'Check out those prints in the snow – they look like bear prints.' The last words had only just tumbled out when Bruce himself was sent tumbling by a large mass that bounded out from behind the stone building. Bruno, a huge St Bernard dog, bigger than most bears, looked apologetic before moving onto the next cyclist. This was Sicily, not Switzerland.

It is the largest island in the Mediterranean; the football that sits off the toe of soccer-crazed Italy and the place the *Lonely Planet* guide starts by describing as 'a sun-kissed island in the Mediterranean'. Our mountain bike tour with Australian clients was on the fifth day of a 600 km traverse of the island, and we wondered whether the guide was a work of fiction. By the time we met Bruno we'd experienced biting winds and horizontal rain, and now, high in the Madonie National Park, snowfalls. But we'd also been overwhelmed by the hospitality of the Sicilians, drunk their fine wines and been stuffed – absolutely the right word – full of the most gorgeous of foods.

As our ride across the island progressed, the looming mass of Mount Etna drew us on. Mount Etna, at 3,350 metres, is Europe's highest active volcano, a smoking white cone atop a black lava base. We climbed steeply up the northern side to 1,400 metres to join a series of tracks across the lava along the west face. Some trails narrowed to bizarre single tracks twisting across the black lava fields. We climbed enjoyably and steadily in hot sun to over 1,900 metres. By now we were crossing occasional snow fields dropping from the summit slopes. Snow, lava, blue sky, dead grey trees, living green trees all came together in a cacophony of contrasting colours. Descents on recent lava deposits gave opportunities to drift the wheels wide on corners, like skiing on bikes. Higher on the summit slopes at 2,700 metres, it was desolate country, devoid of vegetation; black lava striped with snow. I sat apart from the group for a while. It seemed an appropriate place to reflect upon my *mediterr année* journey, which was starting in exactly three weeks. Sicily is located almost centrally in the Mediterranean. From the snow on Etna I looked across the Mediterranean Sea disappearing away to unseen Malta and Africa beyond. I had no inkling then that close to a year later I would be travelling across that particular stretch of it.

Back in the Italian Alps and to all the *mediterr année* gear, Marco Costa applied sponsor stickers to the sea kayak with typical Italian flair. The kayak model, from British company Tide Race, was a Pace 17 Tour. Marco peeled off the 17, telling me it was an unlucky number in Italy.

My back had tormented me for much of the Sicily ride, but now Elena worked hard to keep me moving. On 15 April it was Marco's birthday and the two of us celebrated with a magical ski tour under a clear alpine sky to reach 2,500 metre Col de Rima with Switzerland's highest mountain, the Monte Rosa, dominating the view from the col. Good Friday marked one week before I planned to kayak away from Gallipoli. For the first time I had an empty feeling in my stomach and I certainly hadn't been fasting for Lent. It was a certain fear, a trepidation. A feeling I'd known before other expeditions. Everything was accentuated by the issues I was having with my back. All I could do was keep my head in the sand and keep the rest of my body moving toward the start.

The next day Anna and Alberto, who ran Casa Dolce, a small guest house next to Marco and Elena's tiny cottage, put on a farewell dinner in their house that had become my base. Glasses were raised to my journey with 'In bocca al lupo' (In the mouth of the wolf). If that wasn't bizarre enough, Marco followed with another Italian toast 'In culo alla balena' (In the bottom of the whale), and its riposte 'Speriamo che non caghi' (Let's hope it doesn't shit). A toast to a whale seemed fitting for my voyage around the sea. Awash with wine that night, we named my kayak *Miss Grape*.

★　★　★

'Unless you can prove you own this van you will not come into Turkey' said the border guard. After 1,400 km of driving across Italy and Greece, with a 15-hour ferry trip in between, Marco and I had arrived at the Greece–Turkey border near Enez. Marco had bought a new minivan from a motor dealer friend of his only days before, and the van registration document was still in the dealer's name. 'You are smuggling this van perhaps into Turkey. Perhaps it is stolen. And why is there a ship on the roof?' she added. For half an hour Marco argued: it was Easter Monday and he could not contact the dealer. 'You cannot come in; you must return to Greece' the guard continued. Then, gilding the lily a tiny bit, I stepped up.

'The Turkish government are supporting my journey and tomorrow morning I meet with a Turkish and Australian television crew,' I told her. The last part – the Australians – was true.

'Where is your proof?'

I searched back on my phone for the best email to show her. It was true that Gulara, a very helpful woman from the Turkish Ministry of Tourism and Culture, had organised and paid for a hotel in Çanakkale for the coming nights. I showed the email to the border guard. She made a few phone calls then pronounced 'OK, you can come into Turkey, but don't you ever try to do this again.' I felt it unlikely.

It was late at night when we crossed the Dardanelles on the ferry from Eceabat to Çanakkale and found the welcoming Hotel des Etrangers, set back one street from the water. I was in Turkey for the first time. I was close to Gallipoli.

The following morning Marco and I were back on the ferry and heading to Gallipoli. We met the film crew from Australia's Channel 7 at Mimosa, a few kilometres south of Anzac Cove. On a beautiful blue-sky day, *Miss Grape* was lifted off the van and put into the Mediterranean for the first time. I climbed in and paddled around in circles for the camera, realising this was only my second time in a sea kayak since Corsica 10 months

Sign for Anzac Cove, Gallipoli

earlier. I felt good, felt positive, and I dived into the cold waters of the Med for the first time.

After the film crew left, Marco and I spent some hours visiting the various memorial sites commemorating the Anzac landings: Ari Burnu, Lone Pine, Chunuk Bair. Despite the busyness of the rehearsals and preparations going on for the Anzac Day services, I felt the sadness and desolation of the place; the narrow beaches ending at steep earthen cliffs, the scrubby plateau, the lines of graves. I told Marco the story of Gallipoli and how it had come to mean so much to Australians. At Lone Pine, to the sound of a choir practising 'Advance Australia Fair', the national anthem, I tried to explain the words of Eric Bogle's emotional ballad of the Anzac story, 'And the Band Played Waltzing Matilda'. I had first heard it when I was a young man of 16 or 17, a regular in the Dog & Partridge, a real Irish pub with good Guinness and good music guaranteed, in the northern English city of Sheffield where I lived.

I knew nothing of Gallipoli or the Anzacs, and I had no idea then that I would end up as an Australian. I was decades away from dreaming up a plan to circumnavigate the Mediterranean from Gallipoli to Gallipoli. Tom Boulding, my English teacher, was the first person I heard sing that song, and the words hit home that night in the pub. I remember becoming quite emotional, as I have many times since, and as I did when I sang it to Marco: the song tells the tale, with no romance attached, of the true horrors of the Gallipoli campaign: the horrors both during and, for the survivors who made it back to Australia, after their homecoming.

Marco told me not to worry about my tears, and related how an old Italian World War I song about the Alpine troops made him tear up and have *pelle de'oca* (goosebumps). Returning to the minivan, he found the song, '*Signore delle Cime*' ('Lord of the Peaks'), sung by his father's choir. As it played on the stereo, it was Marco's turn to shed a few tears.

Back in Çanakkale I went on a fruitless search for maps whilst Marco drove to Istanbul to pick up Elena who was flying in to see me off. At the hotel, Sanam, an Albanian studying in Turkey and working at reception, advised me not to cross the border to Greece: 'Last week the Greek coastguard shot a man in a small boat crossing the border.' It came home to me there was much I had thought little about for my journey; minor details like crossing international borders by kayak.

On the afternoon of 24 April I pedalled Marco's bike across the Gallipoli peninsula to join thousands of others sleeping over at the Anzac Memorial site in preparation for the dawn service. Packed like sardines on the grass, there was a great spirit amongst everyone and to be there for the service was a special thing. That said, to really appreciate what happened 99 years ago you needed to imagine the place without grandstands, PA system and ceremony. To reflect on a place where there was nothing but sand, scrub, gunfire and war. Keith from Adelaide told me his grandfather landed at Gallipoli on 25 April 1915. He survived and then went to fight on the Western Front. He never once spoke of his experiences, right up to his death at 89. Keith's father, too, had fought in World War II and he too never once spoke of it to his son. At dawn as the last post sounded, a crescent moon hung over the peninsula, a fitting symbol for Turkey.

I read Ataturk's famous words before taking *Miss Grape* down to the water at Gallipoli

I was already tired from little sleep overnight, so the remainder of Anzac Day passed in a haze of packing, replying to messages and calls, some rather entertaining:

Now I'm absolutely sure that you're completely nuts! I hope you don't get a leek* in your craft.

I think that this is very, very dangerous, given your bad habit of putting your foot in your mouth. I can't imagine the Syrians (or heaps of others as well) being too impressed. Shit, even I've been seriously insulted by you more than once! If the sharks and the terrorists don't get you, the only thing I can really be sure of is that you won't be taken hostage and sold into the sex trade. Best of luck with the project. I'll have a look at the Save the Children site and see what the donation options are. Please make sure that Wendy gives me an invite to the funeral so that I can stand there and say I am not surprised; I just thought you'd be dead years ago!

*A reference to my Welsh heritage.

The weather forecast was looking a bit average, with strong winds and rain, for my first few days on the water. Talking with Wendy, I had feelings of guilt wrapped in excitement. By the end of the day I was so stiff I could hardly bend over. Elena got to work trying to loosen me up. I knew that despite feeling as I did, I had to start the next morning. I was in Turkey, *Miss Grape* was in Turkey. I'd said nothing to anyone apart from Wendy and Erica, who was doing my PR for the trip, and communicating

I set off from in front of this small cemetery at Anzac Cove

Feeling nervous and excited in the last hours before setting off

Elena hands me a tiny shell from the beach at Anzac Cove, with instructions to place it back there on my return a year later

with Save the Children. She needed to know just in case I started then pulled out soon after.

On a grey morning, Elena, Marco, *Miss Grape* and I again made the trip back across the Dardanelles, back across the Gallipoli peninsula. Parking by Ari Burnu Cemetery, I carried *Miss Grape* in front of the monument displaying the famous words attributed to Atatürk, down through lines of small headstones and onto the rocky beach. There were very few people around, and that felt right. A group of Kiwi kayakers, on a Gallipoli sea kayak tour, landed and ogled *Miss Grape*. One of them flew the New Zealand flag from the rear deck of his rental kayak. I'd forgotten to bring an Australian flag, and having heard stories of border insecurity, I felt that showing my colours would probably be not a bad thing. So in the Anzac spirit of cooperation, he gifted me his flag. Now, a New Zealand flag, a flag of convenience, fluttered on the back of *Miss Grape*. Given the flags' similarities, I wondered who, when I said I was from Australia, would be the first to ask why I was flying a New Zealand flag.

I gave Marco and Elena one last big hug. Elena reached down and collected a tiny shell from the beach. She pressed it into my palm, instructing me to place it back in 12 months' time.

EARLY DAYS

At 12.30 p.m. on 26 April I pushed off from the beach, my head filled with emotions. I swallowed hard, just thinking about what was in front of me. I thought of my beautiful wife and family in Australia who I would not see for a year. I started shivering. Shivering, as I looked up at the earthen cliffs behind North Beach. Shivering as I kayaked close to shore, past workmen dismantling the infrastructure from the Anzac Day commemorations. I knew that my excitement and trepidation was nothing compared to the feelings of those young Anzac soldiers who had landed on those beaches 99 years ago. I was embarking on a dream; they were entering a nightmare. It was why I was shivering. I turned away and paddled toward the headland that formed the northernmost point of Suvla Bay.

It didn't start too well. A couple of hours out from Ari Burnu, I rounded the headland to face a strong nor'easter full in the face. After bashing into it for a couple of hours I gave up and camped on a rocky beach no more than 15 km from Gallipoli. A tiny patch of grass was just large enough for my tent. Putting the stove on for the first brew of the journey, it felt more than good to be on my way. But here I remained for the next 40 hours. During that first night I woke with an unbearable and painful need to pee. This went on all night along with chills and shivering. I assumed I had a urinary tract infection and started straight on antibiotics. I lay utterly wasted for the next 24 hours, unable to move from a tent that was also being battered by storms. Strangely birds sang all through that first night, not breaking as usual before starting up their own dawn service. Perhaps it was a reminder the soldiers had continued day and night; never letting down their guard.

As if things up front weren't bad enough, an itch behind then signalled an infestation of threadworms; a very real pain in the arse. By the third day I felt a bit better. Fortunately the wind had dropped, and as I packed slowly a pod of a dozen or so porpoises frolicked just offshore. It was the good omen I needed. I set off along a beautiful coast under grey skies with torrential rain at times – there was nothing like

My first strokes away from
Anzac Cove with the Anzac
Memorial site at North Beach
in background

My first camp of the journey presaged not quite the start I had planned

Rainstorm on my third day, but at least I was paddling again

getting some contrary doses of weather so early in the journey. Apart from the odd few fishing shacks the seashore was just cliffs and occasional beaches. Not wanting to overdo it I pulled up to camp mid-afternoon beneath an old concrete sentry box, another reminder of the battleground this whole peninsula had been 100 years ago. I had no appetite but forced a small amount of pasta down and a cup of tea, knowing I needed the energy. Carried by the wind across the Gulf of Saros, the muezzin's voice floated, calling the faithful to prayer. As in Muslim Kashmir in 1991, I had got to the start line, and other worries buried the issue of my back; *mediterr année* had begun.

At Erikli, Yusuf, town planner at the local government, called me in from the jetty construction he was supervising. In his black trenchcoat two sizes too small, he cut an interesting figure in the wind and sand. Soon a small crowd had gathered, each wanting a photo, each proffering help in some way: the most useful was the weather forecast. Finally they pushed me back off the beach – but I'd only been going for half an hour when I heard, above the wind and waves, a horn beeping madly. I looked over my shoulder to see a car bouncing down a dirt track behind the beach, the driver hanging out of the window beckoning me into shore. The car buried itself on the sandy beach and a young man ran to the water's edge. An older man followed slowly. As the bow of *Miss Grape* hit the sand, the young man tried to hand me a large glass jar whilst dancing deftly to keep his shoes dry. I climbed out of the kayak to greet them and accept the large pot of honey that was their gift. The father explained in mixed Turkish, Italian and German that they'd seen me paddle past some kilometres earlier; seen the flag flying on the back of my kayak. They chased me down to wish me well wherever I was headed and to give me a gift. Necedet Arsu had a tear in his eye. I knew his name, as he'd ripped out the personal details page from his diary to hand to me. Now I had not only his contact details but also his driving licence number and blood group. This first random act of kindness since my journey began presaged a year of endless kindnesses.

I certainly sensed the strong bond between the Turks and Australians, expressed to me a number of times and born out of that time as enemies at Gallipoli when respect for each nation grew amongst the carnage. Already I was looking forward to being back in Turkey at the end of my journey.

This Turkish father and son chased me down the coast just to give me a jar of their honey: the first of hundreds of random acts of kindness that marked my journey

MAY

I curled closer to May,
comforted by her warmth.

Kiera Cass

A week from Gallipoli I left Turkey behind, paddling across the Evros river delta into Greece: my first watery international border crossing. This time I had no errant minivan to delay my exit from Turkey: Ramazan, the coastguard commanding officer in the Turkish border port of Enez, made some phone calls before declaring I was free to go to Greece, telling me 'Greece and Turkey are not friends.'

I always find river deltas eerie places – the mixing of salt water with fresh, brown with blue, sandbanks and shallows, everything so flat except waves that seem to have risen from nowhere.

I cleared immigration at Alexandroupoli. A dozen coastguard officers gathered around me. Finally, once they'd accepted that kayaks don't come with shipping registration papers, I was marched, along with a man arrested for smuggling shellfish from Turkey, to the police station for passport control. Paper was key here, with the photocopier the most popular thing in the station. Endless toing and froing from offices but always a stop to pay homage to Xerox, the Greek God of paper.

Alexandroupoli offered the first pharmacy since I'd began my journey. I went in search of a remedy to kill off my worms, which were now most irritating. The pharmacist spoke no English. I pointed at my rear end and wiggled my finger, but she just smiled a puzzled smile. Then, as chance would have it, I realised I had a pack of Wurmis, jelly worms from Haribo, that omnipresent European sweet brand. I pulled one out and dangled the 5 cm green worm behind me. The smile became broader, almost a laugh, and she placed a pack of tablets on the counter. I offered her a jelly worm along with some euros and a big smile of my own.

Greece, a country then diving headlong into economic crisis, was to embrace me for the next seven weeks and 2,000 km of coastal kayaking. Greece was a country of reducing salaries and increasing costs. Evi, the daughter of a taverna owner at Nea Roda, told me about her job in a hotel; seven days a week for €700 (AU$1,000) per month. Sheltering from a wild thunderstorm in his office near the ancient city of Polistilo, Constantinos, a Greek coastguard officer told me his salary had gone down by 20 per cent – whilst the repayments on the house he had proudly built kept increasing. He was a proud member of the Pontic Greeks, who for centuries had lived around the Sea of Marmara and Istanbul. He told me of the great transmigration of 1922, when the borders of modern Turkey had been drawn: a million or more Greeks went west and half a million Turks east. The architect of this population exchange was renowned Norwegian polar explorer Fridtjof Nansen. In those first weeks in the Greek regions of Thrace and Macedonia I met many who still believed Istanbul was Greek, was still Constantinople.

A sense of decay in northern Greece – unfinished buildings everywhere along the coast, rubbish, derelict picnic areas, stinking toilet blocks; people still shat in there, though nothing now got flushed away.

The Mediterranean was quiet with only the early migrating species showing up. I spied the occasional Bulgarians in bikinis or board shorts as I paddled along lonely beaches, but most hotels and bars were closed. The fishing boats were out but I had yet to see a yacht or powerboat.

Greece, a country that I grew to love and one whose hospitality is unparalleled. The battle to maintain the rhythm of my journey started here; a 15-minute stop on a beach to stretch my legs out of the kayak so often became a three-hour lunch. At times I feared stopping, feared that *mediterr année* – one year in the Mediterranean – could easily become *mediterr deux années*, two years. It is not surprising perhaps that in the Greek language *né* means 'yes'.

With worms banished and the agony of pissing now easing up somewhat, I was dropping into the comforting daily rhythm that for me marks any long journey. I'd set off each morning soon after dawn, and when the Med threw up its winds around midday I'd paddle through the waves or sit on a beach and wait for calmer waters, then continue. Late afternoon or often well into the evening I'd start to think about camping; whether I was on a quiet beach or close to a town. I'd drag *Miss Grape* up the sand or rock and start the process of unpacking and setting camp. Soon the stove would be brewing or a bottle of cheap red opened.

'We are here to take a painting back to our church in Romania, prepared for us by one of the monasteries of Athos,' Sylvia informed me. I was in Nea Roda, a small village at the neck of the Athos peninsula, the most easterly of the Halkidiki peninsulas; three fingers that reach down into the Aegean Sea. Athos is home to the holy mountain of that name that soars over 2000 metres straight up from the sea, and upon the peninsula are some 20 Orthodox monasteries that make up this autonomous region of Greece. Permits are required to visit the peninsula – and none are available to women, who are absolutely forbidden to enter. Sylvia was a man. Were I to visit the peninsula, it would be a great opportunity for me to pick up some time – the monasteries follow the Julian calendar and I'd step back 13 days, thus immediately putting me almost two weeks ahead of schedule.

But I preferred the way of the Persian king Xerxes. In 500 BC his fleet of invading warships was sunk by wild katabatic winds sent down by the gods off Mount Athos. So Xerxes had a canal dug, some 2 km in length, across the narrow neck of the peninsula from present-day Nea Roda to Tripiti. Little remains of this incredible engineering feat from 2,500 years ago save a few depressions amongst the farmland. A road however does follow the line of the ancient canal and, using the kayak trolley I carried with me, I wheeled *Miss Grape*, my own warship, across the peninsula. This bit of route canal therapy saved me over 100 km of paddling and also avoided the issue of illegal camping on the peninsula.

Some absolutely stunning – and challenging at times – sea kayaking followed around the middle finger, the Sithonia peninsula. From one perfect beach camp on Sithonia, I looked back across to Mount Athos and realised that despite my relatively simple life and possessions on this journey I was still cluttered (burdened?) with stuff that connects me to my world. In the corner of my tiny tent lay two phones, a laptop, VHS marine radio, spot tracker, two cameras and a twisted spaghetti of chargers and leads. I thought of the ascetic monks on Athos and their simple life, eschewing modern possessions. Or have they too suffered the insidious creep of 'stuff' into their lives? I have railed against so much of this for so long, and I realise how lucky I am to have experienced adventure and misadventure that cannot be brought to a halt by pressing a button. There is no doubt that whilst the physical adventure can still be as strong, the real connection to country can never be as powerful as it was. That perhaps I am of the last generation that could enjoy reasonably pure adventure where, once we stepped off the beaten track, we really did disconnect from our modern lives. And once disconnected we start to use the senses that we all have but don't use any more: the sense of direction, of danger, of what is inherently the 'right' choice to make without knowing we are making that choice. Now, the knowledge that we can make a phone call or that we can press a help button – even if we don't – removes that self-reliance forever.

Another fine beach camp. This time on the Sithonia peninsula, northern Greece

Of course the shores of the Mediterranean are not a place of wildness in the way that, say, some of my previous wanderings had offered. There I had gone for some weeks without seeing anyone, contacting anyone. Around the Mediterranean it is hardly possible to travel a couple of days without meeting someone. I am by nature a sociable being but the outdoors had always been for me a chance to essentially be away from people. I liked journeys with others but equally, probably preferably, enjoyed the time alone. If I had been concerned at the outset that I would perhaps tire of all the humanity that lives and recreates in the 22 countries bordering this great sea I needn't have worried; I embraced it and found myself continually in its thrall.

★ ★ ★

But you don't have to be remote to feel adventure. Going around the tip of the Sithonia finger with strong winds behind me and a choppy sea rebounding off huge cliffs made for exhilarating paddling. My glasses were fogging up – a sure sign of nervousness and adrenaline – in much the same way as the car windscreen steams up when you pull off an overtaking manoeuvre you probably shouldn't. My stomach was aching from a huge lunch at Kalamitsi, head spinning a little from evil ouzo, a drink I think is best given away as a gift. I'd landed to stretch my legs before rounding the cliff-lined headland which would offer no respite, only to have Costas, a man in his 70s, help pull up my kayak and absolutely insist I join him and his wife for lunch in their house. Again I succumbed and heard how his father had been taken prisoner in World War II by the Germans and somehow they were resettled in Tashkent in Russia. Costas had returned with his family to Greece in the 1970s. Many Greeks still hold the Germans in poor regard and consider the economic bailout led by modern-day Germany to be nothing more than imperialist self-interest.

Once around the headland I outran a fast-approaching storm and was glad to land in dumping waves at Destinia on the west of the peninsula, at a not yet open campsite and taverna. That didn't stop me receiving a very warm welcome. When I told Nicky, the owner, of my fundraising, she slipped off her Bvlgari wedding ring and showed me the inside engraved with the Save the Children logo. It turns out this luxury brand was a worldwide partner of the charity.

The neck of Kassándra, the final Halkidiki peninsula, offered the still-existing Portes Canal which I was happy to take. Once out of the canal I found the wind blowing hard against me, waves breaking over *Miss Grape*, so I took shelter in the harbour at Nea Moudania. At the back of the harbour was a small beach and just behind the only house. As I pulled *Miss Grape* onto the sand an old man came from the house toward me.

'Australia, Australia. *Yiassou, yiassou* (hello)!' Like most people Theo, 86, did not recognise I was flying a Kiwi flag. But he knew Australia well enough. He had moved there in 1953 and for six years worked at the steel mills of Port Kembla and for the Hydro Electric Commission in Tasmania. He had met a Greek woman and they were married in Sydney's Hyde Park. He went back into his house and returned with faded photos: their wedding, the Three Sisters in the Blue Mountains, the 1956 Melbourne Olympics. I looked beyond Theo to sheets bowing like spinnakers on the washing line, wondering if perhaps his wife were still alive. 'You see my Hills eh? I am proud of my Hills' he smiled. 'I did not want to leave Australia but my wife was homesick and in 1959 we took the ship back to Greece. On the ship I bring some Australian things and I bring my Hills.'

Vegemite, Victa lawnmowers, Speedo swimming trunks and the Hills Hoist would be on the list of most people's iconic Australian inventions. In 1945 Lance Hill returned to Adelaide from the war and his wife whinged about her clothes line getting in the way of the lemon tree in the backyard. So he got to work to invent a rotary clothes line: the Hills Hoist. On a windy day in Halkidiki I'd happened upon quite possibly the only Hills Hoist flying the washing in Greece, if not the whole of the Mediterranean.

When I returned from buying some supplies in town, Theo was stood next to *Miss Grape*, holding my flag in one hand and a torn and faded map in the other. The map was of Asia Minor, western Turkey. He pointed out the names of towns around the Sea of Marmara near Istanbul – Greek names like Moudania and Kallikratia. He explained that was where his family was from, before the forced transmigration. Many Greeks settled in 'new' towns with the old names like 'Nea' (new) Moudania where Theo lived now.

I'd raised some emotions for Theo and as I left, watery eyes bade me farewell. 'Ah, Australia, good Australia ... *Yiassou, yiassou* ...'

Possibly the only Australian Hills Hoist
rotary clothes line in Greece, if not Europe

At least Theo had experienced the real Australia. Throughout the length of the Greek coastline, in fishing harbours and on tiny boats, I met many older Greeks who told me they had visited Australia. Their visits had been fleeting ones to the ports of Fremantle, Adelaide or Sydney. They had journeyed the world aboard the ships of Onassis and Niarchos; Greece, despite being a tiny country with a population of only 13 million, still ranks as the number one owner of ships worldwide.

I had no desire to paddle to the top of the Gulf of Thermaikos past Greece's second city, Thessaloniki. A better plan was to cut straight across the gulf but, aware of the busy shipping lane, I decided I'd inform the Greek coastguard of my plans and request them to ask shipping to keep an eye out for little *Miss Grape* as we cut across the channel. With this in mind I kayaked into the harbour of Nea Michaniona and was soon in the coastguard office, at afternoon prayer time with a large number of officers taking offerings from Xerox.

It all started well enough, with an informal conversation with Nick; he had been born and brought up in Melbourne, then after his family had moved back to Greece in 1997 he had joined the coastguard. But my request for some assistance turned into a grilling, with Nick translating for his superiors. How had I got there? By kayak, I replied. But did nobody stop you? No. How had I got to Turkey? Why did I not have a support boat shadowing me and did I have permission from the Australian government to do this journey? Did I have permission from the Greek government? Did I not know it was illegal to kayak more than 300 metres from shore? (This is quite a common rule in Europe, with the distance varying in some countries. Five hundred metres in Croatia, one mile in Italy. It is, however, a rather unwise rule, given that in rough water the rebound from cliffs often makes it more dangerous for small boats to be closer to shore than some distance out.)

Officers were feverishly taking notes (and then photocopying them), numerous phone calls were made including to the Chief Poo-Bah of the Thessaloniki Port Authority. I was ushered into an office where Nick translated the words of his boss: 'You are OK to go across the channel in the morning but it is at your own risk. We do not want to know. The port authority will not let the ships know you are crossing.' So the agency responsible for safety at sea was not prepared to acknowledge my existence at sea.

'Please call us in the morning to get the forecast,' said Nick.

'Sure,' I responded, 'I will call you up on the VHF radio.'

'No, no, don't do that in case the port authority hears us talking to you. Use your phone to ring us.'

Such a response is sadly only too common when you engage with agencies who have little understanding or interest in your activity. It really does give the lie to the oft proffered advice to tell someone before you go. On so many occasions in Australia and elsewhere it has been thus.

Early the following morning I slipped safely across Thermaikos gulf, waiting for a few cargo ships to pass before heading across the channel.

★   ★   ★

By late May things were warming up a bit and I hit the Pelion peninsula in a spell of good weather. On my watery highway I wandered at will, overtaking nothing but the land. Rest areas were plentiful if I dared to take them, but I was always conscious of the endless Greek hospitality. Other than on hidden beaches, wherever *Miss Grape* landed there were questions, cold beers, invites... *mediterr année* was finding its rhythm and I was loving it. I took my first swim of the journey.

The Pelion was the most impressive section of coast since I'd left Turkey. Forest-clad mountains, stunning cliff scenery and dozens upon dozens of sea caves, all accessible in the millpond conditions. Mount Ossa, Pelion – familiar names in this unfamiliar environment. Mountains I'd climbed back in Australia, in Tasmania, take their names from these in Greece. But here these mountains crouch respectfully beneath snow-capped Mount Olympus (2,911 metres), the party room of Zeus and his fellow ancient Greek gods and the highest mountain in Greece. Olympus had been my companion for much of the past week in the same way that Athos had been the week before. Indeed as the one faded into the background the other grew bolder each day. As I looked up at the mountains I thought forward to my planned traverse of the Alps which was getting closer, albeit still two months away, my legs progressively weakening in the kayak.

Many mornings I woke to a deep diesel engine thud, thud, thud floating across the sea from the trawlers, along with the musical clanking of the plastic floats of nets being winched in across their metal reels. And now too the beach bars were waking, were opening. Expanses of sand were spawning ranks of blue or white sunbeds. Still only a tiny smattering of bodies added contrast, most still waiting for the summer 'occupation'. In whatever country I kayaked through – Greece, Albania, Croatia, Spain – Bob Marley was king of the beach bar. 'No Woman No Cry' or 'One Love' were the common European currency. And once on the water my own classic songs took over. Inane anthems that I had sung to Wendy, annoyingly repetitive. But despite singing the same words a thousand times, I never could sing them now. But indeed many were the same words I sang on journeys 10 or 15 years ago. I'd love them and hate them. Aside from shouting out my love they had the purpose of keeping me awake. Too often, usually in mid-afternoon but sometimes sneaking up at other times, I'd start yawning, banging the side of the kayak or my head, singing, shouting. Anything to stop me drifting off, which occasionally I did for a second or two. Usually I could work through the doziness for the half-hour or so it lasted, but occasionally a run for shore and a nap was the only answer. Coffee could be the answer. But if Greek

A boiling hot spring pours into the sea on the island of Evia

coffee gives caffeinated beverages a bad name second only to Red Bull, they have now excelled themselves with frappé, a disgusting concoction of iced coffee made with Nescafé.

Most people think of Greece and the sea and think of the Greek islands. But my journey was following the mainland almost in its entirety. The only section I planned to bypass was the Peloponnese, the bulky, many-tentacled peninsula hanging by a thread, the Isthmus of Corinth, from the rest of Greece. The spectacular 6 km Corinth Canal cut the thread, and by going through it I would save some 250 km of paddling. On the day I actually crossed to Evia, my first island and Greece's second largest, I received the news from the Corinth Canal Company that they would grant me special permission to kayak through the canal. It would be the last, longest and most special of my route canal therapies.

The Mediterranean rarely has any tidal flow worth the mention, but the west coast of Evia is renowned for the largest tidal range in the eastern Mediterranean; up to a metre and up to 2.5 knots of current. The tide races took me by some surprise as wind against tide put up some funny water that *Miss Grape* enjoyed setting herself against. Archimedes was rumoured to have thrown himself into the waters off Evia, frustrated by his inability to explain what was going on. I just went with the flow. It was the 29th day of the journey, my longest sea kayaking trip to date, surpassing my paddle along the incomparable Kimberley coast of NW Australia. There, tidal flows of up to 13 metres offered huge challenges daily.

Lona, a Swede, Wilhelm, a Norwegian and Adar, a Kurd, took to following me down the coast shouting encouragement at beach and headland. Then another finish in the dark after a hard-fought battle against waves and wind on a 15 km open crossing. The following day, near Skala Oropou, the sea went from smooth calm to the wildest of white water in a matter of seconds. At one point I tried to leave the beach but *Miss Grape* was pushed time and again to shore.

The Mediterranean is an uncomfortable sea – short and sharp with no real rhythm to her ways and waves. People who don't know her come expecting serenity, but those born with her or who have acquainted themselves a little, know better than to be taken in by her undoubted charms.

Perhaps it is as it should be. We have blasted and bastardised her coast, we have plundered her depths and we have rubbished her shores. Perhaps her anger is all she has left to fight back with. Perhaps her anger is her defence mechanism against the domestic violence she suffers. Every open water crossing I did I was aware of the possibility of this angry sea getting up to test me. Sometimes it did. She kept me on my toes.

Whether large or small, Mediterranean waves invariably, I'd noticed, came in sets of three, often a bigger one bookended by two smaller. This phenomenon has a name in Greece – *trikimia*.

A combination of too much time to concoct plans and paddling ever closer to Athens gave me an outbreak of marathon fever. In 490BC the vastly outnumbered Greek army had defeated the mighty Persian army in the Battle of Marathon, thus saving Athens from capture. Legend, or perhaps just Robert Browning's poem, has it that a runner, Pheidippides, was despatched the 42 km to Athens to announce the victory. And thus the marathon was born. Always thinking of different ways to boost my fundraising for Save the Children and obviously not satisfied with my own 12-month marathon, I alighted upon the idea that I should attempt to paddle 100 km in one day, well over twice my average day's paddle. Looking at the map I noted that once I had passed through the Corinth Canal beyond Athens, the Gulf of Corinth was about that length.

Then, some days after hatching this plan, I saw that my route down the coast would soon pass within 10 km of the inland town of Marathonas, where Pheidippides had started his run. Surely, given how close I was, I should follow the classic marathon route to Athens? After over a month sitting on my butt it was time my legs got a good shake-out. My legs actually needed it. Years earlier I'd gashed my right shin on a piece of rusting steel. Despite course after course of antibiotics it leaked litres of plasma over the following months. This included a trip to India where overnight it would form a thin skin, allowing me the unpopular breakfast party trick of touching it to release a jet of clear fluid that would shoot a metre or more out from my leg. The end result of all this was a damaged lymphatic system and lymphoedema in my lower right leg. Now, after periods of inactivity (long flights, long lunches or a month in a kayak), my right foot puffs up badly and can become most uncomfortable. A marathon walk would do it good.

Then, the day after I thought of this walk, I received a message from Stavros Georgarakis. This bear of a man would, for many reasons, become a legend amongst many legends for *mediterr année*. He had been following my journey on social media and, it turned out, is very much the glue that holds Greek kayaking and canoeing together. For the past 20 years he has run Cannibals Kayak House, which, I was to discover, is the finest kayak shop in Greece. Stavros was inviting me to be a guest at the Surfers for Life Festival, a day of kayaking, biking and running taking place the following Sunday at Schinias, the location for the rowing/kayaking events at the 2004 Athens Olympics. It just so happened that Schinias was the closest place on the coast to Marathonas. This was all too much of a coincidence. I resolved to try and reach Schinias by Friday evening, then on Saturday walk the 10km to Marathonas and the 42km marathon course to Athens. Once there Stavros would bring me back to Schinias for the festival and afterward I could continue my paddle.

On the Friday I left Skala Oropou far, far too late to make it to Schinias. Mid-afternoon I landed on a beach near the tiny village of Sesi. The intention was to stretch my legs for 10 minutes before pushing on as far as I could until dark. Intentions. The sounds of a bouzouki floated down from a taverna. I could do with a quick cold drink …

A group of six men, the only ones in the taverna, sat around a table full of mostly empty plates and bottles. Andreas, Costas, Georgios and the rest didn't invite me but instructed me to join them for a late lunch. My quick stretch turned into a long, long one. By sunset we were still going. Despite the additional distance, Sesi was as good a place as any to start walking. Leaving *Miss Grape* locked inside the taverna when the party finished, I strolled out into the darkness. The climb straight up from Sesi for 500 metres was not what I needed for legs that had done little but amble along beaches that past month. After walking 10km to the town of Grammatiko, I slept a few hours in the family house of Costas, the Sesi taverna owner, who had given me the key.

Well before dawn on Saturday morning I left and walked the 7km to Marathonas. As I reached the outskirts of town my phone rang. It was Andreas, the bouzouki player, who it transpired was also postman of Marathonas and coach of the Marathonas soccer team. He was inviting me to breakfast with his family. When I was full of pastries and coffee, he took me to the start line. I was the only one there. At 9 a.m., the crowd roared (Andreas cheered), the gun went off (Andreas clapped) and I was away. It started well enough – but a third of the way in, my training programme of sitting down in a kayak for 35 days was starting to pay back. My quads started to pain me, initially just twinges. By 21km, the halfway mark, they were bloody sore. Rain began to fall on a day when I had hoped to stay dry after all that time in a kayak.

The route of the Athens marathon is not quite as it was when Pheidippides had skipped along it 1,500 years ago. For those familiar with Sydney roads, I'd liken it to spending a day walking down a combination of Parramatta Road and the M5 motorway. I took my chances on the road itself a few times, but was usually scared back onto the verge and into the bushes by close calls with cars.

Pain increased as the kilometres passed ever slower. Would I break 10 hours? At one point I was thinking how much of a beer desert Greece was – so very little choice – and pondered whether there was any move to craft beer brewing, a trend sweeping the world. As I did, on the other side of the six lanes, I spied The Beer Corner. But in my state the 50 metres might as well have been 50 miles. Thirty kilometres in, a tortoise passed me on the trail.

The closer I got to Athens, the more the blue line, painted for the 2004 Olympics, faded from the tarmac, the result of more and more tyres screeching across it. My legs

Given the voracious appetite for seafood around the Mediterranean, it is surprising there are any fish left. Fish farming has expanded massively in recent years

felt dead and I wondered how, after 90 days in the kayak, I would cope for the first days of the Alps trek. I even started looking for laybacks on the pavement to avoid stepping the 20 cm up onto a kerb.

Then, just before 7 p.m., I looked to my left and there was the Panathenaic Stadium, the home of the first modern Olympic Games of 1896: the finish for the marathon that year, again in 2004 and now for me. But the crowds had left save for a few milling around inside. 'Can I go in?' I asked an attendant taking down some barriers. 'We are just now closed,' he replied. So with 300 metres to go around the stadium track I was stymied but done. After announcing 'We won!' to the Athenians, legend has it that Pheidippides promptly collapsed and never recovered. I knew how he felt, but at least I was still alive.

JUNE

*In early June the world of leaf and blade and flowers
explodes, and every sunset is different.*

John Steinbeck

A n hour or so after my marathon triumph Stavros found me in a bar rehydrating.
We drove back to Sesi to pick up *Miss Grape* and then onto Schinias, arriving by
midnight. He offloaded me into a hotel with instructions to relax and come to

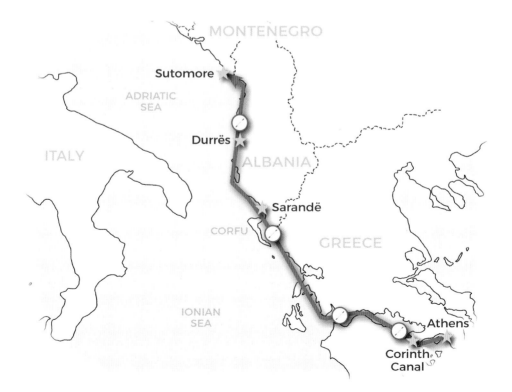

the festival the next day when ready. A leaf blower pointlessly chasing seaweed off the beach woke me too early the next morning. By then I'd smeared the walls of the room with my blood, and the floor was littered with the carcasses of the little buzzing bastards who had kept me awake much of the night; I was still alive, but even so I wondered who had really won the battle. I ran out of the shower to take a call from Wendy, slipping on the water that poured across the floor from bathroom to bedroom. Rather aptly she told me how things were going pear-shaped with the renovations. Our builder, who like all builders had started off the nice guy, was starting to show his true colours: apparently the fall in our new bathroom was about as good as the one in this hotel in Schinias. Not for the first time I felt bad about leaving her with all that to deal with.

It seemed the only other people staying at this soulless hotel were an Australian couple taking a few days' holiday after a conference. I joined them for breakfast before walking the couple of kilometres to the *Surfers for Life* festival. I didn't feel too bad given my marathon effort of the day before. A team of young Greeks under a sign offering 'Free Hugs' began a day wrapped in great spirit – races, food, dancing – raising money for children suffering from cancer. To date on this trip I'd not met another kayaker, a famine that had surprised me. Here at Schinias was a feast of 100 or more. *Miss Grape*, on display, was receiving a lot of attention. Dimitris Kokkoris – laughing, shouting, smiling – was one of the key organisers and welcomed me to the festival. Like Stavros, he would ultimately feature prominently in my year around the Mediterranean.

After saying a few words and presenting the medals to the winners of kayak races I spied Andreas heading for the microphone. This postman of Marathonas had come with the president of the football club to hand deliver a club jersey and flag to me.

With force 7 southerly winds forecast for the next couple of days I reasoned there was no point trying to paddle to Athens. I'd got there by human power already so took a lift back with Dimitris after the festival. Anyway I had another flag presentation ceremony to get to. As I'd kayaked through Greece, the Australian embassy had become aware of my journey. I was invited to the embassy to receive an Australian flag to replace the New Zealand flag of convenience fluttering on the back deck of *Miss Grape*. Aptly the ambassador, Jenny Bromfield, was en route to a major shipping conference that same day. The staff of the embassy assembled in the lobby and Jenny was handed a tiny flag on a thin stick. It was one of those given out to wave on Australia Day processions or other jingoistic occasions. Jenny, rather embarrassed, enquired of her staff if that was the best they could do. Having suggested that the large one hanging in the lobby might do the trick, or the Aboriginal one next to it, I gratefully took my little flag, later packing it away inside Miss Grape and continuing as a Kiwi imposter.

I spent a couple of days in Athens. Stavros and Dimitris couldn't do enough to help; running me everywhere I needed to go. I'd elected to stay in a hotel in order to focus on some work and when it came to time to check out I discovered Stavros had paid the bill. A totally unnecessary gesture but so typical of the man and the people. I tried to force euros back at him but he was genuinely insulted.

I bade farewell and relaunched *Miss Grape* at Perama under a 50-shades-of-grey sky, some I'm certain caused by the pollution and the nearby oil refinery. Sea kayaking and big cities rarely mix. As darkness fell, I landed at Pachi and went in search of a hotel. This small

Jenny Bromfield, the Australian ambassador to Greece, presents me with a rather small Australian flag to replace the New Zealand 'Flag of Convenience' I was flying on *Miss Grape*

After berating me for not cutting up the tomatoes the 'Greek' way, Dimitris Kokkoris gives my Greek salad the thumbs up

town had bars aplenty but hotels none. I couldn't believe it when, unknowingly paraphrasing from Little Britain, one bar owner told me 'There are no rooms. This is a local town for local people.' I pitched camp amidst the tables of a harbourside taverna as rain bucketed down.

The next day, the Peloponnese came into view, the only bit of the Greek mainland I planned not to visit. Tucked away was the Isthmus of Corinth, and as I approached it I got in touch with Olga Tzimos-Zarris. Olga had answered a call put out by the Australian embassy for people who might help my next marathon attempt: the Gulf of Corinth. Originally from Australia, Olga had married Antonis, a Greek, and now lived in Kiato on the gulf, 20 km beyond the Corinth Canal.

Late afternoon, a couple of days' paddle from Athens, I weaved *Miss Grape* through a large number of anchored ships to arrive at my ultimate route canal. For thousands of years boats had been hauled across the 6-km wide isthmus on logs, thus saving the time and treacherous 250 km journey around the Peloponnese. For thousands of years thoughts had turned to building a canal. Indeed Roman Emperor Nero had one started, turning the first sod himself with a shovel made of gold. It was French and Greek companies who finally completed this magnificent engineering feat, in 1893. It is 25 metres wide with walls up to 76 metres high, and it was a real privilege to be permitted to pass through the canal in a kayak, alone, for free. In high summer up to 150 vessels a day pass through the canal, down to 20 or 30 in winter. A medium-sized cargo ship pays upwards of €1,000 for the pleasure.

I was invited up into the control room at the eastern end of the canal. 'How

Having permission to kayak through the Corinth Canal, nearly 80 metres deep and 6 km long, saved me 250 km of paddling around the Peloponnese. I didn't know then I would wash up on the Peloponnese nine months later.

long will it take you to canoe through?' asked the duty officer. I reckoned about an hour. What I wasn't including in that reckoning though was time spent taking photos and just allowing the current to take me slowly in the silence whilst I looked up and along in awe. At one point the silence was broken by echoing off the cliffs: 'Aussie Aussie Aussie!' I looked up at one of the bridges high above to see massive Australian and Boxing Kangaroo flags hanging down, and Olga shouting and waving.

Toward the end of the 6 km my phone rang a number of times, but then and there was not the place for conversation. As I approached the control room at the western end, a man in uniform was stood on a jetty waving vigorously, whilst an agitated, perhaps a little angry-sounding, voice bellowed out of a PA system. It was all Greek to me though as I passed the man, who was now shouting and throwing his hands into the air.

'I've been trying to call you' said Olga, waiting on a little beach where the canal enters the Gulf of Corinth. 'You took too long and all these big ships have been held up waiting for you to be clear of the canal.' She translated the PA message as basically 'Stop taking photos and get a bloody move on!'

Olga headed home and I headed out into a sun lowering itself into the Gulf. Taverna Vounalakia was my camp for that particular night and, as was so often the case, Athena and Michael refused payment for dinner. Despite not cleaning up until after the last diners left well beyond midnight, they were both there at 7 a.m. just to make me coffee before I left.

★   ★   ★

On 5 June, World Environment Day, I paddled past yet another plastic bottle bobbing in the sea. Discarded plastic on our coasts and seas is now a pollution epidemic. Not only is it ugly, it kills and maims millions of birds and marine creatures. In the Mediterranean the problem is essentially out of control. The plastic, which takes hundreds of years to break down and never truly disappears, has nowhere to go in a sea that has only one natural, and very narrow, connection to the world's ocean currents: the Strait of Gibraltar. One country blames another. 'It is Tunisia's fault' says Italy. 'It comes from Greece' says Egypt. But the reality is the winds and waves move the plastic from one place to another until finally a big sea dumps it out of reach up coastal gullies or to tangle in coastal vegetation. It piles up metres deep and thick on beaches and rocks.

Millions depend on the Mediterranean, millions take pleasure from it. Few care for it. For the many sun-seeking holidaymakers who move little further than a room-bar-pool-beach circuit, their gaze is limited to just the cleaned-up bit of beach in front of them while the plastic remains piled up around the corner. While I was kayaking off Albania some fishermen called me over. As I bobbed at their stern they served me coffee and we chatted in a mixture of arm waving, Italian and Greek. Each of the men, when his coffee was finished, tossed the plastic cup into the sea. I tucked mine under the kayak deck elastic. They admonished me and signalled for me to throw it into the water. I refused. They were insistent before ultimately shrugging their shoulders and laughing at me. Many times I've seen those who make their livelihood from the Mediterranean treat it with such disrespect.

At the *Surfers for Life* festival I had sat down with Konstatinos Kavagiannis, a media entrepreneur who began to reassess the important things in life after a cancer scare. He told me about Beach Invasion, an initiative of his for World Environment Day. Schoolkids in sailing dinghies would land on beaches around Athens and, bin liners in hand, proceed to pick up rubbish. A great initiative – but to stand any chance of winning the battle the whole Mediterranean needs a huge multinational army of people to invade and occupy the beaches for longer than one day a year. And then of course there's the plastic that has sunk, out of sight, continuously killing off whatever is left in the sea after the fishermen and liquid pollution have taken their toll.

I was in Igoumenitsa for a couple of days just before I left Greece. All day, each day I would see a homeless man of Demis Roussos proportions walk up and down the main street picking up stray plastic bags and bottles; emptying bins of them too. He'd stuff them in his pockets and down his trousers, making his already portly frame even grander. Each hand carried a number of plastic bags full of other plastic bags he'd collected. Whilst there may have been some psychological impairment to the man, it manifested itself in a one man battle against plastic. Perhaps an obsessive-compulsive disorder we could do with more of.

The stunning coastline of Croatia was perhaps the cleanest I paddled along during my year. A number of Croatians explained to me that this was an upside of the financial crisis that gripped most of Mediterranean Europe. Croatia had introduced a container deposit scheme in 2006 and apparently many unemployed people now scoured the beaches for containers in an effort to make a little income.

With over eight billion beverage containers used annually, Australia has been slow to enact such positive legislation – despite its proven success in South Australia since 1975. The battle against the proposed legislation has been waged by the beverage and beverage container industries with typical obfuscation of the facts. The tide may however be turning, with New South Wales and Queensland both promising to bring in legislation in 2017.

Plastic pollution in the Mediterranean is out of control. This is a beach in Albania but it could be anywhere along the shores of the 22 countries that have a Mediterranean border

The Mediterranean coastline – beautiful but abused

Kayaking past another empty plastic bottle looking for a shore to call home

Back in 2009 I wrote an article in the quarterly magazine of my home town, Bundanoon. In it I put forward the idea of our small town of around 2,000 people becoming the first town in the world to stop selling plastic bottles of water. At the time I owned a bike shop and cafe in town. The madness had struck me for a number of years: why would you pay as much as twice the price of petrol for a product that comes essentially free from the tap? It seemed like the ultimate con job, proof that we offer ourselves up as fools to the gods of marketing, gods that overcome common sense. Bottled water is now a massive industry with a global market worth over US$100 billion. It takes 200 ml of oil to produce a one-litre plastic bottle. Then it takes some three litres of water to produce one litre of bottled water. It takes massive amounts of fuel to transport this stuff around a country or, even more insanely, around the world. And a very large proportion of the bottles end up as rubbish spoiling our beaches and seas, our parks and roadsides worldwide. The Mediterranean Sea offers but one sad example.

My article, 'A Town with no Bottle', sparked much interest and the planets aligned to see a group of passionate and talented community members and others come together to take the idea forward; health professionals, graphic designers, business owners and researchers. *Bundy on Tap* was born.

At a town meeting on 8 July 2009, Bundanoon voted 355 to 1 to go "bottled water free" and a worldwide media storm erupted. The story ran across the media worldwide – from the *BBC*, *China Post*, *New York Times*, the *Guardian*, *Le Monde*, *Al Jazeera*, the *Kazakhstan News* and just about every other media outlet in between. *Bundy on Tap* was the number one news story across Australia and over a few days I did more than 200 interviews. We had no idea that the actions of our little town would have such a profound global effect.

In town, water drinkers were provided with conveniently located fountains, and retailers were provided with in-store chilled water dispensers and a supply of re-usable bottles to sell. Contrary to headlines that proclaimed 'Bundanoon Bans Bottle', there was never any ban: rather a voluntary understanding that commerce would support the community in the venture. On 26 September 2009 the last bottles of still bottled water were taken off the retail shelves of Bundanoon and from the fridges of the cafes.

Bundy on Tap would go on to feature in numerous documentaries, as a case study in various books, inclusion in school curriculums and much more. Various awards flowed through, including my being listed as one of Time Magazine's *25 Worldwide Responsibility Pioneers*.

Whilst many towns, universities, schools and others have taken steps to reduce bottled water usage it remains a massive issue worldwide and there is a long, long way to go.

★ ★ ★

I had hoped for an easy couple of hours to Kiato that morning but a vicious force 5–6 headwind was up and I hauled into it at less than 2 km per hour, soaked by the breaking waves. Eventually, when I found the sanctuary of a small harbour on the eastern edge of town, I gave up. Olga went there to meet me and, after we had stored *Miss Grape* at a local sailing club, drove me into town to meet the mayor before we sat down to a sumptuous meal she had prepared.

The following day, 6 June – the 70th anniversary of D-Day – was a week since I'd hobbled my way along that thin blue line into Athens. Now I planned to attempt another marathon: to kayak 100 km from Kiato to the Rion-Antirion bridge at the western entrance of the gulf. I was already tired. My hoped-for rest days in Athens had been far from it as I had worked late into the nights trying to keep up with work issues at home, the continual forward planning for the journey, and more. How was my schedule? Could I find ways to keep up? Indeed I don't think there was one day during *mediterr année* where I truly rested mind and body. Every time I stopped moving there was a list of things to catch up on, always the black cloud of downloading images, chasing the internet.

Olga waved me off at 5 a.m., but when dawn broke and the sun rose, the wind rose with it, full into my face. I hadn't gone two hours when I started to yawn, pulling faces to stay awake. The westerly wind didn't relent all day, and pushing into it meant that in nine hours I'd hardly done half the distance I'd planned. I spun the filigree silver bead Anna and Anders had given me at Sydney Airport for strength. At one point the skies darkened; I thought to just stay where I was, a kilometre or so offshore, but something told me to head in toward the coast. I'm glad I did as within seconds a storm cell had whipped the sea to white and rain absolutely hammered down in gale force winds. I landed on a pebbly beach with nowhere to shelter, waiting for the storm to pass. Then when it did I struggled to stay awake and, blaming a bad case of wind, admitted defeat after 70 km in my own marathon battle.

George Kaltis met me on the beach at Nafpaktos. George, 28, was an international class white-water kayaker who had missed out on competing in the Beijing Olympics due to an administrative error by the Greek Canoeing Federation. For George everything was stupid: stupid federation, stupid man, stupid mountain, stupid day, dog, beer, kayak.

With 45 days of solo paddling behind me, it was nice to have his company the following day, nice to get kayaking photos of something other than the bow of *Miss Grape*. With Marathon Week over, it was back to my own marathon. Kayaker and local resident he might be, but it was the first time George had paddled the coast west of the Gulf, into the Ionian Sea, my final Greek sea. Then I would trend north toward Albania, toward Montenegro, Bosnia, Croatia, to Slovenia and Italy. In the Ionian and the Adriatic the prevailing summer winds are northerlies and I feared they would slow my progress for the final 1,000 km of this paddle section. But early summer had already been turned upside down; rain instead of sun, southerlies not northerlies.

George left me at Missolonghi, near the start of the delta of the Achelous, one of the longest rivers in Greece and the place where Lord Byron had died of fever in 1824. From a kayak you often see things that turn out to be not what you saw: when you get close, large castles turn out to be little sheds, a village tumbling down a hillside turns out to be rocks. These cases of mistaken identity are amplified in flat delta country. At one point I saw a couple on a beach – fishing, I thought. Then as I got closer one sat on the other. There was nothing too unusual in that: as I'd gone along the coast I'd

My first day on the Ionian Sea, near Messolongi, Greece

passed quiet beaches with lovers in embrace and more. I would usually avert my gaze and glide quietly past but would sometimes, if feeling a bit cheeky, shout out a cheery '*kalimera*' (good morning) with a wave and a smile. As I got closer to this couple, the man got up; not off his wife but a chair. Some things were clear though. A small herd of cows, each sat individually under a beach umbrella, all except one who was stood chewing on the umbrella palm fronds. Perhaps an early summer break working on their tan before being tanned?

The point where I finally turned north, Ak Scrofa, overlooked the site of the Battle of Lepanto. Here, in August 1571, a sea battle involving over 500 ships had seen the Ottoman Empire roundly defeated by a Catholic fleet put together by the Vatican. This success was credited with ensuring that the Ottoman Empire would expand no further into Europe.

The delta became cliffs and islands; all great paddling. Hot days, calm seas, squeezing sponge-loads of seawater over my head. While I consumed water, becalmed yachts consumed diesel in the search for wind. The sea sparkled against a backdrop of grey rocky mountains. I had dinner on board a yacht with Canadian couple, Miles and Sarah, sailing for a year in the Med. Sinking a few beers before eating, Miles confessed he realised he needed to cut down his drinking when that day he had the urge to open a can in the supermarket before he reached the checkout. It's one thing to burgle a few grapes or even a plum, but another to arrive sober and leave half-sozzled, holding empty cans at the checkout.

★ ★ ★

An engine woke me up on my first island camp in the Ionian Sea. It was 11.30 p.m. A small boat came close, the engine cut and it drifted into the shallow bay, bumping up onto some rocks a few metres from shore, a few metres from my camp. I climbed out of the tent into the glare of a torchlight beam and shone my own back in retaliation. The fisherman couldn't understand a word I said, I not one of his. He beckoned me to get into his boat. I shone my light onto the kayak, the tent and indicated I was going nowhere. Then he started using his arm in a snaking motion and hissing, using his hand to 'bite' his other arm. He kept repeating this. He kept beckoning. In the end he gave up, shrugged his shoulders, pushed off from the rocks and disappeared back into the night. For all I could work out, he was warning me of snakes on the island. Warning an Australian, home to eight of the top 10 most venomous snakes in the world, about Greece's only poisonous snake, the viper, perhaps? Still I could not be 100 per cent certain and slept fitfully that night.

In my Corinth Canal excitement I had forgotten that Greece had one more canal for me: the Lefkas Canal, separating Lefkada from the mainland. It might have been as long as the Corinth but, cut through swamp country, there was nothing spectacular about it. I briefly touched the left bank of the canal, remembering Lefkada as the island where Wendy and I had had our first holiday together in 1998; my last visit to Greece.

Miss Grape and I were into our final week in Greece. There was no doubt the country had been a very generous and beautiful host over the past seven weeks and 2,000 km, and I had feelings of both melancholy and excitement as I got closer to Albania.

My melancholy though was not just about leaving Greece, nor that perhaps, with summer arriving, holidaymakers were starting to take over 'my' Mediterranean. Friday 13 June, my 50th day out of Gallipoli, was the last day of my 50th year.

I camped that night in a beautiful spot south of Parga, in a white sandy cove ringed by red cliffs. It was reminiscent of the beach in Australia's remote Kimberley where I had celebrated my 40th birthday as I paddled that wild and gorgeous coast. I was missing Wendy and the family but was also a bit upset. Things were not going too well with aspects of my business back home. I wanted to do my bit but also didn't want it to cloud my journey, to bother me. I'd trusted my second-in-command, Danien, and the team enough for me to go away for a year but, as in any small business, it was difficult for the owner to let go. This was even more the case when things were on a downturn. A large chunk of the activity of my business, Wild Horizons, was running mountain bike events, something that we'd done for nearly 20 years. During that time mountain biking and cycling had boomed. But now it seemed that just about every mountain bike event in Australia was on the decline, in part due to the sheer number of events, and we were not immune from the downturn. Financially it was making things a bit difficult.

But my mood was sour more for another reason. I was angry with Wendy. We'd had a couple of narky conversations in the past week and then, on my birthday, she told me her parents were with her, enjoying our newly renovated house. For many this would be no big deal, would be welcomed, but her parents had utterly refused to acknowledge my existence for the past 17 years. Ever since Wendy and I had got together, her parents had blamed me for breaking up her first marriage regardless of how happy she was now. This was tough on Wendy for sure. I'd accepted it on the basis that they were small-minded, ultra-critical people cutting off their noses to spite their faces; the sort of people I didn't need in my life. Wendy had made some rapprochement in recent years, now back visiting her elderly parents in their home. I respected that, it was her mum and dad after all. But they had never been invited to our house and now I was angry it had been done while I was away, and all the more so that she had not discussed it with me.

Wendy argued that it was time to move on, that they were her parents and she had the right to have them in our house. And, in any case, it was me who had buggered off for a year. She had a point, of course. But I still felt badly let down and our physical distance apart did not help the emotional distance.

Out on the water I did my first and only Eskimo roll of the journey. It was poorly executed. I sang 'Happy Birthday' to myself at full volume with only some spectacular rock formations as an audience. I surfed in turquoise water onto a beach for a birthday lunch at a taverna and sat under a eucalyptus. The leaves floated down to the table in the Mediterranean breeze to give an Australian essence to my Greek salad.

I lost a bit of focus that day: didn't know whether to go hard or have an easy day, be with people or alone, to camp or find a room. In the end I flipped and flopped, paddled hard and paddled slow. I reached the town of Igoumenitsa, wheeled *Miss Grape* up the main street and found a room in the Jolly Hotel.

Sagiada was the last Greek village, my last night in Greece. Spirigula, the very friendly and alert female coastguard officer there, recognised clearly the issues with the Greek coastguard. 'We do too much paper and not enough work, too much time in buildings and not on boats,' she told me. I paid homage for the last time to Xerox and paddled off toward Albania, my third country.

Grey skies, strong winds and a choppy sea were there to bid me farewell from Greece. I landed to take shelter and looked across the whitecaps to Albania. Wendy and I had continued a bit of a stand-off in recent days but I wanted to talk to her before I crossed the border, to a place with perhaps more uncertain communications. It was not

a good conversation: both of us standing our ground, me on a windswept pebbly beach, the last in Greece; her in the garden at home, her elderly parents in our house. As we spoke a vicious Rottweiler came from nowhere toward me, snarling only metres away. I'm not great with animals and he'd arrived at far from the best time. I put the phone down and admit to crying in the wind. I was as confused as the sea in front of me, as uncertain as any time I had been on the journey to date. SMS messages came and went as did the bloody dog.

Then Lady Luck obliged, the wind began to drop and I had no excuses. I pushed *Miss Grape* off the pebbles and paddled to Albania. Within minutes I felt strangely energized; a contrast to my moribund feelings only minutes before, and paddled strongly into the chop, into Albania. Things became clearer; I had to let it pass for the imperative of my journey but more importantly for our relationship. In a month or so Wendy was coming over. That's what I needed to look forward to.

The coast was low and rocky, and I was only a few hundred metres into Albania when I came upon the first one; soon after, another; and 100 metres further, a pair. Like daleks crawling down to the sea, Hoxha's mushroom-shaped concrete bunkers were everywhere. There were more bunkers in that first kilometre of Albania than on the Old Course at St Andrews. Just over 20 years ago it would have been near-impossible to enter this country, let alone just float across its border. Offshore sat the large Greek island of Corfu, and looking across to it, I thought back to my trip there in 1982 as a 19-year-old; as I had partied, drinking way too much ouzo and cheap beer, I didn't even realise that just across the water lay this inaccessible dictatorship.

As I kayaked across the delta of the Butrint river, I came across an anchored German yacht. The sole occupant waved me over for a chat. When I asked him why he was flying the Greek courtesy flag he replied that he was in Greece. He was rather surprised when I told him he was in Albania. Most yachts I met give Albania a wide berth, sailing direct from Greece to Montenegro or Croatia, or across the Adriatic to Italy. Their skippers were put off by stories of bureaucracy and entry difficulties, and of course by history.

Albania had me intrigued. The country had been ruled by the self-proclaimed King Zog up until the outbreak of World War II. Zog sounded more like a piece of Ikea furniture than such royalty. (I've often thought that one of the best jobs in the world must be a position on the Ikea naming panel. I imagine, in the six-month darkness of an Arctic winter, they retreat to a cabin complete with a crate or two of vodka. There, as the snow falls and the shots are drunk, the suggestions ring out in the cold air: 'Tockarp!' Perfect for a cupboard perhaps? 'Leirvik!' For that comfy bed?)

After Zog was deposed, communism took over and for over 40 years up until 1992, Albania closed its borders. Ruled with an iron fist by Enver Hoxha, it slowly retreated from the world, alienating firstly its Russian allies then its Chinese friends. The country neither welcomed nor sought contact with the outside world; 700,000 concrete bunkers were built – more than enough for one for every four Albanians. Now the country is open again, visitors are welcome and the economy is finding its way on the international stage after some desperate teething troubles. Many Greeks warned me to be careful and travel quickly, but the travellers I had met who had been there said it was a fine and hospitable country. Understandably the Greeks may have some residual mistrust, having lived with a neighbour whose door was so emphatically shut for so many decades.

I paddled north past headlands and small beaches, some sporting what seemed a measure of Mediterranean progress; the beach bar. I glided past one, Bob Marley taking his rightful and omnipresent place on the speakers. Bars are fast replacing bunkers in Albania. I even came across bunkers that had been converted to bars.

The town of Sarandë was my port of entry. Battalions of beach umbrellas in front of hotels protected this cosmopolitan town. A quarter of a century ago there had been no beach culture whatsoever in Albania; the communist regime would not allow it – except, of course, for holiday homes for their party officials. I paddled into a small harbour and shouted up to some police on a veranda. A reply, in English, was to beach my kayak and bring my passport up. It was a simple process and a warm welcome. I found a hotel for *Miss Grape* and I was soon drinking great Italian coffee on a terrace. Eric and Sonny joined me: he a manager of a Nascar racing team in North Carolina, his wife of Kosovan descent. They were in Albania for a big family gathering and a wedding. It was a beautiful conversation until a big cloud loomed over the table: Armend, the imposing figure of Sonny's father, joined us. He didn't know who I was, where I was from or what my religious interests might be, but straightaway launched into the foulest of anti-semitic invective. The 'fucking J.E.W.S' (he spelt it out each time he said it) were apparently responsible for the cost of university fees in the US through to the global financial crisis and everything in between. He was ugly in presence and word.

By contrast I dined that night with a gentle German couple, from Hamburg, who had braved the uncertainties of bringing their yacht into Albania. As I walked back through Sarandë, three large outdoor screens set up in parks and on the waterfront played silent films to empty audiences. The Sarandë Silent Film Festival was running for four nights. But there was nothing silent about all the bars and cafés, packed to overflowing, people crammed around widescreen televisions. Nothing trumps soccer around the shores of the Mediterranean, and no film festival organiser in their right mind would run up against the 2014 FIFA World Cup.

From Sarandë I headed north-west along a rocky shore broken by occasional beaches. At times conditions were challenging, with rebound from the cliffs causing confused seas. Superb-looking mountain ranges dropped to the turquoise sea. I pushed into a strong headwind for some hours before giving up near Qeparo, beneath Mt Gjivlash. I found an excellent little

Miss Grape and the holidaymakers, Shëngjin, Albania

hotel for 2000 lek (about AU$20) before going for a wander through the villages up in the hills behind. I kept trying to imagine this place – the North Korea of Europe – before communism fell, before contact with the outside was allowed. A couple of old ladies ducked down a laneway before me and I wondered how they had coped with the change. Indeed, even people of my own age would have lived half their life in isolation – and then suddenly, freedom. Is it any wonder that when the gates opened, many Albanians did not know what to do with their freedom, did not have any understanding of its unspoken boundaries? People ran amok, crime flourished, the country became home to Europe's car rebirthing industry. Hundreds of thousands of stolen cars found their way into the country. The Italian mafia moved in to both add to and take advantage of the turmoil and the vacuum. In the mid-nineties various pyramid selling schemes brought the country economically to its knees and civil war ensued, brought to a halt eventually by a UN force. Around a million people, nearly a third of the population, fled Albania to Italy, Greece, Germany and beyond.

I walked back to the beach past a fence woven with an intriguing collection: a plastic model of King Kong, two handguns, a couple of vehicle hubcaps, a hand grenade, ammunition belt and a bearing race.

After a restless night wondering about Wendy and worrying about landing options on the Karaburun peninsula, I was away by 8 a.m. in calm conditions. My road map of Albania, at a scale of 1:350,000, told me little. Once I was past the blinding white sand beaches of Dhermi there was 50 km or so around a peninsula that, for the whole period of communism, had been locked away from the people. Like many of the best parts of Albania it had been reserved for the military, which had, strangely, given it some environmental protection. The Karaburun was a place of cliff and cave that I hoped would offer at least a couple of landing spots if the weather changed for the worse.

The wind stayed low and it was spectacular sea kayaking. I looked to my left to see a small warship offshore but thought nothing of it. After some hours I came to Plazhi i Gomes, a tiny horseshoe-shaped cove hidden by a narrow channel through cliffs. I paddled in through the entrance and was surprised to see a number of tents on the small beach and some RIBs, Rigid Inflatable Boats, pulled up. I almost didn't go any further, slightly disappointed my quiet bit of coast had been burgled, but I was keen to stretch my legs. Once fully inside the opening, I was further surprised to see a couple of powerful police patrol boats. An officer shouted something across to me and I kayaked closer. The only things I understood were the words American Ambassador and a waving of hands. I ignored the latter and landed on the beach by one of the RIBs.

'G'day Australian, you're very welcome,' drawled an American, having spied my New Zealand flag. It turned out I'd gatecrashed an R&R weekend for the staff from the US Embassy in Tirana, Albania's capital. I introduced myself as the Australian Ambassador for the Mediterranean and spent an hour or so chatting with the Americans and enjoying my first US Military ration pack. This included the obligatory M&Ms and a sachet of peanut butter and the non-obligatory but very welcome addition of a can of Albanian beer.

After I moved on from the party, the Karaburun continued to deliver what was probably the most spectacular and most remote bit of coast I'd yet seen. Tiny entrances led to deep, narrow coves and into huge sea caves. After 60 km for the day, as the sun dipped low toward the horizon, I turned into a little cove to camp. The following morning I continued around the nose of the peninsula and into the largest sea cave I'd ever paddled into; at least 100 metres across and 50 metres high. I sat for nearly an hour on a rock in the middle of the cave, in awe.

Earlier that morning I'd seen a yacht sail down the peninsula, a couple of kilometres offshore. I was keen to get a weather forecast, so tried them on my VHF radio. 'Yacht off Karaburun peninsula, yacht off Karaburun peninsula; this is Australian sea kayaker Huw Kingston,' I called.

'Australian sea kayaker; this is Australian yacht *Solero*, Australian yacht *Solero*.' It was hard to believe: the first time I'd had any response to a radio call since Turkey and it was some fellow Aussies, from Newcastle in New South Wales.

I wanted to make a beeline 15km straight across a gulf, to bypass the city of *Vlorë*, but the wind was putting up a very nasty sea. As was now my pattern in the Med, I pulled *Miss Grape* onto a beach in the middle of the day to wait for the wind to drop, which it often did by late afternoon or early evening. The beach was steep and rocky and I fell asleep in the shade of an overhang. Suddenly I was woken by a clatter of stones and a big splash. *Miss Grape* had made a run for it and had slid down the beach into the sea, all hatches open. I dived into the water and swam after her. The wind was pushing her further out but eventually I grabbed hold of the kayak. I thought to climb in but realised my paddle was back on the shore. Slowly I swam her back to the beach. It was the only time on the journey *Miss Grape* tried to escape. Finally I judged the sea safe enough for the crossing. I left the peninsula behind and landed on the far side just as darkness fell.

The coastline, the delta country of the Vjosë river, was now flat and featureless. Along the 20 km of beach before the river mouth, the amount of plastic in the water and lining the shore was depressing. Albanians were swimming amongst it. Didn't it bother them? But I was more focussed on a 'now you see it now you don't' phenomenon up ahead. In the distance I saw what I assumed to be the roof of a beach bar, a green canvas sail type structure, quite common in the Med. Then a few minutes later, when I looked up again, I couldn't see it. This went on for nearly an hour. There it was. There it wasn't. How could it be I wondered? Was I suffering in the heat? Was there some weird perspective at play?

As I got closer to the stubby headland holding the main river channel the mystery of the disappearing bar roof was solved. Every 15 minutes or so a huge green fishing net held by thin timber poles would rise above the land in front of me. Then, a few minutes later it disappeared from view, dropped into the river waters behind the spit of land. The age-old method of pole fishing. I laughed at myself as I paddled across the river mouth and looked down the channel to see it all working together: a complex system of poles, pulleys, rope and netting.

I was now in the Adriatic Sea proper, and camped fittingly at Adriatika, a ramshackle collection of plastic-sheeted, bamboo-poled beach buildings in front of a mosquito-infested swamp. It was 23 June, the ninth birthday of Anna, my eldest grandchild. I rang her to sing 'Happy Birthday', realising just how much I missed them all.

Near Spille a few Muslim families were enjoying some beach time; some of the women dressed in the full burka. Albania had been 70 per cent Muslim before communism banned religion, and now perhaps people were freer to express their beliefs again. I rounded Kepi i Lagit into the big bay that held Durrës, Albania's second city and most important port. Within minutes the sea was a mass of whitecaps from a wind that had suddenly sprung up. Fortunately the wind was from the south, behind me, and I surfed the short, sharp waves toward the built-up waterfront.

The winds of chance again worked well for me. Realising there was little option to camp south of the main city, I landed in front of some hotels in the suburb of Mali i Robit, the 'mountain of the man.' From the water I'd seen a hotel with big letters spelling out what I thought was Hotel Papa. As 'Papa' was what my grandkids called me, it seemed as good a place as any to stay. But as I came in to land on the beach I realised it actually said Hotel Fafa. The surf-in had *Miss Grape* almost land on some sun loungers, and a few older Albanian gents moved quickly. We talked for a while and they called for Rajmonda, the owner of the smaller Hotel Dea next door, who was soon followed by Bjorka, her daughter. Bjorka, a law student in Tirana, had perfect English and soon had me fixed up with a room.

Rajmonda and Bjorka joined me at a spectacular dinner that night. Over a beautifully presented rocket, walnut and crumbed cheese salad, seafood risotto and smooth Albanian red wine, Rajmonda, with Bjorka translating, explained how the hotel, named after the Albanian goddess of beauty, had been the first to open on the strip 15 years ago. She and her husband had a love for food, particularly Italian food. He and their son were currently away in Italy, sourcing produce. The Italian influence in Albania was very strong. Before communism the Italians had colonised the country, and after communism fell Albania turned to Italy for many things: coffee, food, mafia…

Bjorka, 20, was a highly intelligent young lady with a perception well beyond her years. When communism fell many Albanians were lost, she told me. They went out into the world but found that freedom was not in any sense perfection, and poverty existed everywhere. They didn't know how to behave – some turning to crime, others to building a new democratic nation. She was proud of her country and was keen to enter politics but aware of its corrupting influence.

'Albanian people thought only of surviving, not living, before the fall of communism,' said Rajmonda. 'But the good side of communism was that there was fresh produce, power and drinking water. Now in some ways it is harder; the factories have closed, the farms are now non-productive and corruption is everywhere.'

Bjorka organised her class at university to donate their coffee money to buying bedding for a Tirana orphanage. They actually bought the bedding directly, not trusting to give money. Not for the first time I heard that in Albania you often had to pay €5,000 or more to a middleman to secure a job. I loved Rajmonda and Bjorka's passion for everything despite the challenges they faced.

★ ★ ★

It was a grey, rainy day when I said farewell to Rajmonda and Bjorka and cut across in front of *Durrës*. A big swell was running and the waters off the port entry were confused. The port authorities radioed me to come into the port to visit but I declined, knowing

These bunkers weren't in the sea when Albania's communist dictator
Enver Hoxa had built them. Rising sea levels perhaps?

that most ports had nowhere for a kayak to land; kayakers need beaches, not high walls
and jetties. Some decent waves were breaking as I picked my way north and around
Kepi i Pallas. Bunkers of all shapes and sizes were along the coast and on the north
side of the cape a small harbour containing an old warship was backed by tunnels
leading under the cliffs. It was one of a number of such underground entries I saw;
hidden bases, perhaps, for small boats and submarines during Hoxha's paranoid reign.
Interestingly quite a number of the small mushroom bunkers I passed along the coast
were now actually in the water when they would have been built above it. I wondered
if this perhaps was a result of rising sea levels: I could think of no other reason.

The weather remained unsettled as I made my way up the Albanian coastline; foul
winds would rise and then just as rapidly fall. At the tip of the Cape of Rodon, I surfed a
little sandy bar, pretending I was racing a yacht I'd seen running parallel to me offshore.
It beat me, and I found it, the *Pela*, anchored on the north side of the cape off another
crumbling military installation of stone jetties, gun emplacements and bunkers in the
cliffs. One of the bunkers had been converted into a remote restaurant. I joined the
yacht's crew, Swedes Ray, Marie, Joahann and Anneka, for a bunker lunch. The front
10 metres or so of the bunker was the restaurant, but it went back a further 25 metres
into the cliff before a wooden doorway blocked further exploration. 'Through there
is 20km of tunnel,' the restaurant owner told us. After a long lunch of fresh fish, we
walked the short distance across to a lovely grassy clearing that held a beautiful old
church. It had been restored in 2001 by the Germans and stood in such contrast to the
military paraphernalia.

I was reaching the end of my near 400-km traverse of the Albanian coast. Amidst
rapid and sometimes rapacious development, the people were overwhelmingly friendly
and the coffee perfect. Nowhere was this development more apparent than in Shëngjin,
the last real town before Montenegro. Where 20 years ago there had been nothing

but a military harbour, there was now an ugly strip of hotels and apartment blocks lining the beach, a beach itself that was unappealing. The sound of bulldozers hid the laughing of Kosovan and Serbian beachgoers, the beat of jackhammers drowned that of the beach bars.

Miss Grape nudged into the harbour and we glided past the rusting hulks of Soviet-era torpedo boats, minesweepers and a destroyer. Their war paint had run and was now streaked with as much rust brown as battleship grey. Everything was rusted in that harbour. Everything bar *Pela* with my Swedish friends aboard. Their gleaming yacht was moored incongruously next to some very tired-looking, reflagged coasters with their previous Scandinavian names – *Bergstrom* and *Lilleham* – painted over. The Swedes were waiting for clearance to leave Albania, and had spent the night bobbing in the oily water, being mauled by mosquitoes.

A policeman waved me over and soon I too was bobbing around in filthy, oily water, looked down upon by a dozen very puzzled police officers. They were trying to decide if the kayak was called Paddy Pallin, Save the Children or Anzac, depending on which sticker they were looking at. *Miss Grape* was, I'm sure, the first sea kayak they'd ever seen, and they looked unbelieving when I told them where I had come from. The rotund and very friendly harbourmaster implored me to tie up and come with him to his office. However I figured the clearance process might be quicker if I feigned an inability to climb up onto the jetty and stayed in *Miss Grape*. I passed my passport up to one of the police officers now lying on the jetty reaching down to me. When he stood up, my passport in hand, he tried to brush the rust stains from his white shirt. The harbourmaster and all but one of the police disappeared with my passport, returning half an hour or so later to present me with a special clearance paper for my 'ship'.

Whilst I had official permission to leave Albania and should have done so that day, the weather gods had other ideas. Now a very wild nor'wester was blowing. I sheltered for hours by an old military establishment, now mostly covered over by a modern hotel. The juxtaposition of the two was intriguing: beach umbrellas and sun loungers marching across what was formerly a parade ground; a dozen young boys diving into a deep channel leading to a tunnel with massive doors holding back its secrets. Finally, around 6 p.m. a thunderstorm sent people and umbrellas scuttling – and then all was calm and clear, so I set off, passing the largest sand dunes I'd yet seen, and continued until dark.

★   ★   ★

'Here, speak to my brother in Detroit,' said Alfred. This was not the first time I'd been handed a mobile to speak to a relative in some far-flung place. The Albanian diaspora was responsible for funding much of the recent development. Beach bars, hotels, restaurants were often owned by Albanians in Canada, the US and Germany, and run by family members. Detroit-based Anton welcomed me to his bar in Albania and invited me to camp there for my last night in this country. I pitched my tent next to the bar whilst great pizzas came out of the oven and ice-cold beers from the fridge. Alfred would take nothing for it. I had mixed feelings about the generosity that marked my journey. So many people wanted to help me, were inspired by my journey. But so many of these people throughout Greece and Albania also told me of the economic woes. Much of me wanted to contribute to the economy but to refuse the hospitality or to thrust money their way was, I had learned so often, to offer insult.

If Alfred and friends had provided a very human send-off, Albania itself ensured I wouldn't forget my last night there. A violent katabatic wind got up during the night and smashed down from the mountains, so my tent was lifted up on more than one occasion. But it was the sandblasting that I'd remember most. The mesh inner tent acted only to sieve the finest dust upon me and I was covered; ears, eyes, nose all full of sand. Around 2 a.m. I wrestled the tent onto the veranda of the bar for meagre protection.

With hardly a wink of sleep behind me, I packed to leave on a still -windy day. Pjeter Logoreci and his young daughter Mara came along the beach. He had left his village nearby 18 years earlier, as a refugee to Austria, and he now worked for the UNHCR as an advocate for the resettlement of the refugees from Syria.

Pjeter claimed that much of funding for the building boom in Albania came from money laundering by the Italian mafia. I had heard this a number of times as I travelled up the Albanian coast. When I asked him for an estimate of what percentage of the economy was honest and what corrupt he threw the figure 30/70 at me. Whilst he tried to bring his family back to Albania each year, Pjeter had little optimism for the country of his birth.

As I bounced my way toward the mouth of the Bune river, which formed the border between Albania and Montenegro, a RIB headed toward me at speed. When it got close I could see 'Police' written on its side. They refused to let me paddle on. I handed across my passport and customs clearance from Shëngjin. A few phone calls later and I was free to go.

Once I was across the wide and deep green river mouth, the first couple of kilometres in Montenegro were along a long, lonely beach. Then I spied my first naked body, sheltered from sun, sand and wind behind a shade tent. Then a naked couple strolled up the beach toward me. We all waved as we passed in opposite directions. The deeper I went into Montenegro the more naked people there were; I began to wonder whether when communism fell, clothing had fallen with it.

It was getting harder and harder to make progress into the sea with waves breaking regularly over me. Up ahead more pink and brown beach life came into focus, as did my first building in Montenegro. It was time for morning coffee. I picked a line carefully in the dumping surf and landed next to a blonde-haired lady lolling at the junction of sand and surf. Maria was from Serbia, a journalist on parenting in Belgrade, and naked as the day she'd been born.

Clothed and over coffee, Maria assured me that this was one of the few nudist beaches in Montenegro. When I came to pay I discovered that whilst Montenegro was not in the EU, the euro was its currency. How did that work? I sat all afternoon with Maria and her naked friends, waiting, waiting for the wind to drop.

The wind, generally most prevalent in the afternoon, was becoming a frustrating factor in my schedule. So many times I'd need to sit it out, wait impatiently. So many

End of another day, time to camp, Karaburun Peninsula, Albania

Miss Grape appears as a ship of the desert on this beach in Montenegro

times the wind would die away in the early evening, allowing me to paddle to sunset and beyond. Those last few hours were often the most invigorating; evening light on the cliffs and sand, a darkening of the sea, fish jumping. I realised I was spending too much of my time being disappointed in progress, so needed to get into my head that what would be would be. That I would miss places, be delayed by weather. I needed to be more accepting, to push and push but also to accept the need to go with the flow.

Montenegro, the smallest of the Balkan republics, became a country in its own right only in 2006 when it split with Serbia. It has a coastline of only 120 km, so my visit would be a brief one. The summer season was really kicking in now. Humans basked like seals along the rocky shore – indeed some looking alarmingly like seals. Much of the coast was still relatively untouched but an equal amount was scarred by extensive, often insensitive, hotel development.

I remained an illegal immigrant for a couple of days until I reached the well-named port town of Bar. En route I kayaked past a dive boat called *Down Under*. Not only was this a great name for a dive boat but Goran, the owner, told me that the year he had spent in Australia in 1987 still ranked as the best year of his life, hence the naming of his boat after the land down under. I was ready for a drink after too long being grilled by the customs officers as to why I'd been in Montenegro for two days before checking in with them (answer – I can only paddle so far in a day. I have no motor). I spied a sign for the Ferry Terminal Bar but couldn't find it and had the same problem with the Bus Station Bar. Then it hit me; there should have been a comma before the word Bar on the signs.

That night I arrived just on dark on a mirror-calm sea to a rocky beach beyond Sutomore. Here, tucked on a rock shelf above the beach was a real bar. The night watchman, Goran from Belgrade, pulled out a couple of beers and we chatted for some hours. He explained the animosity still between Serbs and Croats: 'If I go there for a holiday now, we fight. We have always fought.' Although Albania had dealt alone with its transition in the early nineties, the rest of the Balkans had fought a series of the most vicious of wars. Nearly a quarter of a century later, travelling the length of the former Yugoslavia, I would hear plenty of comments and tales as to how the sores of that time had not healed. Perhaps they never would.

Up until now on my journey, wild seas had always been accompanied by strong winds. But I was woken the following morning with dumping waves but no wind. Soon the waves built up, and deckchairs and umbrellas were being washed into the sea in front of my tent. This began a day where many beaches facing south received a lot of damage from powerful waves – single waves, not sets – smashing onto beaches with some force. I stayed put, knowing that to go was to risk *Miss Grape* being severely damaged heading out or attempting to come back in.

JULY

It's July and I have hope in who I am becoming.

Charlotte Eriksson

The first day of July was my last full day in Montenegro. A large group of Russians saw me off the rocky beach and I dodged a few sun loungers out at sea. It was a beautiful stretch of coastline north but I was keen to make good progress and stayed well offshore, bypassing Petrovac and Budva. Beyond Budva and around Cape

Platamuni it got even better along a cliff-lined coast, where only one small rocky cove offered a marginal camp. On the rocks sat a young woman and her two babies. She was from Budva and had an Australian passport but had never been there. She told me her husband was fishing off the cliffs. The tranquillity of the place was ruined when he and a friend returned. Dressed in army fatigues, they ran around gesticulating and shouting. Testosterone was practically oozing into the air. Then one of them, the friend, dived into the bay and dragged out a huge net bag bulging with dozens of fish. He brought it over to me, pride in his face, pulled out a couple of large fish and offered them to me. 'Good fishing, huh?' he almost snarled. 'Boom! Boom!' he followed up, throwing the fish into the air. Their haul had come about not by the cunning of the hunter with hook or speargun but by the chaos of dynamite. I didn't need to dine on fish caught in such a way. What chance does the Mediterranean have? It is loved but not respected, used but not looked after.

Montenegro saw me off with some excellent sea cave exploration before a crossing of the entrance to the fiord-like Kotor, to find myself in country number five. After six hours' paddling I came to the first village in Croatia: Molunat. A natural harbour dotted with rocks and boats backed by a couple of bars and some houses. It was a good introduction to what would turn out to be the country with the prettiest of all the Mediterranean built environments. A large police boat was moored on the jetty. I considered whether to say anything about my arrival in Croatia. Perhaps I shouldn't have…

Pasjaca beach, my first camp in Croatia, and as an illegal immigrant

Me: Hello. I've kayaked in from Montenegro. Do you want to see my
    passport?

Him: No. You must go to Cavtat for immigration.

Me: OK, I'll go there and will hopefully reach there tomorrow.

Him: No. No. NO! You go now, you go today.

Me: But I don't have a motor, only arms.

Him: That is not important. You go today. TODAY!

Having learnt from my own mistake, I shrugged my shoulders and said that of course I would go there today.

I had no decent map of Croatia and no idea of the nature of the coast north to Cavtat, some 35 km away. A young waiter in one of the bars reckoned it was all cliff, apart from perhaps one, maybe two, small beaches. It was 4 p.m. when I left Molunat, wondering if my police friend had contacted his colleagues in Cavtat, a place I had no intention or indeed chance of reaching that night. The waiter was right; for over two hours I followed vertical red cliffs, their colour accentuated by the low sun. I followed them to a narrow strip of sand with a spectacular track cut through the cliffs behind it. If Montenegro had surprised me with its initial nakedness, the Croatian surprise was cross-dressing: on the sand was a small group of young people surrounding a boy dancing in a bra and bikini briefs. I landed *Miss Grape* by them and joined Danko's 27th birthday party. Before they left me to camp in this beautiful spot alone, they welcomed me to Croatia with a smooth pebble painted with the place and date: Pasjaca, Croatia, 2/7/14.

★ ★ ★

'I arrived by kayak from Montenegro.' I told the surly-looking border policeman in Cavtat, a rather pleasant town, south of the famous walled city of Dubrovnik.

'You can't arrive by kayak,' he responded.

'But I did. Look, I'm here and look out the window; that's my kayak over there.'

'It is not possible; it is not allowed. You can't,' before then making a number of phone calls. Then he got back to the questioning. 'Where is your boat made?'

'In England.'

'Did you sail from England? Where in England?'

'No I kayaked from Turkey. The kayak is from Penrith.'

'Where is Penrith? I don't know Penrith. I write London on the form. Where are you from?'

'Well, I live in Australia.'

'Did you sail your boat from Australia?'

'No, I kayaked from Turkey,' I repeated.

Then finally, after more inane – or despairing – questions the officer threw my passport back toward me. 'You can't ever come here again by kayak, you understand? You must never come to Croatia again in that ship.'

Very strong winds held me in Cavtat for the rest of the day, and it was dark when I left to paddle across the bay to find somewhere quiet to camp. Landing on a small beach, I wandered up to a shack above where a light was shining. I thought it best to ask if I could camp. I opened the door of the shack to find a huge table groaning under the weight of food, the centrepiece being a large ray that was half devoured. I was beckoned to the table and was soon enjoying a late dinner and too much wine with a bunch of Hungarian doctors on a dive holiday.

They were keen for me to join them diving but I needed to make progress, to try and keep to some sort of schedule. The wind was frustrating me at times, but there was nothing to be done but wait for windows of opportunity to go hard. The following morning it was up early again, and into hugely strong gusts that on a couple of occasions ripped the paddle from my hands. I ground into it, making very slow progress and staying as close to the shore as possible to reduce the fetch. As I inched my way onto the north side of the bay, a few multi-storey grey buildings came into view. At first I thought they were unfinished projects. So often on the Mediterranean shores I'd come across half-built projects; hotels and apartment blocks, where the money had obviously run out and all that was left was a useless scar on the landscape, a use of resources for no use.

Sick of battling the wind I took shelter in the sandy bay of Kupari beneath the buildings. Three men in their seventies were tanning already leathery hides. One was Josip Ljutic who told me about the buildings: they were holiday hotels built for the elite of the Yugoslav army, mainly Bosnian Serbs, but had been bombed during the war in 1991 and had been derelict ever since. As he spoke I looked up at the hotels and could see all the damage, the concrete peppered with holes from the naval bombardment.

But Josip Ljutic had a much more personal story to tell me. In an attempt to escape communism he and three other Croatians had left from this same beach in a tiny boat in the early hours of 27 September 1960. Foul weather made them turn back some hours later. A week later they tried again on a moonless night and this time the conditions allowed them to get away from the coast, only to run out of fuel. On their second night they signalled to an oil tanker which to their initial horror turned out to be Russian. However the captain was no communist sympathiser and took them on board and on to the Italian port of Ancona. From here Josip spent 18 months in a series of refugee camps around Italy before the USA accepted him. He lived in New York for 25 years, working as a painter and decorator. After communism fell Josip returned to Croatia in 1999 and, whilst happy to be home, was damning of the corruption in modern Croatia, claiming that many of today's leaders were just the sons of yesterday's communist leaders.

Looking out across the Adriatic that Josip had crossed 52 years ago, I could see the whitecaps had died off during the hour I had been speaking with him. As I slid into the kayak he handed me 200 kuna (€30) for Save the Children, saying, 'I was a refugee; this is to help other refugees. It is a terrible time on the Mediterranean.'

I paddled north toward Dubrovnik, reaching this magnificent walled city an hour or so later. As I threaded *Miss Grape* through the tourist boats I felt chuffed to be arriving there by kayak, coming into the medieval port. So much of me wanted to view this site, to spend a couple of days there. But I didn't have the time, and the last thing I wanted to do was run around just to say, 'I've seen Dubrovnik.' It would have to wait for another time.

In one of the rocky bays around the city, some guys at a canoe hire business shouted me in. They insisted on giving me lunch and were even more insistent on checking out the svelte lines of *Miss Grape*. One thing that had been notable about my journey to date was the lack of fellow kayakers. In fact, apart from a couple of people messing about on sit-on-top kayaks, a few hire businesses and the good folk at the Surfers for Life Festival near Athens, I had yet to meet any sea kayakers at all – any paddlers on the sea using a kayak as a means of travel.

Beyond Dubrovnik I hopped between the Elephantine Islands, and at dusk slipped through the narrow gap separating the islands of Šipan and Jakljan. With darkness falling I hoped to find somewhere to camp amongst the rocks. With nothing suitable I pushed on to a large bay and was surprised to see the lights of a couple of anchored superyachts encircled, as if with cleaner fish, by a few small yachts. At the back of the bay, in the gloom, I picked out some buildings. *Miss Grape's* bow bumped onto a crumbling concrete promenade. I hopped out into shallow water to see the buildings were derelict; it was an old overgrown hotel complex that would do for my accommodation that night.

As I started to unpack *Miss Grape*, piling drybags onto the promenade, I looked out into the bay and saw shadows moving across the water. The shadows and laughter came closer... finally, on my 70th day, a group of sea kayakers. Four Irish lasses – Orla, Joanna, Karen and Suzanne – nearing the end of a 12-day paddle from Zadar to Dubrovnik. Our bumping into each other coincided with Suzanne's birthday. That night the craic in Croatia was alive and well.

There were shades of the Athos peninsula the following day when I put the wheels on *Miss Grape* and pulled her 2 km across the narrow neck of land separating the walled villages of Ston and Mali Ston. This saved a three-day paddle around the Pelješac peninsula, but more importantly allowed me to access the coastline, all 8 km of it, of Bosnia and Herzegovina, my fourth country in a week.

In Yugoslavian times, Marshal Tito had given this tiny bit of coastline to Bosnia, a coastline bordered on both sides by Croatia. But as I kayaked along the rough, rocky shore there were no beaches or buildings – no port of any sort – and no indication that I was moving between countries save for a border post on the road high above. What there was were endless numbers of long branches jammed into rocks with plastic bottles or shoes hung off their ends, the purpose of which eluded me. I did see one small boat with four bare-chested young lads which I took to be the Bosnian navy.

I arrived back in Croatia, passing the huge pylon of an abandoned bridge construction. Five years previously, Croatia had commenced building this link from Komarna to the Pelješac peninsula. Currently anyone driving to Dubrovnik and the southernmost strip of Croatia must pass into and out of a few kilometres of Bosnia and Herzegovina, with attendant entry/exit formalities. The bridge would have bypassed this issue, but Croatia had run out of money to finish the project. Now, as a recent member of the EU, Croatia hopes for some European funding to complete the bridge.

Around the corner from the pylon was the small settlement of Komarna, tumbling down toward the green waters. I was only metres offshore when a big cheer went up from the only bar, with: 'You need a beer?' the time-honoured call to a thirsty kayaker late in the day. It was time to stop and celebrate my two countries in one day. Within minutes the good people of Komarna had provided beer, pizza, a 'Welcome to Komarna' T-shirt, a Komarna coffee mug and an apartment for the night.

The leader of my welcome party was Mirko, whose friendly nature was framed by a sour outlook, contrasting with his job as perfume salesman. It was made clear to me that Croats didn't like Bosnians, primarily Muslims, but loved Herzegovinans, primarily Catholics like the Croats. In fact they insisted that Bosnia and Herzegovina was really Herzeg Bosnia. Mirko, himself originally from Herzegovina, told me: 'The Croatians hate everybody,' adding 'We

An apartment for the night, pizza, beer, t-shirts, mugs. Just some of the things the locals of Komarna showered on me when I landed on their beach

are friendly but if we don't like someone then we are twice as good at being unfriendly.' I was being welcomed everywhere I went in the Balkans, but I sensed deep mistrust and centuries-old animosities never far from the surface.

The following day, a Sunday, half the population seemed to be out on the water in little half-cabin cruisers. Just on lunchtime one boat hailed me and I paddled over to where it was anchored. Lunch was served as I bobbed about at their stern. Saying thanks and farewell I paddled on, but within minutes had another boat tooting and hollering as it motored up to me. As one man guided the boat to me, the other hung over the side proffering a glass of cold beer. It would have been rude not to accept. Service was a little slow for dessert but eventually, after an hour or so, another small boat called by to pass some homemade biscuits, cake and coffee across the water. My Sunday lunch was complete without even getting out of *Miss Grape*.

In the first months of my journey the Mediterranean coastline had not yet woken from its winter slumbers. Most hotels were closed, all beach umbrellas likewise. As time progressed it was interesting to see the human tide of summer slowly engulf the sea, and by July the Mediterranean was in high spirits. It belonged to the sun seekers and kids diving off harbour walls; to the yachts and inflatable beach toys. *Miss Grape* even struggled on occasions to find a parking spot on a beach. On occasions, when we landed, it might have been as if the aliens had arrived.

But Croatia was a sea kayaking paradise of endless islands, peninsulas and inlets. It was generally the least overdeveloped of the countries I'd passed through so far. The villages were prettier and the holiday accommodation mostly low-rise, not high. What Croatia did lack was sand, though, the vast majority of the coast being rocky. This had the advantage of making it hard for battalions of beach umbrellas to invade, as they could not penetrate the rock – but it did play havoc with *Miss Grape's* bottom, dragged as she was up rock and pebbles a few times a day.

My plan had been to head across to the large island of Hvar thence across to Brač, but a forecast for some very strong southerly winds had me change to continue on up the mainland to Makarska. From there I could hop the 10 **km** across to the north coast of Brač, where I'd be away from the wind when it arrived. At Makarska another big cheer went up, this time from a bunch of backpacking Kiwis who'd spied my flag.

I made it across to Brač just before the wind hit, and celebrated with dinner in a hidden restaurant far up a sheltered inlet with a dozen lederhosen-clad Austrian yachtsmen. They were from two villages near Salzburg and the friendly banter of centuries of rivalry came out as the wine flowed and the songs got bawdier. One of the group, Chris, a New Yorker, had married into one of the villages and lived in the other. He was an easy target for both.

I've spoken little about the discomforts and challenges of paddling day in, day out for 8–10 hours a day. The rashes and wrenches, the effects of salt and sun, pushing on when you might want to laze on the beach. Since the start of my journey, apart from the two days in Athens I'd not stopped anywhere for more than a day. My body was holding up OK, although it was interesting that whenever I did stop, my back would start to pain me, stiffen up. It was almost as if it was telling me to keep pushing on and I began to seriously wonder, not for the first time, if that was my future. Over decades it had been at its most annoying when sitting at a desk, hunched over a laptop.

A T-shirt I was soon to be given said 'Never too much of Brač and I was to be on this island of rock walls and olive groves for over two weeks; a real knees-up in Croatia. A little pain on the left knee had started the night I arrived on Brač. It felt like an insect bite gone septic; a bit of throbbing, a little itching. But I could find nothing on the surface. I wrote in my diary 'Now into the last 10 days or so of this kayak stage' and immediately regretted the tempting of fate. I should have indeed: on my second morning on Brač, I woke in the tent and struggled to get out of my sleeping bag, struggled to move or bend my left leg. The knee was huge, perhaps twice its normal size, hot to touch. It took me an age to pack up and load *Miss Grape*. Straight-legged, I eventually climbed into the cockpit and pushed off. Only a few kilometres away was the village of Sutivan, where perhaps I'd find a doctor.

Sutivan has to be one of the prettiest Mediterranean villages I've ever seen. A gorgeous little harbour surrounded by old stone buildings, a dominating church and a couple of tiny, narrow pebbly beaches either side of the harbour. It had half a dozen bars but no doctor; the only one on Brač was back at Supetar, a town I'd passed the previous day. I sat on a coffee for ages, deciding what to do. I hated the idea of going back; surely the knee would settle down. I decided, with little conviction, to push on and paddle across to Šolta, the next island. I limped back to *Miss Grape* and sat next to her on the pebbles, deliberating some more.

'Nice kayak,' said a bloke looking down from the sea wall above us. 'Where you paddling to?' I told him where I wanted to go but also explained my predicament. 'Right, let's lift your kayak up here and I'll drive you to the doctor in Supetar.' Ivo Ljubeka ran a mountain bike, kayak and rock climbing business on Brač, based in Sutivan. This proud son of Brač, with a warm smile and a twinkling eye, took me to the medical centre.

It was not my plan to visit the city of Split on the mainland and if I should have to, then not to spend time in a little-loved attraction, Split Hospital. But the doctor on Brač insisted I go there, worried about a thrombosis (of the *knee?*). Ivo took me down to the port and I was soon on the hour-long ferry ride to Split. After six hours and all manner of tests and scans, the consultant proclaimed a case of bursitis, and prescribed rest, ice and antibiotics. I told him the last two were possible but that the idea of resting was unlikely, at least not for long. I was already behind schedule and needed to push on, to get to the Alps; the trek through the mountains I expected to take some three months, and I needed to complete it before winter hit. And, more importantly, Wendy was heading over in a few weeks, the first and last time I'd see her in the year. Our plan was to have some days together at the end of the kayaking and before I started trekking. It was a deadline too important to miss.

Bursitis is more commonly known as housemaid's knee, a throwback to women scrubbing floors where the regular pressure on the knees inflamed the bursa, little fluid-filled sacks. In more modern times it is common in carpet layers and plumbers or anyone who spends too much time down on their knees. So how the hell did I have it? I could only put it down to the upward pressure of my knees bracing against the inside of the cockpit and the thousand upon thousand tiny rubbing movements over the past months.

When I was back on Brač, Ivo and his lovely wife Eti made me very welcome in the harbourside home that doubled as the base for their business. People, staff and customers, came and went, hiring bikes or heading out on canoe or climbing trips. If I was to be stuck somewhere then it could be far worse than such a beautiful place as Sutivan, with such a beautiful family as the Ljubekas. Theirs was a business not dissimilar to my own back in Australia. I liked their approach and we compared and consoled each other with remarkably similar stories about battles with bureaucracy in our desire to give people adventures. I loved the name of the adventure festival they ran on Brač each year: *Vanka Regule* (No Rules).

My original plan was to rest up for three or four days at the outside and then push on. I sat around with my leg up, ice pack on, mixing my time between the house, office and one of the half-dozen cafes around the harbour. It was good to catch up on a backlog of emails and more, and even better to observe the village life, both locals and holidaymakers.

A cousin of Ivo's, an orthopaedic surgeon from Zagreb, was one of the latter. He gave a second opinion on my knee and made it very clear that unless I gave it enough time, two weeks or possibly more, then it could get worse, go septic and then require an operation. I had no choice but to stay put, not wanting to jeopardise the whole of my journey.

There was a long way to go on this journey, and in reality fair winds had been with me in spades since I had left Turkey. Rough weather was to be expected, too.

My knee seemed to be slowly getting better but was still troubling. Every day that ticked past, as pleasurable as it was, was starting to bother me. The *Vanka Regule* festival was only days away, and whilst it would be great to be there I hoped not to be.

Daniel Lasko arrived on Brač to help at the festival; he is an adventure journalist with a fine sense of humour. In 2011 he had set out to create the 'Biggest Welcome in the World' and, over 45 days, kayaked, walked and rode the length of Croatia spelling out the word 'WELCOME' with a GPS track, turning it on only at well-choreographed moments to write the word across Google Maps. I thought it an excellent idea and how good it could be to write 'Climate Change is Real' across Australia.

The past weeks on Brač had been the slowest of my life in recent years, and offered me a chance to observe. Sutivan was like my Hotel California; I'd arrived but I couldn't leave. And despite the undoubted beauty of the island, my endeavours to rest my errant knee ensured I did not explore it, but observed just the village of Sutivan. Innumerable coffees were drunk at each of the six bars. Meals were taken multiple times at each restaurant, and soaks in the Med occurred at both beaches.

I observed a lot of sun, some wind and on one day, a cracking good thunderstorm that shook buildings and turned cobbled streets into white-water rivers. My thoughts wandered ...

> Every morning a blonde, long-haired, long-legged Englishwoman left her apartment set back from the small pebbly beach. On the wall above the beach she stopped, hands on hips, and waited. Slowly, generally two-by-two, out wandered blonde, long-haired girls. Long-legged all, from 6 to 16, at least ten in total. They joined the Englishwoman and descended to the beach.
>
> A tall, long-legged, short-haired adolescent boy came into the office after 6 p.m. each day and put his palms together in the prayer position to Eti or Ivo, to borrow one of the long skateboards racked up on the wall. For the next hour he sped up and down the asphalt around the small harbour. At some point, most days but not every day, a tall, long-legged, long-haired adolescent girl swooshed past on her roller blades. The two crossed over in different directions, smiled coyly but never spoke nor ever travelled in the same direction.
>
> As the setting sun made the old stone buildings around the harbour glow orange, an old man, tall and gaunt, always in navy pants and pullover, always in a navy beret, climbed aboard his small, blue open boat. Boxes of ropes lay scattered unkempt around the deck. He slowly, methodically tidied the ropes, coiled them and sheeted them. When done, before the sun had fully set, he climbed off the boat and disappeared up a narrow lane. One day he threw me; he took the boat out to sea.
>
> Around the same time as the skateboard was being borrowed, a small trolley, painted up with *'pancake/palecinken/creeps'* rolled past from its daytime position behind the beach on the eastern side of Sutivan and set up for the night by the harbour. However, the man who walked past mid-morning in short shorts, pushing a luggage trolley holding an ice-box, offering corn cobs for 10 kuna, I only ever saw once. But twice I'd seen him in the supermarket ordering from the delicatessen counter only the middle section of a loaf of bread (what happens to the ends?) and four slices of cheese.

Between the harbour and the small pebbly beach on the western side of Sutivan there were some steps down from the road to a narrow concrete path across the rocks to the water. Every day the same tall, thin, middle-aged man stood in front of his ice-box at the end of the concrete and cast his line into the Mediterranean. No one else ever fished from this spot. In fact he was the only person I saw fishing with a rod. Despite the huge coastline, fishing is not big in Croatia; not the national sport it seemed to be in Greece and Albania.

All day, large yachts and motor cruisers entered the beautiful small harbour there in Sutivan. In the middle of the harbour they did numerous circles at a snail's pace. Eventually a man, the harbour master perhaps, wandered to the sea wall and gesticulated towards them. Some of these boats then threw him a line. He would tie it off, if space allowed, either to a harbour bollard or another already moored craft. Then more gesticulation before, invariably, he would untie the line and throw it back aboard a boat, which then motored out of the harbour and away from Sutivan.

Always, as the sun said thanks and goodnight, at a time when invariably the wind of the day had also said farewell to be replaced by mirror calm, a tiny yacht, no more than 4 metres in length, sped out of the harbour, faster than allowed, small outboard motor screaming. I forgot to watch where it went, only noticing that the skipper was always alone. But he didn't go far, as before dark he sped, faster than allowed, back into the harbour.

Meanwhile a short, middle-aged man with a swollen knee, sometimes bandaged, but not always, strolled barefoot (no one else was ever barefoot in Sutivan except for Ivo and this man), invariably clad in the same faded, grey T-shirt. He stopped often to drink coffee by day and beer by night at one of the bars. For one week he was alone but then, for a second week, he was always accompanied by a blonde, long-legged, but never barefoot, middle-aged woman. He must have got lucky in Sutivan.

I had indeed got lucky. The night before she had left Australia to fly to Europe, Wendy and I had agreed to a change of plan. That she should come to Brač and we would have our time together there, now that I would miss our planned rendezvous in Italy. In the meantime others came to visit. Jim and Penny, good friends from Australia, had seen on the internet that my tracker device had stopped dead for some days. They diverted from their holiday in Montenegro and visited, as did various members of the Croatian media, now able to pin me down in one place.

It was better than good to have Wendy in Sutivan, to be together for the first time since that tearful farewell four months earlier in Sydney. The past month or so had not been our best; the issue regarding her parents had led to a bit of a standoff. Now, together, we could discuss issues directly, and all was good. But things had not finished well with Ben, our builder, with the major renovations I had left Wendy in the midst of. He had proven to be less honest than we believed, and tensions had built as he tried to cover his tracks and on occasions his bad work. Some of this Wendy had tried to keep from me, but there was enough to keep me on his back, even from a distance. By a remarkable set of circumstances Ben and his Croatian wife were on holiday over in Split while Wendy and I were on Brač. It seemed too good an opportunity to miss: a chance to sit down face to face and try and sort out some of the issues. But he ignored all emails and didn't return calls, digging an ever bigger hole for himself.

The week-long *Vanka Regule* festival had started and I was getting too used to the rules and regularities of Sutivan. Wendy's time on Brač was coming to an end. She was flying to England but this time our farewell was tempered by the knowledge we would soon, all being well, have another week together in Italy.

I'd been in Sutivan for 15 days; I couldn't rest any longer, my mind already full of the potential consequences of the delay. The day after Wendy left, I too farewelled Sutivan and brought *Miss Grape* back out into the light and onto the water. I felt strangely uncertain paddling, a disconnection between me and her, a lack of confidence. These feelings were not helped by my attempts to keep pressure off my left knee, which was still puffy and sore to touch. The final section of this three-month paddle, the final 250 km, loomed more as an obstacle than a downhill run to the trek.

On Šolta I took morning tea at the holiday home of Dina, a Croatian lady who lived in Perth, Western Australia, most of the year, and then I island-hopped back across to the mainland. Here I spent my first night on a yacht, in the company of Dutch couple Robert and Christa. It was good to be moving again, to be back not knowing where I'd be each night, or how I would be sleeping.

Croatia continued to deliver all the way to the end with unbelievably fine paddling – along Pašman, Ugljan, Molat, Lošinj islands, and many more in between. It also continued the pattern of the summer of 2014 in delivering very changeable weather. On Lošinj island, 300 mm of rain had my sleeping mat bobbing up and down on the tent floor the same way my kayak did on the Mediterranean. The locals were saying it was the craziest of summers. In another storm a couple of nights earlier on Pašman island, it had taken a sizeable chunk of my strength to hold my tent, with me in it, down to the ground.

My camp there on Pašman was in front of a remote holiday shack occupied by a young Czech family from Prague. Michael was an expert on bats, frustrated that his work on cataloguing the bats of Libya was currently stymied by the troubles there. I too was frustrated that my desire to visit Libya was being stymied. Whilst on Pašman I was contacted by Jogi, who ran a Croatian sea kayak tour business. He lived on the island of Rab. Rab is also the name of an outdoor clothing and sleeping bag company based in the UK. Indeed in a previous life I had visited their factory in Sheffield on a number of occasions to find Rab, the founder, with his big hair and beard invariably flecked by goose down. I had some Rab equipment on my Mediterranean journey, provided by Paddy Pallin, my major sponsor. Paddy Pallin sell Rab gear in their adventure stores across Australia. Robert Pallin, the son of founder Paddy Pallin, is the company chairman. His wife Nancy is a keen studier of bats. In the seventh degree of separation, the previous year, Jogi told me, he had taken Robert and Nancy Pallin on a sea kayak tour in Croatia.

There were, however, some coincidences more useful to my journey. I landed on the small island of Ilovik, just south of Lošinj. I left *Miss Grape* on a quiet tennis court-sized beach at the only village on the island and went in search of fuel for my engine. Over lunch I made the decision to ride across the neck of the Istria peninsula to Muggia, near Trieste, in Italy, in one day. My original intention had been to kayak around all of Istria, following my last piece of the Croatian coast and the full 30 km length of Slovenia's, to finish at Muggia. But the ride overland would save me three days or so; three days that could be important for my schedule.

When I returned to *Miss Grape* an hour or so later, I had to pick my way past sun-worshipping bodies now crowding the beach. Squeezed hard against *Miss Grape*, their sun cream balanced on her bow, were Fabrizio, Vanessa and their young daughter Sophie. Fabrizio was excited to hear about my journey. I explained the past plan and indicated the future one, my fresh-out-of-the-oven plan. 'Ah, this is fantastic. I wrote the cycling guidebook for Istria and we live in Muggia. I will show you the best route and we will meet again in Muggia.' Of all the beaches in all of Croatia.

With knowledge of an approaching storm, I landed that night at a campsite halfway up the east coast of Lošinj. Spying a trailer full of kayaks, I soon found myself camping with a group of canoeists from Bratislava in Slovakia; one a former world champion white-water rafter. Stephan's skill was almost required, because for two days and two nights it absolutely flogged down. Rivers ran through the campsite, hundreds of tons of imported sand forming the beach all but disappeared into the sea, and the restaurant was as wet inside as out with water showering through the ceiling. Some of the thunderclaps were the loudest I'd ever been deafened by.

When the storm had finally passed, Matteo and Stefan accompanied me on my penultimate day of paddling. We said farewell on the island of Cres, my final island. Soon after I was headed for cover from another storm cell and paddled into the embrace of a Slovenian family headed by Peter and Jasna, and a night of flowing conversation and wine. Indeed for the first and I'm certain last time I drank *bambus*, apparently a favoured Slovenian tipple of red wine mixed with Fanta.

In the morning I woke and cast bleary eyes through the tent door. Sometime during the night the wine fairy must have visited, as there in the doorway was a bottle of Slovenian red wine and a note from Peter and Jasna.

The pretty harbour village of Sutivan held me for over two weeks

As I dodged one final storm and paddled across to Istria from Cres, I felt a little melancholic. I was absolutely ready to move on, to move on by foot; but my three months all at sea had been very special, had cemented the fact that my journey around the Mediterranean was a fine reality. So many acts of kindness, of generosity, so many beautiful people and places. Necedet and his son in Turkey chasing me along the coast to give me honey close to my journey's start, and the Slovenian Wine Fairy the previous night bookended such generosity throughout. Dodging storms, enjoying sun, battling winds and running with them, endless conversations, endless kilometres, fish and birds, dolphins and dogs. Being tired, oh so tired. Long days into the setting sun, sore butt, arms, legs, back. I had felt weak at times; at others incredibly strong.

On the last day of July I landed *Miss Grape* on a beach for the final time; this on the 97th day since I had pushed her off the pebbles of Anzac Cove. Mošćenička Draga, on the Istrian peninsula, was the last landing of hundreds on sand, stone, rock, cement; onto beaches and boats, and into bars. In front of me, by coincidence, was the Hotel Mediteran; the *mediterr année* expedition just had to stay there, and I booked *Miss Grape* in for the night too. She'd not only slept on many beaches but had had lock-ins in tavernas and been put on show in a number of hotel reception areas.

What a woman she had turned out to be. When we had set off I had hardly known her; a few pictures on the internet before she arrived to meet me in Italy ahead of the long journey to Turkey. In over three months and 3,000 km together she had never once thrown me out, and that despite my bad singing. As I had darkened in those past months, *Miss Grape* had faded a lot, the strong Mediterranean sun taking a toll on her complexion. Hopefully we would rekindle our affair in southern Spain in December when the Mediterranean would be a very different place, a very different temperature.

AUGUST

August has passed, and yet summer
continues by force to grow days.

Jonathan Safran Foe

arco joined me in Mošćenička Draga that evening, our first meeting since Gallipoli. In fact he didn't so much join as attack me. While I was quietly enjoying a beer in the hotel garden, a shadow came across me and I was hugged to the ground. It was great to see him, to hear how his and Elena's parallel journey was going; she was now four months pregnant with their first child.

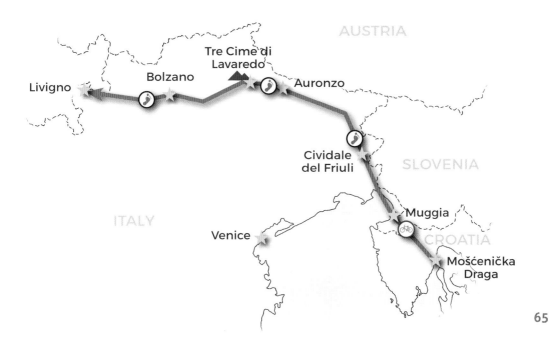

The following lunchtime I climbed aboard my mountain bike for the first ride in four months, the first since I had squealed like an excited kid, careering down the lava slopes of Mount Etna in Sicily. Fabrizio had provided route, map and the words: 'There is a little steep climbing at the start.' I sweated my way up from sea level to 800 metres, worried about unused legs and my recent knee injury. Cake and coffee was provided in the garden of a Croatian family in a tiny village when all I had asked for was water. It was great to be on the bike, but it hurt. Halfway, I was joined by Marco, Fabrizio and Cesare riding from Muggia to meet me. Soon we were rehydrating with my last beer in Croatia, in Jelovice, the last village before the border.

Spinning downhill, I flew across the border into Slovenia, country number seven. A shrill whistle and lots of shouting followed. I looked over my shoulder to see a border guard waving me back. I pedalled back up the hill and fished out my passport. With Croatia only a recent addition to the EU it was not yet part of the Schengen zone and its open borders.

Slovenia was to be too quick a visit, and at the time I had no inkling how important one of its citizens would be to my journey. That said, we did spend a little bit longer than planned riding the 20 km across Slovenia to Italy. Guidebook writer Fabrizio and mapmaker Cesare decided to show off some sneaky trails and we promptly got lost.

Back on track, at dusk we gazed down from the lookout at Socerb across Slovenia to the Italian city of Trieste and the Adriatic Sea. A rain squall hung over Muggia, our destination, and soaked us as we descended into it just on dark. '*Buonasera Italia!*' Three countries in one day.

Muggia is a pretty little town with an ancient core and delightful harbour. We were warmly welcomed by the mayor and others – Fabrizio's family in particular.

In between sorting all my gear so that Marco could head home with *Miss Grape* and all the paddling gear, there were important things to attend to. It was time for a barber. Mario was, as is the Italian way, a man of passion. Not for him the electric shaver as he flourished his scissors. I indicated I wanted it short all over. He got to work, primping here, pushing up there. He went short on the sides and longer on top as was the fashion. He was pleased, his girls came to admire his work. I didn't have the heart to say take some more from the top. It was possibly the first time I had been 'styled' in decades. If it was going to happen then Italy was the right place.

Thence to the shops to purchase some lightweight footwear for around camp on the trek. For years wife, stepdaughters, granddaughter had pushed me toward thongs: very fashionable these days. I always refused, not so keen on the rubber intrusion between big toe and toe. But emboldened with new coiffure and outlaying a mere €5, I went in barefoot and came out thonged.

I had not had a massage for 100 days, not since the night before I had left from Gallipoli, when Elena had eased my tense muscles in Çanakkale. 'Massagio Muggia' was also an Elena. She left me behind the screen after handing me a small foil package with instructions to call her when I was ready. I ripped it open to find a paper thong. Behind the screen I tried it on both ways to try to ascertain which would best cover my own package. After decades avoiding thongs, here I was with two types in an hour. Finally satisfied with my directional selection, I lay down for what was a fine massage on fatigued muscles.

In Muggia I also enjoyed some excellent meals. It was Italy after all, where the passion for all things food and wine is infectious. Marco and I dined with Fabrizio the first night, then with Marin Medak, a Slovenian, on the second. Marin had contacted me weeks before, having been following my journey; a journey he had first learned of from the Facebook page of Stavros Georgarakis, the generous kayak shop owner in Athens. Marin had offered assistance if I needed any when I passed through Slovenia. I didn't, but he drove into Muggia and it was great to meet this young but wise and entrepreneurial man, a keen sea kayaker who had also rowed across the Atlantic a couple of years ago. He had wanted it to be a team of Slovenians making the first ocean crossing for that nation but couldn't find any compatriots keen to take up the challenge. Instead he had led a crew of three Brits from Gran Canaria to Barbados.

On my final night in Muggia, after farewelling Marco, I was alone for dinner but found this incredible little trattoria: friendly, cheap and with no menu other than what Laura, the owner, told me I was going to eat. It was of course delicious. When I had pangs for something *dolce* to finish, the waitress told me they had nothing. Then Laura came out from the kitchen and, with a twinkle in her eye, asked, 'You prefer marmalade or chocolate?' Chocolate was my reply even though I didn't know chocolate what. Soon the most delicate of crepes and an espresso were on the table in front of me.

As I wandered back to my hotel the main piazza was going off. Fully coiffured, and no doubt thonged, beauties were vying for the title of the local beauty queen. It was good to be back in Italy.

★ ★ ★

Late afternoon on 4 August I shouldered my Osprey pack and turned my back on the Mediterranean to walk into the hills, up into the Alps. Away from the sea that had been my home for the past 100 days, a sea I would not touch again until Monaco at perhaps the end of October. One hundred days from Gallipoli on the day that, 100 years previously, World War I had begun. We have of course learned too little in that time.

Apparently there are something like 750 muscles in the human body. Well the hundreds that hadn't got used while paddling ached like hell now I was trekking with a pack on my back. But it was great to be in the hills, where the water flowed vertically as opposed to the horizontal that had been my playground before.

Tjasa from Slovenia National Radio had not been fast enough to catch me on my dash across her country by bike. So she came to Muggia to meet me. During our interview she suggested I should have had at least one night in Slovenia, and admonished me that I had not even drunk a Slovenian beer in Slovenia. She would have been pleased to find that then, on my first night out of Muggia, I took a wrong turn and found myself back in Slovenia. I actually ended up camped in the garden of an old border post, now a holiday home for Yuri. As I pitched the tent on his lawn, Yuri came out with cold Slovenian beers.

Within a couple of days my suffering intensified when a blister, caused by those bloody thongs, formed on the top of my foot. The tribulations of being a fashion victim. The blister then opened up as an infected sore on my right foot – the wrong foot, given it's the one that suffers from lymphoedema. So I hobbled my way on hot days, fat-footing through the Friuli region up from the Mediterranean; foot throbbing, leg muscles slow to respond. It was a sort of purgatory; my body not yet in tune with the walking, the walk not yet in the mountains proper.

One thing to look forward to was Wendy joining me at the end of the week. The third day of my hobble marked her birthday. That day I walked through Prosecco, the village that produces her favourite tipple, and rang her to toast her special day. After our reunion in Croatia, Wendy was in the UK, and was then coming back to Italy to join me for one more week before flying back home to Australia.

I don't like overdone goodbyes, but on the night of her birthday I found myself back close to the Mediterranean, camped on a lookout on the cliffs, tired, hot and bothered. As if to send me on my way inland the heavens opened whilst at the same time, surreally, I was bathed in sunlight. As the beautiful cooling rain squall passed, a rainbow was left across the sea; my first since Turkey. It seemed a sign, an encouragement for me to push on to reach the end of this rainbow of countries, landscapes and cultures.

Soon my own pot of gold was with me. She found me in Capriva del Friuli and I took a day off the trails to rest my foot and more importantly to be with her. I felt bad, though; the first week we'd had together I had been laid up on Brač with a ballooning knee. Now for our second and final week it was a ballooning foot. The rough plan was for us to meet up at the end of each day with Wendy having driven ahead and found somewhere to stay. So much of me wanted to take the week off and spend all the days with her as well, but I was far behind schedule and didn't want to run out of summer to cross the Alps. It was great to be together but in some ways a hard week too, knowing that soon it would be another eight months or more before we'd see each other again.

As the foot went down, I climbed higher into the mountains from the vineyards of Friuli. On one evening Alessandro and his wife Rosie hosted us for a beautiful dinner at their home in Udine. Alessandro headed up Tabacco Maps, who were kindly supporting my trek with their excellent maps of the Alps, the first Tabacco sponsorship I'd ever accepted.

Hard up against the Slovenian border in heavily forested country known for its population of *orsi* (brown bears), I came upon a sign on the trail: '*Passo Carrabile*' (no passage). A healthy disbelief in many such signs from decades of successfully ignoring them made me push on into the forest. After a couple of kilometres I was clambering over fallen trees and pushing through thick bush. Some mighty windstorm had obliterated the track. I pushed on further, relishing the thought of some good old-style Aussie bush-bashing until the whole forest floor was a carpet of nettles beneath the fallen timber. I tried to pick my way over them but my bare legs were getting hammered and eventually I admitted defeat, retraced my steps and took the long, long detour.

The following grey morning Wendy dropped me back where she had picked me up the previous evening. Plenty more Passo Carrabile signs, this time respected, meant more detours, and the sky was almost black as I approached the tiny hamlet of Montemaggiore, tucked beneath the cloud-covered eponymous mountain. Whilst I'd come across no bears, the first thing I saw in Montemaggiore was a big, fat, black pig trussed in a full-body harness; then, soon after, half a dozen young women in formal dress and the highest of stilettos tottered out of the gloom toward me. All this seemed incongruous in the old, cold hamlet. I went into the only bar where a man in his eighties served me coffee and, pointing at his watch, shook his head when I told him I planned to go over the mountain. It was 4 p.m.

Big globules of rain started to fall as soon as I pulled the door of the bar closed behind me. Thunder echoed as stilettos clattered down the empty street and disappeared into a shuttered house. On the edge of the village I met a German couple, the first trekkers I'd seen in a week. 'Where are you going?' asked the woman. 'It is dangerous up there, too frightening in the wind, the rain, the storm. It is too late to go now.'

I actually enjoyed the long, steep climb into the mist and the rain. Then, as I crested the ridge at 1,400 metres the storm hit with its full force. One gust flattened me clean to the ground and the rain felt like hail though wasn't. It was day but it almost could have been night. Where the path went through forested sections, I struggled to see the ground in front of me. I dropped over the ridge and clambered down narrow cliffside paths that became torrents, and felt the ground shake under me from the deafening thunderclaps. It was horrible but had its pleasures in the way mountains offer up in bad weather.

Halfway down the mountain, the track reached a gully. White water blocked the way until I eventually found a spot to leap from water-covered boulders to the far bank. Pleased with myself, I continued only to have the track recross the streamway lower down. Again I searched for a way across. Uppermost in my mind was the fact that stream and river crossings had, over the years, presented some of my worst experiences and closest calls. Again I managed to leap across the torrent, upstream of the track crossing. A third crossing was expected and it came soon enough; faster and wider than previously. I looked for a safe crossing but found nothing and started to think about waiting, about the possibility of spending the night out, even though, as I was meeting Wendy each night, I had only a daypack with me. After sitting on the track for a while in the rain, I pushed again through the sodden bushes downstream, a little further this time, and eventually found a dodgy crossing point.

Eventually I hit the road below the Passo Tanamea on dark and, once over it, found Wendy ensconced in the Cyclamina Hotel, a weird, fairly modern place run by a woman and her two daughters. It had neither drying room nor hot water. The only other guests were a couple in their eighties; he a retired maths professor from Pisa and she his English wife. She told us over dinner that they came here for two weeks every year and loved it. Perhaps it was the twee decoration, in the manner of some English B&B establishments. Each to their own.

As I trekked my way in more rain over to Resiutta in Val Fella, it transpired the region had experienced some of the heaviest rainstorms seen for a decade or more. Landslides were blocking many routes and roads had been torn up. Wendy and I spent our last night in Venzone, a once ancient walled town that had suffered the wrath of natural disasters when, in 1976, a huge earthquake that killed over 1,000 people, almost totally destroyed the town. Rather unbelievably the townspeople decided to recreate the town and, block by block, window by window, Venzone rose up again. The imposing church was rebuilt, as were many buildings in the town to the extent that what was old became new but still looks old.

The mountains were revealing themselves with the sun now out. But a grey cloud was descending. Wendy and I had our last day together, enjoying the restaurants of Venzone but mostly just cherishing our time together. There was talk of meeting up again at Christmas wherever I might be, but I think we both knew it was unlikely. She dropped me back at Resiutta. Tears, hugs and kisses. Repeat then repeat again. We've done it so often before, but it is always so hard. Finally we waved goodbye, I picked up my pack and climbed away up into the mountains. I was ready for the rhythm of the trek; glad to have everything on my back; unreliant on hotels or huts, free to stop where and when I wanted.

So many sections of mountain path had been destroyed, and fallen trees blocked my progress too. One blockage at a track junction saw me take the wrong way on a steep and very narrow track. After crossing flood debris in a river gorge, eventually I worked out what was going on and decided to continue that way. It was a worthwhile mistake as I popped out at the mountain hamlet of Stavoli where two couples from Venzone insisted I join them for wine in their tiny cottage. We toasted that the day marked my longest expedition to date; 112 days. Only 253 days to go.

Some long days, some long, long climbs. I was now in big country, vertical country. But so few other trekkers; Friuli had been so quiet. People I'd seen – shepherds, cheesemakers and the odd tourist – seemed surprised to see me, doubly surprised I was on a long trek, triply surprised I was walking solo. It was as if all these trails are not supposed to be used.

On one day I pushed for 13 hours to make a dinner appointment with Giuseppe and Gabrielle, from an Italian cycle clothing company who produced merchandise for my Australian events. Given they'd driven for two hours to see me, that push was the least I could do.

From the kayak, whatever the weather, I was always under the clouds. Here in the mountains I was under them, above them, in them. The past few days had been too much of the latter. On one day, as I transitioned from Friuli to the Dolomites, I walked at 2,000 metres knowing I was surrounded by huge rocky peaks but not seeing them once in rain and cloud. As each day went past I felt stronger in the legs; I found each climb of 1,000 or 1,500 metres more enjoyable, each descent slightly less painful. The rhythm was beating along the track. Unlike when I landed with *Miss Grape* on a beach, I now just merged in, another walker, albeit one with a larger pack. Now in the Dolomites there were more people out on the trails. Questions only arose when I engaged with others, and often I hid away, enjoying a bit of solitude.

There are plenty of mountain refuges across the Alps, some in the most spectacular of locations. Most people stay in them, but my preference was to camp. For many years I have pondered on whether I walk to camp or camp because I'm walking. I prefer the freedom of being tied to no particular end point on a day, but instead of just putting the billy on; being 'sorted'.

Some of us will know of one or two stunningly beautiful women in our day-to-day lives; women who are the equal in looks to any prissy supermodel, and way beyond in

Tre Cime di Lavaredo; just some of the 'supermodel' mountains of the Italian Dolomites

A tasty sunset camp on the Strudelkopf

personality. So it is with mountains. There are those that everyone wants to ogle at, to climb upon. Then there are those that are more discreet, more rounded, but equally stunning. So it is in the Dolomites. At every turn a rocky spire, a beautiful face. But everyone wants to view the Tre Cime di Lavaredo. Roads have been blasted as close to them as possible to make it easier for admirers to gaze at their bodies. I came from a different direction, only to find them half-dressed – resolutely refusing, despite the wolf whistles of the marmots and the Alpine choughs – to peel off their top halves. I'd seen enough naked mountains – both supermodels and the girls next door – so was not overly concerned.

But that night, as I camped high upon the Strudelkopf, the three of them in unison stripped bare, assuming I guess that no one was watching. As I unzipped the tent to take a leak at dawn, I just caught them before they quickly threw their grey gowns back on. Like a paparazzo, I snapped away. If the truth were known I had camped in that spot in the hope of a full-frontal viewing. Perhaps I'm the same as everyone; taken in by celebrity.

Planning the kayak route had been pretty straightforward: keep the mainland generally on my right, decide on an island or three. Here in the mountains, in the Alps, there were any number of routes that I could take to traverse the range. How was I to decide? A year or more before *mediterr année* started I became aware of the Via Alpina, an initiative of the eight Alpine countries to promote routes across and through the Alps. To date they have linked together some 5,000 km of trails. I liaised closely with Nathalie, the administrator of Via Alpina, on possible routes. As the emails flowed I imagined Frenchwoman Nathalie typing away from a gorgeous high-mountain chalet, in between refreshing walks or perhaps a spot of cheesemaking. I later learned she lived in Nottingham, in the Midlands of England.

So I had the Via Alpina as a framework. I had the Dolomites, Monte Rosa and Mont Blanc as places to be linked in the jigsaw. Then Marco, a man who lives in the Alps, but has no time to make cheese, took the framework, the key points, and weaved his knowledge and his magic across the maps. A orange highlighter line emerged on the maps, often paying scant regard to altitude gain or loss. With the orange line as a guide, I would decide on the day what took my fancy; where to deviate.

Despite it still being August, the month when so much of Europe is on holiday, I was surprised how quiet the Alps were. Before I started the journey I did worry that my Alps traverse might, to some extent, be spoiled by too many people on the tracks. It is after all one of the great playgrounds of Europe. But the poor weather of July and August had obviously deterred some mountain lovers. Guardians at some of the refuges told me they planned to close early; to cut their losses. And, as August moved into September and September to October it would only become quieter for me.

I was enjoying the contrast between rain and sun, even occasional snow. It was superlative trekking up valleys and over high passes through the Dolomites, sometimes threading a route through exposed limestone plateau country. As I wandered down the spectacular Vallelunga, I realised it was four months since I'd wandered away from the beach at Gallipoli in Turkey. Walking down the valley, I struck up a conversation with a fellow trekker. Leandro was from the Puglia region of southern Italy, more specifically from a town called Gallipoli. I loved the connection.

The gash of the Vallelunga in the Dolomites

Four months in and a bit over three weeks of walking had brought me through Friuli, right through the heart of the Dolomites and into the Südtirol/Alto Adige region. Austrian until 1915, Italian since, Südtirol is resolutely Germanic in customs and in language. If you're a non-meat-eater like me, you eat a lot of cheese and eggs. If you don't eat cheese and eggs you might as well make like the Alpine cows; bells optional.

Everything was now in tune, even my songs that echoed across the altipiano. Then I broke a string. I felt a bit sniffly, a tad heavy in the stomach. I walked on. As the day progressed things gurgled and in the late afternoon – a cold, cold afternoon – I descended to Selva Gardena. Thoughts of taking a room were countered by the fact I wanted to be up in the mountains, not down with the tourists. I climbed on, feeling weaker; glad to find a flat spot, glad to crawl into the tent, not interested in dinner. Shivering with down jacket on inside down sleeping bag I tried to sleep, but the runs kept calling; rather apt given my camp was on a ski run. Then as darkness fell I bade farewell to breakfast, lunch and everything else, then slept like a baby.

Fortunately I was out of tune for just a day and continued walking beneath the rock walls of the Sassolungo and up on to the Altipiano dello Sciliar. Tiny, crazy trails clung to the rock and I climbed into the cloud, getting occasional glimpses of peaks above. Then everything closed in completely and I felt my way to Rifugio Bolzano and a refreshing Radler. Wanting a camp with a view I headed down, unable to stop myself from calling into a tiny farmhouse perched on a small alp offering a simple but perfect menu of wine and cheese. The track plunged into a long gorge, and camp that night was actually on the trail itself, the only relatively flat spot I could find.

An early morning trekker woke me, tripping over my guy line whilst trying to step past the tent. Later that day I arrived at the only place I'd previously visited since my journey had begun. The fine Hotel Steineggerhof Bike Hotel, perched above Bolzano, had hosted me a few years earlier when last I had visited Südtirol on a mountain bike. Sonia was a perfect host for a second time.

But my walk to Steinegg that day was notable in a more meaningful way. Although Libya was on my original list of *mediterr année* countries it had been obvious to me for some time that I wouldn't get to play there. The country, like some of the others where the Arab Spring had originally offered hope, was descending into a bloody civil war. And, regardless of the issues, it seemed impossible to obtain a visa to cycle across that vast country. The past month, as I trekked through the Italian Alps, I racked my brain for human-powered solutions. Going south of Libya would have me traversing Algeria north to south, to then head across Niger, Chad and into South Sudan. Not only would this route send me through the guts of the Sahara and completely blow my 12-month schedule, but also it would send me across three countries that were as bad as, if not worse than, Libya.

Then, as I strolled across green alps toward Steinegg, it hit me. While the Libyans were having an argument could I not have a row? Could I not row a boat from Tunisia to Malta, then row on to Alexandria in Egypt? That evening I contacted Marin, the young Slovenian who I'd dined with in Muggia just before the trek had begun. He had rowed the Atlantic, so I reckoned he would be a good sounding board; might perhaps even be keen to join me.

'No one rows on the Mediterranean,' he told me. 'The winds are too fickle, there is no reliable swell to assist. But of course Huw, as you know, anything is possible.' Marin offered to help; provide information on suitable boats, people who might join me. But unfortunately for me, his priority was a new business venture and raising finance for it. He was unable to join me. Still, it was an exciting prospect and it occupied what little spare time I had over the following weeks. Ocean rowing is very much a minority sport, so there were only a limited number of resources to check on; boats for sale, people involved. And Marin was right – there was bugger all about rowing on the Mediterranean.

Bolzano, a large town at 250 metres, was as low a place as I'd been since leaving the sea. I headed straight to a barber, ringing good friends Bettina and Eugen to ask them to pick me up there. Suitably trimmed, I waited and waited until finally Bettina rang. 'We're at the bar, waiting for you Huw.' Bar? Barber? I wandered around to Alessandra and Donatella's little wine bar-cum-gallery; a place I knew well from previous visits.

Saying farewell to them after a pizza lunch, I walked 15 km through apple orchards, stealing a few as dessert, arriving just on dark, to a B&B in Nals. After the 20 calls Bettina had made, it was the only place with room. A red-headed, gaunt woman surrounded by cats greeted me, if greet was the right word. She was right out of the mould of a mad British host. You know the ones; the country is full of them, usually surrounded by cats.

After a quick shower I retreated to the bar next door, where the owner spent much of her time angrily shooing her neighbour's felines away. Then soon after 10 p.m., split by no more than 30 seconds, Marie-Clare and Jon arrived from the UK whilst Marco and a friend Michaela arrived from Germany en route home from a bike show. Marie-Clare

Trekking through the limestone plateau of the Dolomites near Pederù

and Jon were joining me to trek for a week. The last time I had trekked with Marie-Clare was along the Overland Track in Tasmania, during my journey from Melbourne to Hobart 10 years earlier, when we climbed Mt Ossa, Tasmania's highest peak. The last Mt Ossa I'd seen had been on the Pelion peninsula, while I'd been kayaking the Greek coast two months earlier.

The only place still doing food in Nals was a pizzeria. It wasn't like I needed another one; however in past days I'd been craving Asian food, and here they had, almost unbelievably, a Bangladesh pizza. It turned out to be Asian in name only, with nothing remotely Bangladeshi about it other than being thin, but still I ordered it. After dinner I gave Marco some excess gear and he gave me the next tranche of maps for my trek before driving off into the night.

After over four months travelling alone it was great to have company for a week. Plenty of laughs, including every morning when they would both emerge, soaked by the condensation from a tent designed for one person for one night but sleeping two for a week. On our first day we descended a very overgrown trail, clambering over fallen trees and clinging to earthen slopes, to Mitterbad. Trees and vines grew through this long-ruined hotel and spa where a plaque announced that the hotel had welcomed Germany's Kaiser, Otto von Bismarck, in 1843 and the writer Thomas Mann much later.

On that first day Marie-Clare's boots fell apart and on the second Jon announced, in the rain, that he'd forgotten his waterproof overpants. New boots were bought and we headed back to the mountains to cross the Flimjoch in wind that pinned us to the rocks at times, and with a steep descent to camp. Heading toward the Ortler range, the weather crapped out for our climb to the highest point of my trek so far: the 3,110-metre Passo del Madriccio. Fresh snow meant wet, cold legs for Jon, and required delicate foot placement on the rocky ascent where a white-out greeted us on the pass.

Marie-Clare and Jon had picked an ECG week; as soon as we reached one high point, we'd lose all the hard-won altitude almost immediately afterwards. We scrambled beneath the near 4,000-metre-high Ortler, glaciers tumbling from its summit slopes, followed handrails cut into cliffs, and ran down endless scree slopes. The Stelvio was our last big climb together, and we stayed in a little refuge high above this, Italy's highest road, on the Italian–Swiss border. After a beautiful morning's trek over Passo della Forcola and down the valley of the same name, we hugged goodbye to whistling applause from a crowd of marmots. Marie-Clare and Jon began their journey home to Scotland, and I continued mine.

SEPTEMBER

September was a thirty-days long goodbye to summer, to the season that left everybody both happy and weary of the warm, humid weather and the exhausting but thrilling adventures.

Lea Malot

My trek on to Livigno was in conditions just as suited to the west of Scotland as the Alps, and I arrived sodden from head to toe. Livigno is a town at 1,800 metres, tucked up in a high valley with Switzerland on three sides and a

lake that, whilst in Italy, is owned by the Swiss; a town with its own language, Livinsasco, and its own duty-free status. The good people of Livigno municipality gave me a very warm welcome. I was soon in a hot shower and ensconced in Hotel Garni al Plan, the only hotel I've ever stayed in that also incorporates a shoe shop. I dined that night in a fine restaurant with Martina from Livigno Tourism and Ivan, a local lad who, with perfect timing, had just completed an end-to-end trek of the Alps. We had much to talk about as we tucked into most excellent fare, finishing with *sorbetto al Braulio*, a local ice cream expertly folded into a local liqueur made from 23 mountain herbs.

The word 'wellness' marches across Europe. Who made it up, this horrible word? In every tourist town there are resorts and hotels claiming 'wellness' in their offerings. But I shouldn't complain; Livigno had even organised a relaxing and soothing massage to aid the wellness of my journey. Then, before I left to trek into Switzerland, the municipality put on a presentation which saw my pack further weighed down with a lovely framed photo, shirts, hats and a hamper of local wine, cheeses and meats. The wine was soon decanted into my drink bottle, the cheese would go down well as I walked, and the meats were returned with thanks.

With a promise to return to Livigno I pushed on, and within a few hours had dropped over a high pass into Switzerland. Although it is hardly renowned as a Mediterranean country, I felt nonetheless that it might prove a useful addition to my 20 countries list as I looked at the issues of visiting Libya and Syria. Algeria, too, was proving interesting; I had received news that the government would only issue me a visa if a travel agent prepared a full day-by-day itinerary for the 1,500 km across the country. Further, they were insisting on a security car coming along for the ride to shadow me. It was really not my style.

I'd last found myself in Switzerland's Engadine valley in 1990 during a winter when a girlfriend and I had lived in an ancient VW Kombi for four months, driving and skiing our way around the Alps. Thirty-five years later, at a campsite at Silvaplana on my second night in Switzerland, I chuckled when I spied a tent in the design of a full-size Kombi.

The Alps were punishing – 1,500-metre climbs tested lungs, 1,500-metre downs tested knees. Different landscapes, new mountain ranges, rock, tumbling glaciers, trails clinging to cliffs. Marmots whistling at the contorted madness of it all. But madness in a certain type of paradise. I was loving it.

My route in Switzerland took me through some grand terrain on narrow, often exposed paths not regularly trodden. Indeed I'd not seen another trekker in a couple of days when, standing on the Passo de Balniscio, one leg in Switzerland, the other in Italy, I spied two people heading down the mountain slopes above; moving slowly, very slowly down amongst the rocks. As they came closer I noticed one was on crutches. A mountain accident perhaps? But if so, how would he have crutches at the ready? There had indeed been an accident, but some years before, as Oliviero Bellinzani told me when he reached the pass. He had lost his leg in a motorbike accident. Now this one-legged Italian was proving, as his business card stated, that 'the only limitations are in the mind'. He had just climbed the mountain above the pass. I was humbled.

That night I lay in the tent listening to light snow flurries dance on the flysheet. I realised summer was nearly done in the Alps. Some might say 'What summer?' Indeed I wondered what had happened to my plans of lying out on soft grass on a sun-warmed alp drifting off to the symphony of a flowing spring, marmots piping in tune with cow and sheep bells.

Most days I was on the hoof for 10 hours or so, usually thinking, around 7 p.m., of somewhere to camp. Another knee-jarring 1,000-metre descent from the Passo del Trescolmen, through steep gorge country offering no place to camp, brought me in fading light to the tiny Swiss summer hamlet of Valbella. I noted a fine grassy spot between an unoccupied cabin and a tiny church and thought it polite to ask at a nearby house if it would be OK to camp. Danilo couldn't see a problem, so, after chatting a while in staccato Italian, German and English, I set up my tent.

'You ready for some dinner?' he hollered down from his veranda. 'We make fondue for you.' I couldn't believe it. My first meal in a Swiss house and they *do* do fondue! I remember when everyone in the UK had a fondue set in the eighties (or was it seventies?). Like that funky machine that woke you up with a hot cup of tea, these fondue sets could then be found at every garage sale or car boot sale, or residing in some dark corner of a kitchen cupboard. That night, much cheese was washed down with much wine, and Portuguese was added to the linguistic menu; Any, Danilo's wife, hailed from Brazil.

The following morning as I climbed out of the tent; sore head to go with equally sore back, knees, feet; Danilo hollered again: '*Caffè*? *Colazione*?' Breakfast was ready. As I said farewell, Danilo slipped a bottle of beer into my backpack with instructions: 'For the next pass.'

When I climbed away from Valbella, the sun was warm. It had been an age since I'd felt that; perhaps I had been too hasty in my thoughts a few days earlier. Somewhere in the forest I took a wrong track and eventually popped out from the trees beneath a ramshackle cabin perched on the mountain. As I approached, I imagined I'd find an old mountain couple, eking out a living in summer from a few cows and the pigs snorting in the yard. Instead I found the wild-looking Nico, a young Italian man from Florence, who in response to my appalling attempt at Italian, asked if I spoke English. Then I met Malena, a young woman originally of chaotic Sicily, now of orderly Switzerland and busy making cheese. I drank tea with Nico before Malena showed me the racks of maturing cheese and explained the process. There was no road to this place, so I enquired how they sent the cheese to market. 'Three times in summer we call for a helicopter,' she explained. 'At 26 Swiss francs per kilogramme it is worth it to protect the cheese that is damaged if we use the horses.' I left with *formaggi* and still-warm bread for lunch.

Back on track, I climbed to Giumela, where I sat warm and contented on the high pass for lunch, enjoying sun and the fruits of a morning's kindness. On the climb I had also picked handfuls of sweet alpine blueberries, careful to avoid the blue-tinged goat droppings that could confuse.

But now I had a quandary. I was about to head into the corner of three maps; but had only two of them. I could see different trails leading off the edge of the map. But to where? I could second-guess but I'd done that before and regretted it.

From the pass of Giumela, a narrow trail led across the mountain and eventually down to a small alp. Here, 300 metres off the trail, was a small unguardianed refuge hut.

I decided to go check it out, and arrived to find a young lad sat outside: Monster energy drink, T-shirt, baseball cap backwards, baggy jeans with underpants waistband proudly displayed, as was the fashion. I learned that Alain was a shepherd, with 19 cows and a handful of goats in his care. In French and Italian, with two maps spread, I tried to explain my quandary. Alain in return tried to explain a possible route for me that was not marked on any map. Wary of being sandbagged I tried to ascertain the detail. Was there a track? How difficult? Alain placed his hand in the almost vertical position to indicate steepness then more vertically in the downward position. 'But there is rope there' I sort of got from his words. It all sounded a bit risky – no map, no track, fixed rope descent, late in the day.

The Swiss *do* do fondue. Danilo and Any took me to their cabin in Valbella, for one

So '*Je viens avec toi*' (I'll come with you) were words I was very happy to hear. Alain hitched up his jeans and we set off, he stopping every so often with binoculars out to scan the mountains for his errant goats. With three decades on him and weighed down by a big pack, I was far outpaced by Alain as he bounded ahead up the ever-steepening slope. Up on the skyline he pointed out roughly where we were headed and, with a final steep scramble up a damp gully, we popped out onto the Sendo del Bo, a tiny notch on a narrow ridge. As I perched myself and thought where the hell now, Alain nonchalantly sent a few SMSs and then took off over the edge. I followed, of course, to see him sliding down a 100-metre-long ramp through the cliffs, protected by some fixed cables and iron foot/handholds bolted into the rock. This

I found Malena making cheese on a high alp in Switzerland. Is is valuable enough for helicopters to take it to the market

deposited us onto steep slopes below a small glacier and, in the distance, Alpi di Seeng di Sopra, our aim point. A few hours of scree hopping, grass sliding and a bit more cable and ladders to finish saw us there as the sun set. I thanked Alain profusely before he bounded off in the dusk down a well-made track to reach his motorbike parked apparently an hour or more far below. Never judge a book by its cover.

I pitched the tent, watching the last of the sun fade from the rock face of now distant Sendo del Bo. In celebration of another special day I drank the beer Danilo had given me that morning and ate the last of the cheese Malena had given me.

After weeks dropping to no lower than 1,500 metres, I now plummeted from over 2,000 metres at the Passo del Mauro down to the shores of Lago Maggiore at 200 metres. Maggiore is as close to the Mediterranean as Switzerland gets in distance from and height above the sea that named my journey, and in the temperament of its Italian-speaking people. For me, it was an unwelcome but necessary descent to a wide valley of towns and some industry, where at the town of Locarno I needed to pick up my next maps. There was, however, something good about dropping down to Locarno: two days a week, Elena crossed the border from Italy to work as a physiotherapist in the town. Now five months pregnant, she was a very different woman from the one I had last seen on the beach at Gallipoli.

As I made my way across the mountains, the idea of the rowing across the Mediterranean consumed a fair bit of thinking-while-walking time. I'd seen a few boats on the internet and made contact with some people, including a Turkish rower who'd had the idea of rowing from New York to Gallipoli. The reality, however, was that with everything else I had to do for my journey, being on the move up to 12 hours a day, being tired, it was unlikely I could pull off the row. I couldn't afford the time to stop for a week or two, fly to wherever to check boats and equipment. And how would I pay for something that was far, far beyond my budget for the journey? It was frustrating because I saw the row as a clear solution to my north Africa and Middle East problems.

The days immediately following my descent to Lago Maggiore were full of mist and occasional rain as I climbed then descended to low altitudes again, into the Ossola valley to make my way through Italy's Piemonte region. They were days of ancient stone pathways soaked by dripping oak, chestnut and beech forest. Days of passing equally ancient villages clinging to ridge tops, villages often inaccessible by road.

On one of those days I ascended 1,000 metres on such a track, the flagstones now covered by autumn leaves. I arrived soaked to the skin at Rifugio Colma, perched 1,600 metres up on the ridge separating Val Antrona from Val Anzasca. The refuge appeared in the mist and rain, and my plan was to take a short break to dry out. I arrived to find Olindo and Patrizia making pasta, though the refuge had officially closed for the season. My short break became a two-hour lunch of fresh pasta and more. For the past nine years, for four months each year, Olindo and Patrizia had run this small 12-bed refuge. For the other eight months they run a children's music school in the city of Bologna. Patrizia asked me to turn off my mobile phone when I arrived. She was the first person I had met whose life was dominated by an allergic reaction to electromagnetism. High on this Alpine ridge for the summer months was a good place for Patrizia to be. Down in Bologna she suffered from nausea and headaches by day. Then, after their teaching was done, Patrizia and Olindo drove out to the Apennines, into a deep valley with no mobile signal where they slept in a mobile home. A home which had special shielding materials built into its walls.

Olindo, who taught piano, violin and guitar, told me (an individual whose finest musical achievement was playing 'Three Blind Mice' on the recorder) about the importance of teaching the feel of music not the just the playing of the notes. As the rain hammered outside, our conversation wandered into a long discussion of how indeed, modern devices were removing the feel from much of life.

As my 50th day on the trek and 150th day on the trip approached, I was reaching high into the mountains again, trekking south-west toward the Monte Rosa, at 4,634 metres one of the giants of the Alps. I was feeling strong now, legs and lungs enjoying the climbs although my knees still protested the descents. The sun rejoined the party and I celebrated with a high camp just beneath the 2,351 metre Col delle Termo just so I could watch her final dance of the day. I found a grassy knoll with just enough of a flat top for my tent and a tiny runnel of water metres away. There is little to compare in life to sitting at a mountain camp, hot drink in hand and watching sunlight creep up the slopes beyond until everything is in shadow; content in the knowledge there's a sleeping bag waiting when it gets too cool.

The following morning, as I came down from the Col delle Termo to the village of Rima, Marco and Elena and another Marco were walking up to meet me. After the obligatory coffees, the four of us ascended toward Colle Mud, Elena moving slowly. At a small alp Marco and Elena descended whilst the other Marco and I continued up. Two years earlier he had lost an eye to a fence in a terrible, freak cycling accident. Even though he suffered from glaucoma in his other eye, it was incredible how he bounded up the mountain tracks, tracks he loved and knew so well. Like Oliviero, the one-legged climber from two weeks earlier, Marco would not let his accident stop him from travelling through the mountains that were his passion.

Marco and Elena were key to the success of my project. During it they went on their own adventure and little Giole was born eight months in to my journey

By the time we reached Alagna at the head of Valsesia, it was beer o'clock, and Marco and Elena arrived by car at the same time as we did by foot. I left my trekking route for a few days, and descended with them to their home village of Val Maggiore and a warm welcome back from Anna and Alberto at Casa Dolce. This was, if I had such a thing, my base for mediterr année. Here I was reunited with (and gave a little peck to the bow of) Miss Grape. She was as thin and elegant as always. I was no more elegant but a little thinner having shed 8 kg since the start of the trek.

I wanted a week, needed a week, to sort gear, catch up on work, organise the route plan for the coming months. But I couldn't afford the time. Autumn had arrived and I needed to finish my trek across the Alps by late October for reasons both of changing seasons and the rest of my journey. I still felt I hadn't caught up the time spent on that two-week-long knees-up back in Croatia.

It was late September and already the shepherds had started to gather their flocks and herds in readiness for the descent from the high alps to the lower valleys. Their bells would fall silent, as would the squeals of the marmots as they too prepared their burrows for the long winter. Most of the refuge guardians had cleaned up, closed the shutters and, like mountain Elvises, left the building. Many did so early, after their worst summer business for some years.

Indeed it had been a cool, damp, grey summer in the Alps. But in truth I had not found too much torrential rain, at least in the past month. Indeed often the rain drops would darken the rocks across which I clambered no more quickly than the sweat dripping off my brow.

Since I'd left Val Maggiore for Gallipoli back in April, Anna – gentle, elegant Anna – had been diagnosed with breast cancer and so now I saw little of her, as she rested for much of the day. Alberto, an avid follower of my journey, was always keen to proffer a drink, encouraging me to sit in their beautiful garden for a chat. The drinking was nice but I sensed he had a problem. Like many in Mediterranean Europe, he had found himself redundant in his late fifties, had been unable to find a job for years since and had given up. He tried to keep busy in the garden and in the kitchen. He baked the finest of breads. We had few words in common but enjoyed each other's company.

I stayed four days in Val Maggiore. Marco and I pored over maps, planning the next stage of my walk to Chamonix and the options beyond. He had hoped to join me at some point in the journey, on the bike ride through Spain, or perhaps later in Algeria. But now, with a first child on the way, he was not quite so free. I snatched at bits and pieces to do with the row, but made no concrete progress and was becoming realistic that it was not going happen. My other options were much less interesting and involved breaking my human-powered rule: leapfrogging Libya by plane to Egypt perhaps, and taking a ferry, if there was one, from Lebanon to Cyprus to avoid Syria.

Stopping at Val Maggiore those four days did what I had expected, perhaps caused by my subconscious self: my back was locking up, pain shooting down my buttocks and legs. How could it be that I could flog myself day in, day out with 15 kg on my back and be fine – and then this? Once again, as always, I relied on it getting better once I started off again. I joked with Wendy that I just had to keep moving, could never return home.

On 26 September, the first day of my sixth month, I set off again from Alagna, now with a bit more warm gear in the pack. I was headed for Mont Blanc, the highest point in Europe. The week that took me there was a glorious roller coaster through superlative mountain country with rarely another walker in sight.

After views from all angles of the sparkling white molars of Monte Rosa I soon had my first taste of the decaying black fang, the canine, that is the Matterhorn – for many people the most beautiful peak in Europe. And from the nearly 3,000-metre Zube Pass I caught my first views of Mont Blanc.

As the Matterhorn came into view I was chewing on some Thornton's Special Liquorice Toffee. The sticky, gorgeous, black stuff was going down well, but I pondered on its ability to pull out fillings. It had happened to me before, has probably happened to everyone at some point.

Then at exactly the moment I considered such things I crunched down on something hard. I pulled the lump of toffee from my mouth and there, in amongst the treacle, was AU$2,000-worth of crown. I licked it as clean as I could and, given that in olden times crowns went there, placed it in the coin pocket of my wallet. As I trekked

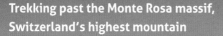
Trekking past the Monte Rosa massif, Switzerland's highest mountain

on I resolved to contact my dentist in Australia for advice. Then, rather unbelievably, that night I saw that this dentist had joined my Facebook page around the same time as I was chewing toffee. Coincidental indeed.

Colle di Nana, Colle di Fontana, Finestra d'Ersa, Fenêtre de Tsan, Col Terray. Passes passed in a haze of scree, scrambling, switchbacks, sunsets, shadows and streams. All under the bluest of autumn skies, the most settled period of weather I'd had on the trek. Only the increasing French nomenclature of the passes, valleys and mountains gave a guide that I was approaching my tenth country. Perhaps it was the ruggedness of the country, the inability to believe my luck or my tiredness, but I felt overawed by the surroundings, felt totally insignificant. I was, of course; we all are. On more than one occasion that week I shed a few tears. But they were tears cried for the sheer goodness of it all; of being in the mountains.

But the goodness of life in the Alpine mountains was tempered by the madness and sadness of death in the Algerian mountains. That week, French trekker Hervé Gourdel had been kidnapped by terrorists aligned with the Islamic State. When the French government refused the demand to pull out of the military intervention in Iraq within 24 hours, Hervé Gourdel was beheaded. I had followed the world news very rarely on my journey, keen to enjoy a year without the endless bombardment. But I could not escape the news that the Islamic State seemed to have taken over from al-Qaeda as the main face of global terrorism, and that the US, the UK, Australia, France and others had returned to Iraq to somehow try to fight against an enemy with no army.

The Vessona valley, like most high alpine valleys, ended in a narrow ravine that eventually disgorged me into the Valpelline, north of Aosta. At Ollomont, Soanna, looking after her mum's bar-cum-general store, looked after me and allowed me to camp in her mum's garden. It felt odd after the wild camps of the previous nights.

On the last day of September the weather finally broke, with fog and light rain all day, and that night was almost my first waterless camp. It is a truism in the outdoors that if you see fresh water and you need fresh water then fill up with fresh water. But still, too often, I believe there'll be more just along the track or around the corner. You'd think I'd have learned the hard way in Australia, where surface water can be so elusive.

Darkness had fallen as I continued along a track high above the valley leading up to the San Bernardino Pass. Everything was damp – but there was no water. On a few occasions I'd divert up or down the slope from the track and ferret amongst the bushes, certain I'd heard a trickle above the wind. Finally, a small stream crossed the track and, given the track was the only bit of flat ground, I pitched my tent across it, happy to get a brew on.

Crossing the Fenêtre de Ferret, I farewelled Italy for the last time and popped back into Switzerland. The fenêtre (window) opened from thick mist in Italy to reveal clear blue skies in Switzerland, and Mont Dolent dominating the views above Val Ferret. Champex that night was quiet, many residents having closed their businesses to take their own holidays before the winter ski season.

Trail marker, Italian Alps

OCTOBER

There is something in October sets the gypsy blood astir:
We must rise and follow her, When from every hill of
flame She calls, and calls each vagabond by name.

William Bliss

O n foot, I'd had a few brief slugs of Slovenian air, then trekked for 52 days in Italy and 8 in Switzerland. Now I crossed into France with Mike, a retired French physics professor and probably the youngest looking 70-year-old I've ever met.

I doubt I'd had a more spectacular border crossing on my journey. Cresting the Col de Balme and stepping from Switzerland into France, I came face to face with Mont Blanc, at 4,810 metres Europe's tallest mountain. Back in the Dolomites I'd declared that I wasn't normally interested in supermodels. But the opportunity to climb up Europe's biggest, was too good to miss; even though Mont Blanc may not be as slender as some, she's a bold and brassy sort of mountain with a lot of facets.

I dropped down into the Chamonix valley where for my first dinner in France – my first night in what some consider the number one gastronomic country in the world – I was served pumpkin soup. Later, Anzac biscuits featured on the menu. It was great to see and stay with old friends John and Anne Norris in their house in Argentière.

It had always been my intention to make an ascent of Mont Blanc during my Alpine trek. It seemed a fitting thing to do – to walk from sea level to the highest summit in Europe. I don't think I've hired a mountain guide before, but conscious of my time limits, not knowing the mountain and wanting to increase my chances of a successful ascent, I did for Mont Blanc; John had recommended that I ask Rick Marchant to guide me. I did that, and was glad, for Rick was great company and we had a ball.

Two days were needed to make the climb. Over breakfast on my first morning, I heard from Rick telling me there was a weather window that day and the next, and we should give it a go. I ran around in freshly laundered clothes trying to get them dry, packed gear for the climb, and made my way to Rick's house for lunch and a quick fit of crampons, ice axe, climbing harness and the like.

We left Les Houches at 3 p.m. on 3 October for the 2,000-metre climb to the Tête Rousse refuge. It was in itself a top walk into the sunset, and we arrived at the hut just on dark. The main refuge had closed for winter a week or so before, but there was a winter room, stuffed overfull with Russians, French, Chileans, Bulgarians and now us. Twenty bodies squeezed into 12 bunks and I slept not a wink. At 2 a.m. the sardine can was opened and four or so were plucked out. The rest of us breathed loudly.

Rick and I rolled out into the darkness at 4.30 a.m. Crampons on, we crunched across some snow and scuttled across the Grand Couloir, a place notorious for stone fall. A steep 500-metre rock scramble led to a snow-covered glacier at 3,800 metres. Sparks from our crampons and head torch beams added colour to the black night.

The first light glowed under the Aiguille du Midi. Soon after, the big cone of Mont Blanc cast her own shadow across the cloud below, stretching for kilometres. What a morning to be where we were. What a day to be where we were heading.

What causes that burst of cold just on dawn? Rick and I reached for down jackets, pulled on warmer gloves. The sun touched us briefly on the Dôme de Goûter, with 500 metres vertical still to climb. But we were soon back in cold shadow on the north-west face of the mountain. Steep, crunchy snow up onto the Bossons ridge led to an ever narrowing, airy snow arête that led straight to sunlight, straight into the sun.

Then this angled catwalk ended and we were on the highest stage in Europe– 4,810 metres above the Mediterranean Sea I'd turned my back on 62 days before. It was 10 a.m. and the stage was empty. I was stoked to be there, to have been given the break in the weather. Beneath us stretched a cloud sea, and looking east across Italy I could trace my route back to the Matterhorn and beyond to the Monte Rosa.

Mont Blanc summit, at 4,810 metres the highest point
in Europe, on an incomparable October day

**From sea to summit. Atop Mont Blanc's summit
ridge, 62 days into my traverse of the Alps**

I fumbled with my phone to switch it on so as to take a summit photo to post on Facebook. A bunch of emails rolled in. I was not about to read them in such a fine place on such a fine day. But something led my eye to just one:

From: Marin Medak

Subject: My plans have changed

I opened it and scanned the words: We failed to get funding for the new business. I want to do the row with you. I will organise everything.

Those words gave me as big a high as the summit itself. Having hugged Rick for the summit, I gave him another huge one for the news. After 45 minutes on the summit we started down; nearly 4,000 **metres** down, to finish a 14-hour day.

I had three days recharging and enjoying John and Anne's fine hospitality. Slotted in amongst this were numerous conversations with Marin. A suitable boat had to be found and delivered to Tunisia; work would be needed on it, equipment made or purchased, and a budget put together. This rowing idea, now a reality, had never been in my original budget. How could it be, given that I'd never in my wildest dreams considered it as a mode of transport? As the spreadsheet totted up I saw the whole exercise could cost me more than €30,000, up to AU$50,000. I hesitated briefly but made the decision that if I didn't go through with it, give it a shot, then I'd regret it in years to come. If I did and found myself in debt then that might bother me for a few years but in a decade I'd have forgotten all about it. And the circumstances of me coming to know it was a reality – on the summit of Mont Blanc – made me feel certain it was the right way to go.

John and I walked together along the River Arve; now I was heading south for the first time in months, on the last section of my trekking arc back down to the sea. He left me at Chamonix; and that night I found a packet of Tim Tams (iconic Australian chocolate biscuits) hidden in my pack by Anne; a final treat to see me on my way.

Despite the time off I felt very fatigued those first days south from Chamonix. The tough trekking to reach Mont Blanc and the ascent of the mountain had probably taken more out of me than I recognised. I calculated that I might reach Monaco in another three weeks and that would put me back on schedule. But then again, the schedule was even more up in the air until we had a timeline for the row. And always I was conscious that any early snowfalls here, still in the Alps, could block my way for days or weeks.

A couple of days out of Chamonix after a long 11-hour day with nearly 3,000 metres of ascent in the legs, I pulled up onto Col de Bresson in light rain and fading light. I debated whether to climb a little higher to the Refuge de Presset and see if there was a winter room to sleep in, or instead to drop down to camp. I decided to ascend – and came upon a very modern refuge with, to my surprise, the guardian, Nicolas, still there. My anticipated winter room turned out to be the full refuge with fire roaring, a couple of beers, a hot shower and a warm doona to sleep under. Nicolas would take nothing for the hospitality.

He had been there 15 years, including overseeing the building of the new refuge. Building had commenced in September and October 2012. A break for winter followed before a final couple of months, April and May 2013. The new Refuge de Presset had cost €1.5 million (approximately AU$2.5 million), with everything brought in by helicopter, just as every packet of coffee, bottle of wine, roll of toilet paper still travels that way.

After breakfast I farewelled Nicolas, who handed me a French Opinel knife engraved with 'Refuge Presset'. On the way down, so often I just wanted to lie down on the track and sleep. My tiredness was not helped by my having taken advantage of the wi-fi at the refuge and so working until 2 a.m. before starting again at 5 a.m; everything had seemed to demand equal priority, whether it was issues with my business back home, forward planning for my journey, driving some fundraising ideas for Save the Children or downloading photos. I could hardly complain, though, sat as I was looking through the picture window at the stars and the black, curving finger of the Pierra Menta rock spire.

After living the high life with Nicolas at Refuge de Presset I descended nearly 2,000 metres to find myself in the lowlands of Landry, a stone's throw away from Bourg St Maurice. First I found a chambre d'hôte with the lights on but no one home. Thinking I might stay, I burgled some wi-fi before moving to the only shop in town: a butcher with a bit of a general store tacked on. A lovely old couple, blood-stained aprons and all, indicated they had a campsite in the paddock behind.

I checked it out – only to find the small area full of cows and the spots without cows full of cow dung. It looked like it had been months since anyone had actually camped there.

Sensing my concerns with the bovine infested site, the old lady, leaving the tripe and the grim, grey pâté behind, showed me into the amenities block. She led me straight past the gents, into the ladies toilets where, in the corner, was a sofa and table. 'Vous voulez dormir ici?' (Would you like to sleep here?) she suggested. Over the years I've called a few toilets home. My preference is for the disabled units: usually clean, spacious and seldom used, they've offered me good shelter in a storm on more than one occasion. Here, dog tired, I crashed onto the sofa, not waking until dawn to the sound of rain and wet cows grunting by the door.

The weather cleared as I climbed up into the Vanoise, fresh snow on the ridge tops and summits. Since I had turned south, the high passes had not reduced in number. But it seemed I was more following the lie of the land, if there can be such a thing in this tortured and twisted landscape. The climbs to and descents from the cols were longer – and still steep, but less so – than when I had been trekking west. Or perhaps my knees and quads were past caring any more.

That night in the winter room of the Refuge du Col du Palet I shared good conversation and a warming fire with five young Frenchmen out for the weekend. The conversation was at its most animated when it turned to the relative merits of Beaufort versus Abondance cheese, both of which were spread out on the table. What I do know is that after a surfeit of *fromage*, that night I had the worst case of wind, which did leave me wondering if the cheese had anything to do with the Beaufort scale.

The near 2,700-metre Col du Palet serves as a watershed between the natural beauty west of the pass and the nightmarish scene east. Tignes and Val Claret represent

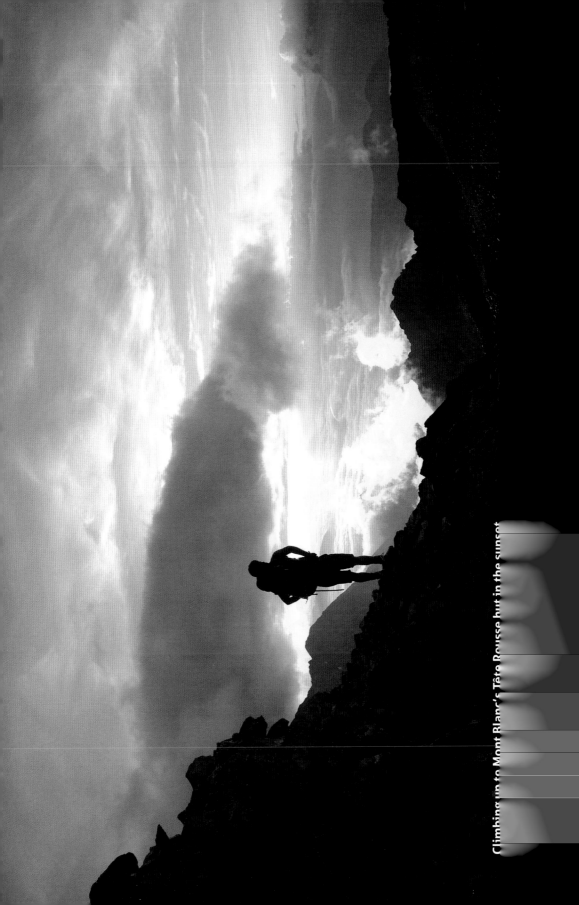

Climbing up to Mont Blanc's Tête Rousse hut in the sunset

the worst of insensitivities visited upon the Alps: a suburb's worth of ugly apartment blocks transported high into the mountains for the benefit of skiers. A suburb that lies essentially empty for eight months of the year. France, more than any other Alpine country (although Italy isn't far behind), has excelled in building the ugliest ski resorts in the most beautiful of locations.

Two of the Frenchmen, Pierre and Nicolas, set out westwards with me. We were through the col and climbing away with our backs to it within minutes. While Nicolas struggled through lack of fitness, Pierre and I strode on, energised by the pace and the conversation. In his late teens Pierre, from Paris, had set up an online education portal which had in the past six years grown to employ over 30 people; this system was, he was certain, the future of education. Where the glaciers of the Grand Motte stood stark against the blackest of skies and snow began to fall, I said goodbye to Pierre, who stopped to wait for his companion, and spent a day soaked until a late camp.

The following day I escaped to lower levels to avoid the snow up high, and dried out a little in the village of Termignon. At the Hotel la Turra, David and Séverine, who had recently jumped from corporate life in northern France to owning a small hotel in the Alps, looked after me with a fine lunch and an offer to stay, but I carried on down valley toward Modane.

After 171 days, after asking at innumerable houses, shops, bars, boats and more if I could camp, I had my first refusal. I found myself in the large town of Modane in the rain, in the dark. I wandered up to the nearby campsite. '*Fermé* (Closed)' said the gate. It was pouring rain by now, so I knocked on the door to ask if I could throw up a tent, no facilities required. A straight '*Non*' met my request. Really? 'Go find a hotel,' was his only suggestion. October/November is the dead season in the Alps; after summer and before the ski season. Most places, including hotels, were now closed and understandably people wanted a break. I found a spot in the nearby industrial estate behind the campsite.

After another knee-jerk descent, this time from Col de Girardin, I wandered into the four-house hamlet of St Antoine. Michel was moving rocks in the garden. I asked if I could camp '*Bien sur* (of course),' he replied. His wife Annie came out, and within minutes I was ensconced in a little garden cabin overlooking the gorge below. I'd just come through the Queyras region of the French Alps, enjoying some clear days of blue skies and autumn colour. Most of the village festivals celebrating the return of the herds and flocks from the high alpine pastures had been held. Occasionally I'd hear a single bell of a goat or sheep that had somehow missed the train to lower levels and would now suffer alone when the winter snows arrived. The tinkling of bells was now replaced by the tinkering of men preparing ski lifts for those hoped-for snows: re-attaching chairs, hanging Poma poles, checking snow-making equipment.

Since leaving Mont Blanc I'd generally been following the GR5. This long-distance walking route starts at the Hook of Holland in the Netherlands on the cold, murky North Sea and finishes at Nice on the warm, clear Mediterranean. But most people trek the section from Lake Geneva south. In these last weeks on foot, so much of my body was protesting: my left knee twinged, as did my groin, I couldn't lie on my right hip for the pain, my back ached. I felt simultaneously both so strong and so weak.

Autumn colours as I trekked through the French Alps

You know the situation; you're sat in a restaurant, you're the only one there and you wonder if there's a reason you're the only one there. Is the food inedible? Should you go someplace else? So it was in St Etienne de Tinée. I'd come through from the bar to the restaurant, passing junk everywhere and a woman ironing sheets in the lobby area. I was shown to a table, surrounded by empty tables and left with a menu. The young waitress closed the door behind her. Was I trapped? Should I dine or dash? But I'd already put down roots; I'd given her my phone to charge.

Anyway there was little else open. I ordered pizza and salad. It was France, but you could almost frisbee a pizza base from St Etienne into Italy. The pizza was perfect, the salad just right and the dessert to die for. Sadly the aftertaste was ruined by my strawberry-flavoured toothpaste. Two things I'd learned in Europe; the only small tubes of toothpaste you can buy are sweetly flavoured for kids, and it is almost impossible to find a breakfast cereal that doesn't have chocolate in it. The dentists must love them both.

I'd hoped that dinner in St Etienne might be a celebratory one – but that day, sat upon the Col de la Cavale with an impressively horned chamois looking on, I had received a message from Marin. Our offer to buy a row boat in England had been knocked back; beaten by a higher one. It had seemed a good boat at a good price but we were back to square one. My budget was limited and within it so was what was available in the rather niche sport of ocean rowing.

Traversing the Maritime Alps, my journey across the mountains was entering its final week to Monaco, my tenth and smallest country. At the 2,500-metre Col du Rousset, my last high pass, I looked south over the lesser and lower ridges between where I sat and the sea. A sea that was still well out of sight, though. A herd of some

25 chamois hopped across below me, spotlighted by the last rays of the sun. Mornings were frosty and ice hung on the tent. I'd timed it well, been lucky again. In a few days the clocks would change and I'd lose an hour of evening light to trek into. Luck was with me again when with only a couple of days to go I tripped over myself and tumbled head first off the track down a steep slope. It seemed an age before I finally came to rest upside down in a bush. Those autumn days I was as likely to slip on the fallen chestnuts that littered the track as on loose rocks.

Soon after my fall, camp that night was again right on the track itself, perched above the Vésubie valley, my tent half on rock, half on earth. The following morning I strolled into the tiny village of Belvédère for my first *Tourte de Blettes*, a tasty sweet and savoury combination of beet, nuts and raisins; a speciality of the region.

I'd been stuffed full of fine and rugged mountain scenery for nearly three months and was now ready for some more open country. I love the mountains, love the vistas – but in the great mountain ranges of the world so much is hidden. That had never bothered me before; in fact it is part of the appeal. But I was starting to crave some wide horizons and smaller undulations. My penultimate night was in Moulinet, a pretty town in the Bevera valley. The country was drier here, still high but influenced much more by its position close to the Mediterranean. On a warm day snakes would come out for a final pre-winter flourish; I saw four. The hunters were out too and I met a couple grinning about the *sanglier*s (deer) they had shot. Descending to Sospel, I walked through my first olive grove since leaving Muggia, and into a town celebrating the 70th anniversary of their liberation from the Germans by American troops.

At the Col du Farguet I went over 1,000 metres for the final time. I'd already dropped off the col when I realised I hadn't looked back. So I climbed back up to the pass and bade farewell to the Alps. I looked back, looked back for the first time in some

A leaf falls to the ground as autumn takes over in the French Alps

A chestnut opens amongst the autumn leaves

hours, and saw only a cloudy haze hiding the mountains. It was the first veil across the mountains in more than 10 days. It was as if the mountains were telling me to move on, the curtain was closed, the show finished; telling me to get on with the next stage of my journey. A man was sat 50 metres away and I rather self-consciously waved at the haze, blew a kiss in the direction of the mountains, waved at the man. Then I turned away and walked down from the Col du Farguet for the second time.

My last camp on the trek was at a picnic area at the Col de St Pancrace, on the edge of cliffs 600 metres above the sea. In the morning, haze and fog kept the Mediterranean still hidden. I'd walked less than a kilometre when I came to a gateway etched with 'Make your life a dream and your dream a reality'. The statement was a little trite – life is rarely that simple – but it suited my mood that morning. Behind the gates were a Porsche 911 and a top of the range Mercedes. Different dreams, different realities.

As I wandered out of a *boulangerie* in the village of La Turbie a man waved from the other side of the busy road. It was Robert, Secretary of the Monaco Alpine Club. With him was Margaret Cooke, an old friend of my parents who I had not seen for a quarter century or more and who now lived in Monaco. We sat down for coffee and *Tourte de Blettes*, and were soon joined by Pierre, president of the club, his wife and a few other club members. All had come to escort me the final kilometres of my trek into Monaco. We wandered down tracks and streets, and I hardly noticed the transition from France. First stop was the Exotic Garden, for me to sign the Via Alpina visitor's book and to be given a presentation from the club. Then lunch at the markets before the final steps to the Place du Palais, where a sign, located just beneath another pointing to the toilets, marked the start/finish of the Via Alpina.

On 26 October, exactly six months and almost to the hour since I had kayaked away from Gallipoli, I had reached Monaco. I arrived after the most satisfying of alpine traverses; 84 days, something well over 2,000 km. At least 130,000 metres of climbing; the equivalent of ascending Mount Everest from sea level about 14 times, Mont Blanc 25, or Kosciuszko (Australia's highest) 65 times. All my gear had held up remarkably well. Indeed it was only on the final day into Monaco that a button gave way on the Ex Officio shorts that had marched with me across the Alps for every one of those 84 days.

To date my journey had exceeded expectations on every level; the physical geography, the human geography, the sheer physicality of keeping going for eight to ten or more hours a day, month after month. Coincidences and acts of kindness had touched me time and time again. If I'd been concerned at the outset that I would perhaps tire of all the humanity that lives and recreates in the countries bordering this great sea, I found myself, and continued to find myself, in its thrall.

I really appreciated everyone giving up the best part of a day to welcome me to Monaco, which is, after the Vatican, the second smallest country in the world, the most densely populated and the wealthiest. Both Robert and Pierre were true Monégasques, a minority in the principality. Margaret gave me the run of her apartment, and I would have stayed longer than one night but needed to get back to Marco and Elena's to prepare for the next leg; across France and down Spain by bike. Whilst Marco would have brought everything to me in Monaco, I wanted some time to rest up, do some detailed planning for the following months. I'd allowed 100 days for the trek, and had

always planned a week back at Val Maggiore, back at Casa Dolce, so was now back on schedule.

Marin told me he had found a row boat, languishing on the Cape Verde islands off West Africa. The price seemed right, partly because of its location, half of what it had originally been listed for. The boat was sitting on some scrap land and had not seen water for three or four years, the current owner, a Portuguese, having abandoned her there during a planned attempt to row to Brazil. Marin negotiated a price of €6,000 on condition of inspection, and was preparing to go there in November to check it out. If all was well he'd close the deal, start work on the boat and prepare her for shipping to Tunisia. I was in a bit of a dream with all this; excited that *mediterr année* looked to be maintaining its human-powered integrity.

Wendy and I talked as often as we could in those weeks. We were both glad that the halfway point had passed and we could look forward to being together again, hopefully in less than six months. But the situation with our errant builder had gone from bad to worse, and we were now preparing for court action to jolt him into action. It was hard on Wendy, and I felt rotten that I was not there to fully fight the battle.

NOVEMBER

November is usually such a disagreeable month . . . as if the year had suddenly found out that she was growing old and could do nothing but weep and fret over it.

L.M. Montgomery

After a foie gras-style week of eating, the scales rose some 3 kg. I was ready to get back on the tracks, get on the bike. First, though, Marco and I had to deliver *Miss Grape*. An old friend, Mark Turner, had driven up from his home near Barcelona

to meet us at Nîmes in the south of France. He would take her back to Spain and ensure she was waiting for me in Andalucia, where, after 2,500km on the bike, I planned to start kayaking again. I confess that despite my own journey being human-powered, the logistics of moving my gear around was hardly environmentally friendly.

It was a hellish journey to Nîmes and then back to Monaco; 11 hours of driving through driving rain. I was grateful as ever for Marco and the time he was giving me to make my journey work. After offloading *Miss Grape* at Nîmes, Marco and I were starving, and I succumbed to my first fast food of the expedition. We laughed at the paper placemats featuring cartoons of Marco the old fart and Hugo the cool young dude on a skateboard. The names were the wrong way round.

Another three hours in the foul weather had us back in Monaco at Margaret's apartment. The news that night showed the damage across the south of France from the storms; rivers flooded, buildings collapsed, beaches dumped up on boulevards. Marco was joining me for the first day and night on the bike, and in the morning we rode back to the Place du Palais. I leaned my bike up against a wall.

'You cannot let go of your bike; it is the law.' A young gendarme of Prince Albert's guard had run up to remonstrate with me. I responded that cars were parked in the square and their owners were not required to be with them. It made no difference and he put his wrists together in the handcuff position. I asked was it OK to put my bike where the cars were parked. He glowered at me: 'You cannot let go of your bike; it is the law.' The journalist from the *Nice-Matin* newspaper who was with us was as intrigued by the regulation as I was. So eventually, unable to sit down and have a last Monégasque coffee without breaking the law, Marco and I pedalled the few hundred metres back to France.

We dodged a lot of debris along the coast to Nice. The wide Promenade des Anglais along the Nice waterfront was in places piled high with sand and trees. On one occasion we swerved past a navigation buoy that had broken its moorings. From Nice we climbed away into the hills, riding well into darkness until we found a place to camp, near Peymeinade. It was the first time I'd shared a tent on the journey and now knew how Marie-Clare and Jon had felt.

Helmets on, we ram-raided the local boulangerie the following morning and kidnapped half their morning bake of *pain au chocolat* and brioches. Then, pleased and full from our endeavours, we gave each other a big hug and said goodbye. Next time I'd see Marco he would be a father; he was setting out on the biggest adventure of his life.

While he set off back to Monaco, I slugged another coffee in Peymeinade and looked at the next to useless tourist map in front of me. Marco, being a young lad, lives by the GPS while I'm a paper sort of guy. It was then I decided to go back to the sea to apologise.

I realised that I'd not given *la Méditerrannée* much attention in that past week. I'd come down to her in Monaco, but amongst the welcomes at the end of the trek I'd hardly glanced at her let alone touched her. I'd actually got pretty excited when 10 days earlier, on the top of La Batterie I finally saw her again as I came toward Monaco. I even peered over the cliffs on the Rock in Monaco and also stared at her from the balcony at Margaret's apartment at sunrise. But it was a bit like an old flame you see at a party that you don't acknowledge as much as perhaps you should. Even the previous day I had focused more on what she'd thrown up in the massive storm than on the sea itself.

Now I felt lethargic; every time I stopped I'd find an excuse to stop longer. I threaded a pleasant route back down to the coast where the Mediterranean was calm now. Near St Tropez, in what seemed a very brave piece of marketing, I passed some billboards advertising the resort of Maxim Plage. The boards showed a swimmer on the surface with a vicious-looking shark coming up from beneath. Mind you, if marketeers can make people want to pay twice the price of petrol and 2,000 times the cost of tap water for a plastic bottle of the stuff, then perhaps they can make swimming at shark-infested beaches become all the rage.

At Plage de la Douane I found myself in a bar by the beach. A quick beer was the plan, and then to find a camp before dark. But Michel the bar owner and Mohammed, a St Tropez chef of Moroccan heritage, were insistent I sample the 'best rosé in the world'. The local wine was good, very good, but finally I made my excuses. I need not have worried. A full moon cast a silvery highway across the sea and shone plenty of light as I put up the tent on the beach. Small waves rolled onto the sand, and I was happy to be reconnected with the sea for the first time since my last beach camp in Croatia at the end of July.

Soon after I'd set off, in the town of Cavalaire-sur-Mer one of my pedals fell off the bike, leaving it attached to my foot. I took my shoe off with pedal attached, and a man stopped to enquire if he might help. Laurent, suffering badly from multiple sclerosis, asked me to follow him and we were soon in his garage, a garage full of old bikes and bike parts. He explained how he was, before the disease had stopped him, a keen bike racer. The best we could find was an old road race pedal that, whilst I could not clip into it, gave me enough platform to pedal on to Le Lavandou and a bike shop.

The day after, I was somewhere east of Toulon when I pulled up for a coffee mid-morning. *Var Matin*, the local paper, was on the bar and the front page shouted to me that France were playing Fiji in Marseille that evening.

I did some quick calculations. I had never planned to go through Marseille, but with a rugby game on, could I now make it? I pedalled hard through Toulon and onward and, after 130 km, as the sun dipped low in the Calanques, flew down the hill into Marseille, France's most cosmopolitan city. With 45 minutes to kick-off there was no time to find accommodation so I weaved amongst the crowd heading to the stadium, all the while wondering what I'd do with my gear. So I asked a policeman who asked a security guard and soon the bike was behind bars.

As I was lining up for tickets the ticket touts saw a likely target: 'Only €60 for you.' It only said 20 on the ticket. 'OK, give me 40.' No thanks, I'll wait in the queue. 'How much you want to pay?' By now a tall, slightly scruffy bloke had approached me. 'I've a ticket; my friend can't make it.' Yeah right, I thought, but he seemed genuine.

For €15 I was in, and Gilles and I headed for a pre-match beer. He turned out to be a Breton, a marine photographer now based here on the Mediterranean. 'The stadium; it's beautiful, yes?' he asked and stated at the same time. 'It opened one month ago. It is named Vélodrome.' I'd fittingly and unknowingly arrived by bike in a country where they name a football stadium after a bicycle stadium.

As we sat down I received an email from my father. It was 21–21 at half-time, Wales versus Australia in Cardiff. I hadn't known they were playing; he didn't know I was at a test match too.

The Marseillaise is one of the most rousing of national anthems. To hear 60,000 Frenchmen sing it in Marseille brought a tear to my eye. Quietly, 'God Bless Fiji' was sung. I cheered for them but nothing could save Fiji. They were hammered. Wales were just unlucky.

Late that night I found a cheap hotel in the old port area, the Hôtel de Rome et St Pierre. Pulling back the sheets in one room revealed a bed full of stray hairs, then there was a full toilet in the bathroom. I was 'upgraded' but the electronic key didn't work, so I was upgraded again. I was tired and hungry and didn't need an hour of this. I refused to pay, they grudgingly agreed (I said it was a cheap hotel) and I shovelled in a meal at a cheap Tunisian restaurant nearby.

The following day was foul. I eventually forced myself out into the downpour, into a nightmare leaving Marseille. Being sprayed by passing cars as much as by falling rain, I was glad to get out alive. The weather eased. Then it absolutely hammered down. Within minutes roads were flooded and awash with gravel. At the village of St Julien, after kayaking ... sorry, riding down a river ... I mean road, I decided enough was enough and took shelter in the local community club. It was packed for the monthly bingo session. Focus was intense; this was France, there was food to be won. I listened out for 'two fat ladies' but this was France. I camped under an awning by the club while the fine couple running a food van for the bingo just kept bringing *crêpe* after *crêpe* to me. It was an unsavoury dinner, but all the sweeter for that.

In improving weather I pieced together a route that took me eventually to the Rhône, one of Europe's great rivers, which I crossed near the end of its journey to the Mediterranean. I was in the Camargue, the great Rhône delta country that took me back to a geography project as a young kid. I recalled being told about the wild horses of the Camargue – but not the wild mosquitoes. A superb camp on the edge of the Étang de Vaccarès was, as many camps can be, spoilt by the little bastards.

My 200th day since Gallipoli coincided with Armistice Day. At the eleventh hour of the eleventh day of the eleventh month I stopped at the ancient walled town of Aigues Mortes to observe a minute's silence.

At le Grau-du-Roi I rode along the sand on a very windswept beach, surrounded by hundreds of kite surfers and windsurfers taking advantage of the public holiday. After being sandblasted along some bike paths I stopped at Carnon to watch a sailing boat go out, capsize and be dismasted before eventually being smashed up on the beach. In the conditions, there was a certain inevitability to it all.

As I cleaned sand from my ears and watched the carnage on the water, I received an email from Marin: 'You now own an ocean row boat. Congratulations!' My dad, Bernard, who had brokered the payment from the UK,was copied into the email: 'PS Bernard, I promise I will take good care of your son, but any tips on how to handle him, if he won't be rowing hard enough, are more than welcome.'

Marin had been in Cape Verde for some days, checking out the boat *Paraguacu* and meeting with its owner. He reported it was in good condition and would, after a bit of

A windy Armistice Day 2014 in the South of France keeps wind and kite surfers happy

work there and in Tunisia, be fit for our purpose. He also assured me that when I sold it I'd get my money back and some. This was real now, an experienced rower, a boat soon to be put into a container and shipped to Tunisia. I still couldn't believe my luck with Marin. It was all too good to be true – indeed so much so that I was racking my brain as to what sort of scam this young man, who I had met only once, could be trying to pull off with my money.

Beyond Sète, still following the coast, I met Victor coming the other way. You couldn't miss him on the bike track, given he was taking up more than half its width. I like to travel as light as possible on the bike: a couple of small rear panniers, a backpack and a handlebar bag. But Victor, an Austrian, had three spare tyres (I carried none), a ukulele and a three-person tent. I asked him if that was in case he got lucky. 'Of course not; I thought I might want to put my bike inside with me.' I asked him if, in the three months he had been on the road, he had ever done so. 'Of course not' he replied.

I left the Mediterranean behind to follow the Canal du Midi, pleasing riding along the old towpath and occasionally ducking out onto narrow country lanes, to a camp beyond Béziers. I left late the next morning, but still enjoyed a beautiful winter's day riding through vineyards on quiet roads south west of Narbonne into Roussillon. In fading light I crossed over the Col d'Extrême – which, at 251 metres was hardly so – and continued in the dark to Estagel, arriving around 7 p.m.

In 1984 I'd hitch-hiked to the south of France and found myself at that village. I'd wandered out to the vineyards of Cotes du Roussillon and, at the first one I came to, asked for work in the grape harvest. Within 10 minutes I was cutting sticky black bunches from the vines. Jean and Annie were the most beautiful of bosses, and I worked for them that year and the next. But a decade or so later I lost touch with them.

Now I had arrived back in Estagel. I went to a bar in a village which seemed bigger than I remembered. This time I asked not for work but for Jean and Annie – but for the life of me I couldn't recall their surname. Soon the whole bar was focused on the names I'd given, including the only other clue I had: their daughter was Françoise, a gendarme. Most in the bar had probably not been born when I was last in Estagel. Finally an older man who had come in said 'Jorda! Jean et Annie Jorda.'

That was it; that was the name. I was getting somewhere. But, '*Ils sont morts*' (They are dead), said the older man. I was getting nowhere. I was saddened but not totally surprised, given what would be their age now. Apparently Françoise was now a nun, which did surprise me. I finished my beer, pedalled out to the local rugby stadium and pitched camp.

That night I wondered, though. Perhaps, maybe, possibly there were other Jordas? Had something been misunderstood in translation?

The following morning, as every morning in France, I went into a boulangerie for a *pain au raisin*; health food for cyclists. The woman serving was quite old. '*Je cherche Jean et Annie Jorda.*' Conversations ensued with two other customers. '*Oui, ils habitent Rue Michelet.*' I couldn't really believe it. So much so that I then rode around to the tourist office where a very helpful lady made a few phone calls and confirmed the address.

I pedalled around to Rue Michelet and at locked gates, pushed the intercom bell marked by a nameplate *M et Mme Jorda*. There was no answer, so I pressed again. Nothing. My heart sank. Then a woman looked out from the balcony above. 'Oui?' Stupidly, I just said their names. She looked confused, understandably with a bloke on a bike at her own gateway apparently asking if she was who she knew she was. '*Attend*' (Wait), she said. Minutes later Jean appeared. This time I said my name and mentioned that I had worked for them years ago in the *vendange*. The gate opened and I went up to the door. A moment's confusion before huge smiles and hugs.

It was a beautiful few hours of laughter, showings of family photos, remembering. Both now 80, Jean said they had talked about me only a few months earlier. They were emphatically not dead. Annie was in good health whilst Jean had suffered some heart attacks and some accident with an exploding bottle that had damaged his eye and part of his face. Françoise was certainly not a nun but was still working as a customs officer in Dijon. It was Patrice, her brother, who was the gendarme.

Jean and Annie wanted me to stay but I had to go. Annie made me a lunch to take. We hugged and said *au revoir*, even *à bientôt*. See you soon. Who knew?

I pedalled away from Estagel and towards Spain in spitting rain, a very happy man. It had been a vine reunion indeed.

The kindnesses that day continued into the foothills of the Pyrenees. At tiny Serdinya late afternoon, a café insisted on feeding me before adding to the weight for my climb with a bag of fruit, cheese and chocolate. The dusk sky darkened some more with black clouds, and heavy rain began but I pushed on over 1,000 **metres**, the highest I'd been since Col du Farguet on the last days of my Alpine trek. I was sodden and cold when I dropped into Fontpédrouse, some sleet starting to fall. At a small but closed campsite I met Philippe, a permanent resident from a caravan. He rang the

'Ils sont morts' (They are dead), I was told. But Jean and Annie Jorda were emphatically still alive when I surprised them for our first meeting in 30 years

owner and organised for me to use the lounge, which was dry if not warm. As I peeled off wet gear, Philippe came back with some wine. Wrapped in my sleeping bag I toasted Jean and Annie Jorda and France. Spain was only 35 km away.

It was a cold, grey day when I climbed up and over to Spain via the 1,579-metre Col de Perche. I thought to divert through the little mountain nation of Andorra but decided I'd leave Switzerland as my only country without a border on the Mediterranean Sea. At least the Swiss had some connection, having chosen Valencia in Spain as their 'home port' to defend their America's Cup sailing victory in 2007.

Spain was the first overseas country I had ever visited, back in 1979. Then it was in the midst of a frenzy of economic growth in the creation of tourist hotspots along the various Costa del Somethings. Now, along with Italy, it was one of the big economic worries of Europe. The relative minnows of Portugal and Greece were bad enough but the debt in Spain, along with some 25 per cent adult unemployment and up to 50 per cent for young people, stood as a time bomb for Europe. In Catalonia, the first Spanish province I would ride through, everyone was watching the independence referendum in Scotland with interest. If Scotland broke away, what would it mean for the UK, for the EU? Would a yes vote lead to others following suit? Catalonia had long considered itself a candidate for independence from the rest of Spain, with its different language and its economic wealth based upon the great city of Barcelona.

I stopped for my first night just across the border in Puigcerdà, a sizeable town on the altiplano. I've mentioned before that Europe loves chocolate in its breakfast cereal – but Spain takes this to a new level. In the cereal section of the supermarket at Puigcerdà the only option lacking chocolate was something called Golden Grahams, sickly sweet wheat pieces dipped in sugar and honey.

In the months leading up to my arrival in Spain, a couple of friends there had sketched out a route for me, a proper mountain bike touring route that contorted its way down the coastal ranges to Andalucia. It was what I asked for. On my first full day in Spain, a bitterly cold day, I pushed and grovelled in the dirt on some very marginal trails that were enjoyable but very time consuming. I finally arrived at Col de Pal to find Mark Turner waiting for me.

Col de Pal sounded like a fitting spot to meet a friend of 30 years' standing. Back in 1985 we had both been mountain activities instructors at a kids' adventure camp in South Wales. This guy, with a shock of red hair and almost luminescent green pants, was my co-instructor as we threw kids off a cliff. They were attached to a rope, although as the summer wore on it was tempting to not bother for some of them. Mark ended up in Spain; not, as many Brits do, for the sun; redheads rarely chase a tan. He had fallen for Isobel, a Spaniard, and moved to near Barcelona where he'd spent the last 15 years on the right side of the tracks as a train designer.

Exactly as he had been 30 years ago, Mark remained committed to clothing and equipment best described as colourful in the true sense. It is probably no bad thing for cycling. Together we flew down an endless descent from the col, and I felt the coldest I'd been on the journey. Snow was forecast for the following days so I decided to go low and stay low. After thawing toes by a heater and hands around a hot chocolate, Mark headed back to his car and home; with a plan for us to meet up again in a few days.

Heading through the quiet back roads of Catalonia was, apart from being so, so cold, most enjoyable. I loved the uncertainty of not knowing where I was going to stay each night; loved the fact that a random decision to go down a particular track or enter a particular bar seemed so often to lead to good things and great people. After dark I arrived in tiny Estaras and started to pitch my tent in the garden of an empty house. Within minutes half the hamlet were out, and soon I was ensconced in the community hall with heating on and the run of the place whilst food arrived.

After climbing to the top of a road sign marking the town of Montblanc, I climbed up into the Prades Mountains to the pretty village of Prades. It had taken me 30 years to reconnect with the Jordas, in France, but much less to reconnect with Jordi a few days into Spain. I had first met Jordi Roch, a physiotherapist from Tarragona, in a violent and vile sandstorm on the first stage of a mountain bike race across Mongolia in 2010. Along with Mark, it was Jordi who had been helpful in planning a potential route through Spain for this expedition.

Jordi met me in Prades and we enjoyed an incomparable day of mountain biking, weaving a magical route on rocky trails and single track through cliffs, vineyards and

Excellent winter mountain biking with Jordi Roch in the Prades Mountains of Spain

villages of the Prioritas region until well after dark. At La Morera de Montsant, Jordi suggested a quick stop for a cold drink on a day so much warmer than those before. Well over two hours later we rode out into the late afternoon sun with belly full from a fine lunch, and mouth still enjoying the aftertaste of the local red. 'We must get our Prioritas right, Huw' said Jordi as we toasted the day. I can't recall actually having the cold drink we had stopped for.

The final laugh of a day of fun came right at the end. I opened my handlebar bag to find it full of pureed tomato. A large, soft tomato I'd forgotten about was sitting in the bag with my head torch on top. Seven hours of rough riding had the torch blending the tomato to a pulp, and I lay in the tent that night sucking tomato juice from the torch headband.

Whilst I would have loved to make my way down Spain on rough tracks similar to those Jordi had taken me along that day, I decided to keep to the back roads, to try and put some days in the bag. My head was jammed full of logistics for the next few months, continually trying to guess dates, trying to fit in a break, perhaps for Christmas. And always aware that north Africa would throw change at me.

To the detriment of Spain, and not its fault, my head was at times too full of other stuff: the endless planning of logistics and timing that would give me a shot at being back at Gallipoli within the year. Too often my eyes were on a small screen, not on the big screen where I actually was.

In Spain more than anywhere, I let this looking ahead, this planning, dominate my ride through the country, but in reality there was probably little choice. Marin and I were in almost constant communication regarding the row and everything to do with it. I was also trying to deal with both getting a visa for Algeria and understanding what the possession of one would allow me to do. There were many conflicting messages coming from the travel agent there, an agent I was forced to work through if there was to be any chance of obtaining the visa. Finally there was more immediate stuff relating to my need to kayak from Europe to Africa once I'd reached Gibraltar – the permissions required and then, once across, the logistics of moving *Miss Grape* from Morocco to Turkey for our final rendezvous.

Sadly train designer Mark arrived a day too late to join me on the Via Verde, a disused rail line I followed through to the old village of Cretas. It was impressive, cutting through dozens of tunnels west into the mountains. En route I rode past the old station at Bot, which seemed a fitting place at the end of a long day in the saddle. In Cretas' Bar Culture I met a couple: he from Switzerland, she from Malta. Four years earlier they had bought land nearby with plans to set up a campsite. Four years down the track, they were still battling local government bureaucracy. It is the same worldwide; governments full of people who do not understand the realities of the outside world, and who are paid regardless of the efficiency or quality of their work, act as probably the key blockage to economic growth. The couple were just about out of money now; stuck with a block of land they could not use and, in the economic crisis of Spain, were unlikely to be able to sell.

I was the last person to leave the bar, about 11 p.m., and came out to frustration. My bike was locked to a drainpipe outside the bar with a combination lock that had worked well up until then. I started to question my own four-number combination as I punched it in time and again with no result. I questioned how much wine I'd drunk. Was this one of those dexterity or memory tests given to see the impact of alcohol? No: my memory was absolutely correct. I was tired, ready for my tent. The barmaid gave me some pliers but they made no impression. Finally, a Spanish couple came past and I enquired as to whether they were local and if so did they have any bolt cutters. They were passing tourists, too, but the young man was obviously well used to such things. He grabbed the pliers and levered the hook open to break the lock and I was free to ride into the night to camp.

At La Senia the following night, I was rejoined by Mark to ride into the province of Valencia. The two of us threaded a route through hills, over passes; riding through small villages and a few towns, drinking *cortados* and *cervezas* along the way. So many places seemed so quiet. With the economy devastated, Spain was hurting for sure. One night we camped in the garden of Jose's half-built house at Costur. He had started building it 25 years ago. Now, having lost his job as a truck driver, he doubted he would ever finish it.

Mark, with his bright orange bike, vivid yellow panniers and clothing to match, had competition from the citrus plantations, heavy with oranges in the Valencia region that names them. But he shone amongst the muted shades of the olive groves where the harvest was now in full swing. Some had machinery to shake the olives down onto shade cloth laid under the trees whilst the traditionalists just beat them down with a stick.

On our second night together Mark and I ate in a cheap bar in the middle of one of Spain's premier olive oil regions. A good salad arrived and with it a little sealed plastic bag containing two tiny sealed portions; one of olive oil, one of wine vinegar. We asked for the good oil; real bottles of the local stuff. The owner of the bar shook her head. An EU directive had banned bottles of oils and sauces in food outlets for hygiene reasons. Only individual sealed portions were to be used. How has it got to this, allowing these bureaucrats in Brussels, Rome, Sydney or wherever to do these things? Fortunately most bars and restaurants ignored this particular madness, and indeed sanity ultimately prevailed and the regulation was later withdrawn.

After our night camping by the waterway with the longest name I'd seen those past seven months – Canal Principal E. del

My old mate Mark Turner joined me for a few days riding and did a huge amount to help with the logistics of moving bike and kayak the length of Spain

Generalissimo B. de Carraixet – Mark left me to ride into Valencia to catch the train home. But the following Friday he would have to leave the train factory in Barcelona for the last time. As I said, Spain was hurting.

A good measure of a country is, I think, the quality of their barbers. For a decade or more I would wait until my annual trip to India in order to visit my favourite street barber in a town in the Himalaya. Before I left from Gallipoli on this journey, a Turkish barber in Çanakkale was magnificent. Without asking I had not only cut and trim but ear candling, nose plucking, head massage all for the princely sum equivalent to AU$3. It was one reason driving me to finish back there in April 2015.

After riding through the rugged Cortes gorge country I chanced upon the Spanish town of Anna, and just had to stay there, named as it was after my granddaughter. It was my first day off the bike since leaving Monaco three weeks and 1,700 km earlier.

In Anna, local barber Miguel trimmed and shaved me whilst his wife Susanna was delicately shampooing her mother-in-law. It turned out Miguel was a keen mountain biker and, by the time he was done, not only would he take no payment, he was insisting I join them for lunch.Some hours later I was tucking into an absolute feast cooked by the freshly coiffed Matilda, Miguel's mum. In celebration and thanks I broke into a rendition of 'Waltzing Matilda' part way through lunch.

Mountain-biking barber Miguel and his wife Susanna gave me a haircut and looked after me in their town of Anna, Spain

Before I left Anna, Rodrigo, a Director of Save the Children Spain, drove down from Valencia to meet me. It was great to catch up and hear about some of the work that Save the Children do there. Rodrigo told me that one in three Spanish children lived in poverty and 90 per cent of their work was domestic. He also told me about his dream: to take a pedalo, one of those ubiquitous beach resort pedal boats, around the Mediterranean. I loved the idea, both how insane it was and how Mediterranean.

My time in Anna also helped bring into focus a new logistics issue I'd been grappling with; how to get *Miss Grape* on her way once I'd finished with her on the far side of the Strait of Gibraltar. My original plan had been to kayak across from Europe to Africa, then to kayak the Mediterranean coast of Morocco. But messages I'd been receiving from Morocco and, to a lesser extent from some kayakers in Gibraltar, were indicating that any attempt to kayak the Moroccan coast would likely be met by being endlessly stopped by security forces. Out of the blue I'd received a letter from El Mamoun Belabbas El Alaoui, the President of the Fédération Royale Marocaine de Canoë-Kayak, offering all assistance. But as we corresponded it seemed apparent this assistance might well involve police escorts and more, which I fancied was a bit hard by kayak. Places are usually much easier than the naysayers or the media portray but I didn't want to get stuck in Morocco with a 5.3-metre-long sea kayak and blockages preventing progress through the country. There was enough uncertainty with my traverse of Algeria, and I was now investing so much in the row across the Mediterranean from Tunisia. I wanted to keep things simpler, to increase my chances of staying on track.

Having juggled all the options over the past weeks I arrived at a plan. If I got across the strait by kayak, I'd aim to catch the weekly ferry that took three days to go from Tanger-Med in Morocco to Genoa in Italy. In Italy I could meet up with Marin, discuss the row and give him *Miss Grape*. She could be put on a ship to Greece, where Stavros would organise for her to be delivered to Turkey to wait for me there. Having done this in Italy, I could fly to UK to have a break over Christmas with my parents. I could then fly back to Gibraltar, take the ferry across the Strait of Gibraltar with my bike and start the riding across Morocco. Simple really.

I felt I needed a bit more of a break than a day here or there. I was trying to monitor my body, looking out for signs as to how I was doing. I'd noticed that I was happy to fall asleep again in the morning after waking up. Normally I'd be up and at things by 5 or 6 a.m. But now I was dozing off again until 7 a.m. or later, keeping my head cocooned in the sleeping bag. Whilst 10 days or so in the UK over Christmas might eat into the schedule, it might be an important rest to set me up for the final four months of the journey. Then news came from Marin that the shipment of our boat from Cape Verde to Tunisia was delayed until 28 January. This was annoying from the point of view of the overall schedule, but it ensured I could take a break without feeling guilty.

As I was travelling through Spain I was also trying to understand what was required of me to kayak across the Strait of Gibraltar that separates Europe from Africa. The strait is the only natural entry and exit to and from the Mediterranean Sea, where the waters of the Atlantic pour in and out. It is also one of the world's busiest shipping lanes. Control of this strategic location had been fought over for centuries but my concern was who controlled it now; who I would need to talk to allow my crossing. Even before I left Australia I'd been in touch with the Gibraltar Kayak Club. Within minutes of sending an email my phone rang. It was Nigel, the club president, calling to Australia. He indicated the club would do all it could to help when I reached their tiny enclave perched at the end of Europe and would most likely have a few club members kayak with me.

However, as I pedalled further south into Spain it had become harder and harder to get replies from Nigel and others, and when they came, they were often rather cryptic; more back-pedalling than taking me forward. The politics of Gibraltar – the war of words between Spain and the UK – was not helping much either. I did glean that the Spaniards had overall responsibility for the strait, and I fired off a speculative email to Tarifa Trafico, supposedly the Spanish authority responsible for traffic in that narrow but turbulent channel of water.

Meanwhile, I was really enjoying the ride through the back roads of Spain in the quiet of November. Making up the route as I went along, up and over ranges – the sierras – of various sizes, practising my non-existent Spanish, 'burgling bars' and bakeries. It was in the nondescript town of Fortuna, north of Murcia, that I first started hearing the volume of Brits; on market day I wandered into a cafe filled with Cockney and Brummy accents. The weather seemed to be the overriding factor for people being in Spain; that, plus the much cheaper living costs. It didn't seem to be for Spain or the Spaniards, both of which I often found people decrying. Nor did there seem much desire to learn the language. In Fortuna I diverted down some side streets and was rather surprised to come face to face with a large crocodile and kangaroo. Both hung from the wall of the tired and tacky-looking Jackaroo Inn. The bar was closed so I didn't have to taste Fosters – Australia's favourite beer. I can't recall the last time I actually saw that beer in Australia, but it must be at least 20 years.

On the last day of November, after riding through the Sierra Espuña, I dropped down to the Mediterranean for the first time in Spain. I parked my bike against a *No Dogs* sign on the beach, sat on the sand and looked east. I hoped it wouldn't be too long before I finally headed in that direction, facing Turkey, not with my back to it.

It was dark and raining by the time I rode into Mojacar, with thoughts of camping on a beach or perhaps under a palm tree in front of a five star hotel. 'Bar San Pedro – Belgian Beer café' caught my eye amongst other cafes advertising the 'Great British Breakfast.' The bar was, unsurprisingly perhaps, full of Belgians and the owner too was a Belgian, Pedro. His parents, despite no connection whatsoever to Spain, had called him Pedro as they liked the name. Now living in Spain. Pedro had come to Andalucia to run road bike tours for a Belgian company and then opened this bar nearly a year ago with his partner Nikita. They plied me with Belgian brews, and before I knew it they had the shirt off my back and my *mediterr année* cycle jersey was hanging in Pedro's Bar. That night I stayed in their apartment, rising early with Pedro and Nikita; they to drive north 2,000 km to Belgium for a break, me to head south through the impressive coastal scenery of Cabo de Gata toward Almeria.

Soon after this photo was taken and after plying me with copious amounts of Belgian beer, Nikita and Pedro took the shirt off my back (to hang in their Belgian beer cafe in Mojaca, Spain)

I met Rolf, from Germany, near Almeria in Spain. He was
walking around Europe on the side of main roads.

★ ★ ★

As I rode above the cliffs I suddenly burst into tears. Nothing had presaged it, but
I found myself sobbing into the wind, and continued to do so for some minutes. I
wasn't upset in any way but perhaps just sub-consciously needed to release some
emotions.

Those past seven months my path had crossed those of very few long-distance
travellers, or at least those moving under their own muscle power. As I rode toward
Almeria I caught up to a heavily tattooed bloke pulling a trailer. Rolf was from Berlin.
In 2005 he had fallen asleep at the wheel of his car and the result was various broken
bits, deafness in one ear, blindness in one eye and a lifetime annual payment from the
German government. He had left Berlin in January and had been walking ever since:
down Italy to Sicily, across to Sardinia, up to France and now down Spain. In August
he had been hit by a truck in France and spent two months in hospital. Now he was
sticking to the coast, following roads busy and quiet, and surprised me when he said
he'd only once been invited to stay somewhere in those ten months. Next he planned
go up the west coast of Spain and Portugal then across France and over to the UK. Rolf
talked about wanting to walk to Australia, talked of how he wanted his name to be
famous for something but didn't know how or what. I rode on, Rolf walked on.

No more than 10 km later I came upon Enrico – bike, luggage, trailer and two dogs.
He'd been on the move for two years; was now on his fourth lap of Spain. I enquired as
to why only Spain. 'It is too expensive elsewhere and too difficult with my dogs.' I rode
on, Enrico too, his dogs pulling him up a slight rise.

Beyond Almeria I looked up from battling into the prevailing westerly wind. A wind I didn't want for my next 10 days back in *Miss Grape*. I looked across a sea – a sea of plastic which merged into another sea; the Mediterranean. Hundreds upon hundreds of acres of plastic hothouses all the way to the edge of the water. I shuddered at the thought of how much fruit, salad and vegetables never saw pure sunlight; only light filtered through plastic. In the wind the plastic sheeting drummed an awful rhythm.

This plastic sea eventually parted to reveal Almerimar. The owner of the bike shop in Almeria, which I'd ridden through 50 km earlier, had recommended it as a good place to meet Mark, who was driving down from Barcelona with *Miss Grape*. I looked down on the dusk lights of a nightmare: Almerimar was a sea of apartments, finished and unfinished. How much resource is ploughed into creating places that are essentially dead for most of the year? Places that have no sense of place, no link with their surrounding landscape.

I met Mark and *Miss Grape* in the car park of a supermarket. They'd driven over 800 km that day. Mark was sanguine about his unemployment – and I was in some ways grateful for it given he now had the freedom to keep my plans for Spain and Gibraltar on track. The campsite in Almerimar was closed for winter and only the five star Hotel Golf Almerimar seemed open. A massive room, soon filled with kayaking and bike gear, came with an equally large TV, the first I'd switched on in months. I assumed the two sinks were so I could wash camp stuff in one and clean teeth in the other. The hotel was none too happy when Mark started washing my bike in the car park, and the ping of golf balls continued from dawn to dusk from the range outside our window.

DECEMBER

It is December, and nobody asked if I was ready.

Sarah Kay

After nearly 2,500 km on the bike over the past four weeks and two nights in some people's idea of luxury, I was ready to set off in the kayak. Unfortunately the weather was not ready for me. My old friend and foe, the Mediterranean wind, was blowing 25 knots from the west, the direction I was headed. Mark drove onto the sand and offloaded *Miss Grape* and me to wait for the wind to drop, while he set off to take my bike the 300 km to Gibraltar.

The kite surfers were relishing the weekend wind, and Aron, an Albanian working in the hothouses, invited me to stay with him. It was a kind offer but I wanted to be close to the sea, ready to go, so in the early evening I pitched camp on the beach, feeling more comfortable than I ever had in the hotel.

That evening I received a strange email:

> Good afternoon sir:
>
> Welcome to the Strait. Congratulations. You are an 'ausi', strong and hero.
>
> I hope and I desire that you will finish your hard trip safely and happy.
>
> I was in your great and good country, Perth, Fremantle, (Australia).
>
> Why do you choose Gallipoli for starting. I suffer pain for your patriots Australian suffering at that Place in the first world war. For me it is very shadow the song 'Matilda.'
>
> A big hug and be lucky.
>
> Julio Berzosa Navazo
>
> Algeciras Harbor Master.

The email was a response to the one I had sent to the Spanish authorities regarding my desire to kayak across the Strait of Gibraltar. It didn't help me much.

The sea was calm the next morning and *Miss Grape* and I got to know each other again after a four-month separation. The plastic hothouses dominated the coastline, and where they came right down to the sea plastic that had been ripped off in storms tangled with rocks and timber to further scar the shore. The hothouses marched ever higher up the surrounding hills which had been carved out to make some horizontal space for them. In this dry climate of Andalucia each hothouse required water to be pumped up from the aquifer below, and I'd heard what an environmental and human disaster the whole operation was. Once the aquifer was depleted all that would be left would be thousands of acres of plastic. Thirty kilometres inland, I could see the snow-plastered Sierra Nevada topped by Mulhacén, at 3,483 metres Spain's highest mountain. Anyone looking down from there to the coast would think they too were looking at snow or ice, not a glacier of plastic. The hothouses had certainly transformed the economy of Andalucia – but at what cost?

After making good progress for four hours back in *Miss Grape* I landed at Adra, a grim town encased by plastic farms and encircled by fine mountains that deserved better footings. I went in search of caffeine and arrived at a nondescript-looking place under a block of flats. Once inside I was transported to a world of ships, yachts and pirates. I found the piratic owner particularly grumpy but his coffee was good and his tapas even better. Whilst I was sipping my first *cortado*, Mark rang. He was on his way north after dropping my bike in Gibraltar. As we spoke I saw that a vicious westerly had blown up – enough to make galleons run for cover and kayakers order a second coffee.

Mark was near and I wasn't going far. Within an hour he'd joined me on his way back from Gibraltar and I was back in the pirate's bar for a second time. I was building up the courage to try my first *cafe bonbon*; an inch-thick sludge of condensed milk topped by an espresso. Perhaps tomorrow.

After a second farewell in as many days, Mark drove off and I walked back down an ugly expanse of decaying promenade.

'Hello my friend.' That time-honoured greeting when you're about to be accosted and sold something you really, really need. This was worse, as a ruddy-faced man was waving a bottle of whisky at me. 'I'm Russian, I'm a crazy guy. It's my birthday. This is my dog,' was his introduction. He had just enough of an innocent smile to make me think he was perhaps innocent. I'll give him a minute, I said to myself. In the end I gave him fifteen. Dennis had sailed somehow down rivers and across seas from Baltic Russia to Istanbul and hence to the Mediterranean. 'I am crazy, yes? We carry your kayak to the port. You stay with me tonight. I have beer and I cook. I have guitar and we sing. We have a crazy night.' He showed me photos of his tiny catamaran, like a Hobie on steroids. Dennis hoisted his large dog to sit around his neck like a scarf. I wished him happy birthday.

By now it was late afternoon and with the wind not abating, Adra was going to be home for the night. By the time of my third visit to his cafe, the grumpy pirate was now my good friend Juan. He was even grabbing marine memorabilia, in an instant transforming himself from pirate to respectable midshipman or a commander with authority. When I left to set up camp below the promenade, Juan handed me a bag of large oranges.

The coast of Andalucia had its moments, and west of Adra I passed some nice sections. I stayed in the kayak until after sunset when a small shark that wouldn't leave my rudder alone and the sudden winter cold had me aiming for a small cove inaccessible from the road above it.

What I've learned over the decades is that if you're in a mountain wilderness or the wide expanses of a desert and have not seen anyone for some days or weeks, your chances of company are much increased by dropping your pants and having a crap. It's happened to me countless times, and talking to others it seems I am not unique in saying a cheery 'Good morning' whilst waving a handful of tissue.

In the world of sea kayaking there are those who, when the time comes, take their paper to a place inland from their beach camp. Here the deposit is made, the paper hopefully burned and all is well. Others, the beach buriers, dig a hole in the sand, make their deposit, burn their paper and all is well. The third group are those who look for an intertidal dump. They head to the wet sand, near the edge of the water and the business is done. Within a short time – and sometimes, if the timing is bad, before the business is even finished – the waves come through to wash it all away. The breakdown is invariably fast and all is well.

I'm a long-time member of the intertidal dump club. Unfortunately the Mediterranean is without a tide to speak of. In my months along its coast I'd finessed my methods. Often I'd find a piece of plywood, polystyrene or plastic on the beach and use this as my pallet. Then it was simply a case of frisbeeing it out to sea where the wind and waves would eventually capsize it, throwing the cargo to the fish.

Just after dawn in my little cove the muesli put out its call and off I went. I managed with some pride to skim the turd-on-a-lid a couple of times until it settled a few metres offshore. Well satisfied, I returned to finish packing up camp. From nowhere four skin-divers came down onto the beach, quickly slipped their fins on and started walking backwards into the water, straight toward the lid. I looked away.

★ ★ ★

The winter sun was pleasant even though the actual air temperature was cool and the water cold. As I went west the hothouses disappeared but apartments and hotels increased, making it harder to find quiet beach camps. I stayed a night in La Herradura, in a smart boutique pension managed by Christina, a large (in the sporting basketballer/discus thrower mode) Romanian woman who almost single-handedly carried *Miss Grape* up to the hotel. Christina's story was similar to many others I'd come across in the economic crisis of southern Europe: she worked seven days a week, on call 24 hours a day, and was lucky to have one or two weeks off a year. Her monthly salary of €1,500 was actually much better than many others, but it was clear that if she complained or asked for more the owner would find someone else. Job security was zero.

I was rather glad I was kayaking the Andalucian coast in the winter months. For well over 100 km the coast west of Torre del Mar was essentially wall-to-wall apartments and resorts – the infamous Costa del Sol that any country keen to expand its beach tourism should study and learn from.

Sections of the coastline seemed dedicated either to the Spanish or foreigners. As I paddled along, I could tell from language – and looks, of course. In winter, the northern Europeans were for the most part of the older generations and of them the Brits were the easiest to spot. They seemed to carry themselves in a way that looked a bit worn out, whether in clothing, poise or both.

I approached the city of Málaga on a very windy day, slogging into the westerly wind, cold from continual salt-water soakings. Marin and I would want this winter westerly to aid us in rowing east, but right now it was a pain for me in Spain. The last time I'd been to Málaga was as a teenager back in 1982. I'd crewed a yacht delivery from London to Italy, and the owner flew in to Málaga to join us for the last few weeks, having missed the rough seas of the Atlantic and Bay of Biscay. Keith's sole intention on the trip was to get himself laid one way or another, and in various ports he'd pay us not to come back on board too early. Finally, on the last night, on the island of Elba off Italy, he met with success and could head home to his wife and kids satisfied with his holiday achievements.

Now off Málaga, I was conscious of not landing too close to the middle of the city so pulled up in the eastern suburbs on a small beach beneath a grandiose building that had seen far better days. Outside were parked a dozen very fancy cars. I stepped, dripping, into the building, into another world: a huge room ornately decorated with a small number of tables and a large number of well-dressed young waiting staff. At one table sat a gathering of a dozen or so men, all in well-cut suits drinking from the finest of glassware. A puzzled refusal of my request for a spot to camp was not unexpected, even if it was only the second such refusal of my journey to date. On the terrace outside, Marianna, a Dutch woman in her fifties, had also stumbled upon the place and was enjoying a glass of wine in the wind. I joined her in both and she mentioned she was staying at a hostel, the Melting Pot, a kilometre or so down the beach toward the city. This was my first backpacker's hostel of the journey. Four Germans carried *Miss Grape* the 200 metres from the beach into the hostel courtyard. Apart from myself and Marianna, they were the only other residents except for an overweight, middle-aged German man who was utterly full of himself, everything he had done and the crimes he'd committed. The following morning Marianna discovered he'd vanished, together with her money and much of her food.

That morning I received another momentous email from Marin. In it was the news that ELES, the Slovenian national power utility, had come on board to sponsor our row boat. I told Marin that I'd always had a soft spot for Slovenian electricity. Joking aside, it was brilliant news and meant that provided I could sell the boat after we'd finished I might come out not too deep in debt from the row.

Marin was delivering on everything he had said he would, plus a whole lot more. By now we'd also decided to change our plan. This had been to row from Tunisia past Libya to Egypt, from where I had hoped to continue by bike somehow through to Turkey. But the troubles in the North Sinai of Egypt, the impossibility of going direct from Israel to Lebanon and of course the issues of crossing Syria itself were all cause for concern. Now our new plan was to go from Tunisia to Malta and then strike out across the guts of the Mediterranean toward Crete, to Cyprus and a landing in Turkey. It was certainly a disappointment for me to be missing some of the Mediterranean countries of north Africa and the Middle East, but I would now gather up Malta and Cyprus instead. Just as importantly, I was about to embark on a voyage so far out of my original planning and so new to me as to make me even more excited about the months ahead.

Passing Málaga port I shot a selfie or two of *Miss Grape* with the Cunard liner *Queen Elizabeth* in the port behind us, knowing which boat I'd rather travel in. A beautiful mountain scene formed a backdrop to the high-rise horrors of the likes of Torremolinos and Fuengirola. I didn't see the need to land all day until I surfed, after sunset, into an apartment-backed beach at Calahonda.

One of the beauties of most of the European countries bordering the Mediterranean is the pride the people have in their regional cuisine, the passion for their food and their style of cooking and presentation of it. Whilst this meant I was well fed on my journey it also meant I sometimes craved another taste. Perhaps it came from living in a multicultural country like Australia where so many of the world's cuisines are on offer. For months I'd been hanging out for an Indian meal – and Calahonda delivered. In a shopping centre set back from the beach I found first a pub run and populated by Brits, and then an Indian restaurant run and completely populated by more of the same. Dal, a malai kofta and naan breads totally satisfied my craving.

The Indian meal that Thursday night celebrated my being less than 100 km from Gibraltar; that meant two more days' paddling to complete a 7,500 km traverse across the width of Europe. Things were happening now that might give me a shot at kayaking the strait. People were working on trying to help me to find an escort boat, but little could be done about the impending weather. The forecast was ugly for the coming weekend and on the night of Monday 15 December the ferry from Tanger-Med would leave for Italy: a ferry that only went once a week and one that I had to catch if my plan to get *Miss Grape* on her way and me to UK for Christmas was to work. It looked like any window to kayak across would be closed by both weather and ferry timetable. And it was still unclear to me if an attempted crossing was legal or illegal.

'But first at all you should take so much care. It looks as you are a brave Aussi gentleman. But at this time of the year as you know is winter and the Strait of Gibraltar nowadays is a very busy traffic from both directions East-West and North-South.'

I was now speaking with Julio, the harbour master of Algeciras, who had sent me that strange but welcoming email a week earlier. This kind man was trying as hard as he could to be helpful within the bounds of his job. He was forwarding me weather forecasts, gently encouraging and warning me. Julio was also contacting potential support boats, as was Karen from Ocean Village Marina in Gibraltar.

My final night in Spain was fittingly at a place called Buenas Noches. An oily-calm sea was painted completely pink by the setting sun as I came around to Buenas Noches from Estepona. Thirty-five km away to the south-west I watched the Rock of Gibraltar disappear into blackness. Friday morning dawned; another beautiful calm winter's day. As I paddled closer to the rock I watched an endless stream of ships go east and west beyond it. I tried hard to enjoy the moment, to forget about what might be in the coming days, and to relish this key moment in my journey so far. A long, lonely stretch of sand, 10 km in length, the most extensive piece of unbuilt coastline I'd seen in the past 300 km, marked my approach to the rock. The end of Gibraltar airport's runway and a fence heralded the border of this tiny outpost of Britain – and my 13th country.

Just before 5 p.m. on Friday 12 December I paddled into the shadow of the huge rock, the northern Pillar of Hercules, 426 metres high. A small gathering was on the beach including the Gibraltar media along with Paul Lyon, chairman of the local Save the Children branch, and two others from the group. After the welcome and interviews were done, Eyleen from the local paper then asked the question: 'So your plans are to paddle across the strait?' I replied that if weather and other things were in my favour then that was indeed the plan. 'Oh, it's just that it's not allowed' she replied. Eyleen was the first person to actually say that outright to me. Neither Nigel from the sea kayak club, nor the Gibraltar Port Authority nor anyone from the Spanish authorities had stated it clearly as such. I was even more confused.

Soon only Paul and I remained on the little beach. Paul was the headmaster of the only high school in Gibraltar, a man well known and well connected in the small community of 30,000 people. Nigel had said that my kayak could be kept in the club shed on the other side of the peninsula. He turned up to help me transport *Miss Grape* the kilometre across the neck of land, while Paul went off to sort some accommodation for me before heading to the school Christmas disco.

In the car Nigel apologised for his busyness that weekend, something I fully understood given the closeness to Christmas. Although he was still saying he was keen to paddle with me on the Sunday if he didn't have too big a night at his wife's work Christmas party the evening before, I felt like there was no real intention to join me. Nigel then went on to say that various club members had said they would not paddle with me. 'They know your plans to cross north Africa and do not want to be part of a bad news story,' he said. Undoubtedly there would have been many over the years wanting to swim, kayak, row, hang-glide or use other esoteric means to cross the strait. It is the same with any iconic crossing: the English Channel, Florida to Cuba, Bass Strait. I could understand locals might be a bit gun-shy, but it seemed so different to the attitude on display in the months previously.

We unloaded *Miss Grape* and put her in the canoe shed, and Nigel gave me a key. Then I realised my sin, my Brisbane River moment. Back in 2002, on the final day of the Sydney to Brisbane leg of my City2City project around Australia, I had biked down to the Brisbane River at Mogill Ferry. Across the river, I could see Ingrid and Graham waiting with my kayak. I rode straight onto the cross-river ferry that took me across to them, to the kayak that I would use for the final kilometres of my human-powered journey. It was not until I was paddling down the river afterwards that I realised my error. The ferry ride, less than 100 metres long, was not human-powered. Without thinking, I'd broken my self-imposed rule – a rule that I had stayed true to for every other step, ski slide, pedal revolution and paddle-stroke of 25,000 km around Australia. And now, here in Gibraltar, I'd taken a car across the peninsula for a kilometre. On realising my error I determined I'd atone by walking across later.

As Nigel drove me to my accommodation, Karen from Ocean Village Marina rang to tell me that the Royal Gibraltar Police had offered to escort me into the strait. The catch was that they were only able to do so as far as the three-mile territorial limit. Beyond that it was for the Spanish to look after me, they said. Karen had tried the Spanish but got nowhere other than learning that they would come and rescue me if it was required.

Emile's Hostel was a pretty seedy place, but it was conveniently located and I had a lockable room. The hostel was run by one brother whilst a nursery, on the same property, was run by another. Backpackers and people fallen on hard times crossed paths with little kids doing Santa Claus and reindeer paintings amongst a scent of marijuana and decay.

I needed to celebrate my 231 days across Europe and also to make some sense of the previous 90 minutes. I found the Venture Inn and was soon sipping a pint of Fullers London Pride and crunching on a pack of Walkers crisps. The Mediterranean was to the east, the Atlantic to the west, Europe north and Africa south. But Britain was all around me. I'd walked past fish and chip shops to reach the pub, and nearby, a narrow main street indistinguishable from any in a small British town was dominated by Marks & Spencer, BHS, NatWest Bank and others. Posters advertising Jumper Day for Save the Children filled the windows. Apt perhaps, with my fundraising focus and the fact that I wanted to jump across the strait.

A sign sat in the urinal of the toilet of the Venture Inn: 'Out of Order.' It was perhaps prescient of my time in Gibraltar. Saturday dawned cold, grey and windy. The latest forecasts indicated that Sunday would be grim and Monday marginal. I met Paul for coffee, our conversation punctuated by every second passer-by stopping to catch up with him. He made a few calls and joined the many people now trying to help. But as the day progressed I felt the likelihood of me paddling the strait slip further away. The weather looked unlikely to fall in my favour, I had an escort boat from the Royal Gibraltar Police but would be abandoned only three miles out. I spoke to the helpful police marine unit and it seemed certain that for me to continue alone, unescorted, might risk an international incident. Even though they were keen to help, they were not keen to pass me directly to the Spanish.

A Spanish charter boat operator had offered assistance – but at a price of €800, which Julio described as modern piracy. That Saturday morning Julio contacted his superiors all the way up to Madrid to enquire if his nation could help me beyond the three-mile limit. The message came back down the chain to say they would not, due both to the precedent it might set and, as with the Gibraltar Police, issues of borders and politics. 'They are all friends of mine in Gibraltar, but you must understand the official difficulties,' Julio told me.

The official difficulties to understand were that the British had captured Gibraltar from Spain in 1704 and despite numerous Spanish attempts to take it back the territory has remained a British colony. In 1967 and again in 2002 the Gibraltarians voted overwhelmingly to remain part of Britain, and this remains a thorn in the side of the relationship between the two countries. For long periods Spain closed the land border between itself and Gibraltar, essentially a partial blockade. And even now, when I was there, long queues formed at the border as the Spanish customs routinely and laboriously delayed people crossing over – an annoyance for the many who worked on one side of the border and lived on the other.

As I was on the phone to Julio in the lounge of the Emile Hostel, Adam, a young Irish backpacker, overheard our conversation. He told me he'd met an American yachtie the previous day who he understood was planning on leaving for Morocco soon. Perhaps, if I couldn't kayak across, I could at least sail across? Wind wasn't human-powered, but it would be better than taking the diesel-powered ferry from Algeciras.

I walked in the rain just before dark to the kayak shed to wash *Miss Grape* and rinse out the still wet and salty gear from my arrival in Gibraltar the day before. By the end of the evening, after a couple of pints of Tetleys and having spoken to Wendy, I was quite sanguine. Yes I was dangling on the edge of Europe with Africa only 13 km away but I couldn't expect Lady Luck to be with me at all times. She had been with me for so long for so far, and now the things in Gibraltar – the mixed messages from the kayak club, the politics of Spain versus Britain, the forecast weather, the lack of a support boat – were all part of the deal.

By mid-morning Sunday I'd made the call that the crossing would not happen. Monday's forecast was even worse. At some point I had to start planning to get myself and *Miss Grape* to Algeciras to catch the ferry to Tanger-Med in time for Monday night's boat to Italy.

First, though, I wanted to visit Europa Point, the most southerly point of Gibraltar and Europe. I realised I had not even looked fully across the strait since I'd been there, had been too tied up in the narrow streets and marina quays. En route I found the American yacht in Queensway Marina, a tattered Stars and Stripes hanging off her stern.

'Beer, rum or both?' was my welcome aboard from Greg. Down in the cabin, in a fog of cigarette smoke, were Greg and Lydia, both drinking both beer and rum. It was 10 a.m., a little early for me.

I listened first to stories of his Atlantic crossings – embellished, I was sure – and so was Lydia. 'You're full of shit, Greg,' she said. 'It took us a month to get here from Barcelona and you can't tell the difference between a cruise liner and an island. You're a fucking useless sailor.' At every opportunity, Lydia would query Greg's stories or pull them down as the rum bottle swung back and forth between them. He was from Philadelphia and claimed to own a large window-fabricating business that funded his sailing. Lydia had been born in Montenegro and brought up in Serbia. She had married a Bosnian and moved to Sarajevo but left there during the Balkan wars to end up in Mallorca. I think that's where she and Greg had begun their disrespectful relationship.

'Look, I need to get out of Europe before I'm taxed €20,000.' I'd heard these stories before: non-EU boat owners were required to pay VAT on the value of their boats if they stayed in the EU too long. 'What do you know about Morocco?' he asked me. 'I'm happy to sail over there with you and the bitch; lash your kayak on the deck. Forecast is for force 11 this week – yeehah! I love sailing in those conditions, and it would make a man of you.'

Eventually I found enough of a chink in the mad conversation to make my excuses and take my leave. I promised to call them back later. 'You bastard, you won't call. Too rough for you, is it?' screamed Greg. He was right.

By the time I'd walked the couple of kilometres to Europa Point it was absolutely pissing down, and on the point itself blowing enough of a gale as to make it difficult to stand up and impossible to keep a hat on. Behind the point was a large mosque, facing across to Muslim north Africa. The waters of the Strait of Gibraltar were wild; a good 35 knots was blowing through and huge waves were ripping past the point. Occasionally the clouds parted enough for me to look across to Jebel Musa, the southern Pillar of Hercules, but for the most part Africa was unseen. I was content with my decision or at least the one made for me.

Then my phone rang. I took it in the bus shelter, out of the wind. 'Huw, it's Shane here from Dolphin Adventures. I hear you're looking for a boat. I've spoken to the boss in England and he's happy for us to come over with you.'

I thanked Shane for calling but told him that the weather was foul and there was no way I could see it improving for Monday, the day I had to go. Shane reckoned the forecast was not as bad as it looked and suggested I call in to see him when I got back to town.

With the rain hammering down, I decided to take the bus back to town. James, the driver, let me on early out of the weather. Instead of asking for money for a ticket he offered me a big bucket of sweets. All the way back to town we talked about the Spain/Gibraltar relationship, my journey and his interest in whether Australia was really a continent or just an island. 'Take a few more sweets. There's no charge for the bus for you,' were his parting words as I stepped off the bus by the Ocean Village Marina.

Shane was just bringing the *Dolphin Explorer* in to the quay, having towed a bloated and decaying dolphin out from the marina. While Shane moored the boat, I went into the dive shop and started chatting with a young lady from Leicester who worked there along with Dan, an English guy who it seemed had recently moved to Gibraltar and was a keen diver.

In the cramped office at the back of the shop, Shane called up various forecasts. The current conditions were expected to ease by Monday morning but there was some conflict as to what might happen next. Some forecasts indicated reasonable winds, 10–15 knots and seas of 1–2 metres. Others were much more pessimistic. But all agreed that conditions would worsen on Monday night. But it's not just the wind that matters in the Strait of Gibraltar: complex tides and currents of up to 4 knots push back and forth from the Atlantic to the Mediterranean, depending on the state of the tide and the phase of the moon. For a slow craft like a sea kayak that cannot push into such currents, you need to aim away from your destination and hope your calculations are correct to ensure you land where you want to land, not be swept past it. For the strait it meant an actual paddle distance of some 30 km to reach the little Spanish enclave of Ceuta, which was only about 15 km distant as the crow flies.

With a waning moon and high tide at nearly 9.30 a.m., Shane reckoned a mid-morning start might work; might allow me enough time to get across before current and predicted weather increased.

There was certainly a chance, and there was now a boat in support. This met the still unclear legal requirement, and offered the ability to warn shipping and, if things got really bad, some safety. I just needed to switch my head from Off to On mode. I enquired how much this was going to cost me. His boss had told him he could do it to meet fuel and crew costs and Shane reckoned £300 (AU$600) would cover it. I realised that was more than fair for a boat of that size with three crew but wondered if I could afford it for what I considered was a less than even chance of success.

'I'll pay for the boat.' Dan had been leaning in the office doorway saying little while Shane and I had talked. 'I can't believe what you're doing and wish I had the balls to do something like your journey.' An unbelievably kind gesture. Boats, bus drivers, bankrolling; everything was coming into order. I had no reason not to give the crossing a go. I thanked both Shane and Dan profusely and we agreed to meet at 8 a.m. the following day.

By now it was late afternoon. I went to the canoe shed to start preparing *Miss Grape*. The shed door was ajar and inside was a man with long, curly, wet hair and one leg. He looked up at me. 'You're the fucking lunatic who plans to get beheaded aren't you?' I was taken rather aback by the introduction. 'You're the idiot who's going to paddle along north Africa.' I introduced myself to Norman and told him that it was certainly not my intention to lose my head. I explained my current plans, as Norman was about six months out of date. He had kayaked across the strait a couple of times over the years but had abandoned his most recent attempt to Morocco due to bureaucracy. I told him how helpful the Fédération Royale Marocaine de Canoë-Kayak had been to me; Norman had never heard of them and was keen for a contact.

With all the things going on that Sunday, eating had been forgotten and I suddenly realised how hungry I was and how I might need some fuel for the following day. It had been years since I'd been into a Pizza Hut, but there was little else open in Gibraltar on a cold, wet Sunday night before Christmas. As I devoured a fluffy-crusted vegetarian pizza I received a call from the national coach of the Fédération Royale Marocaine de Canoë-Kayak. I was remiss in not having kept them updated with my latest plans, but everything had moved so fast. I told him I planned to attempt a crossing to Ceuta the following day. He assured me they would have someone at the Ceuta–Morocco border ready to take *Miss Grape* and me to the ferry port at Tanger-Med. Remembering one other link in the chain, I called Carolina from the Ceuta Tourist Office. I'd assumed the border with Morocco to be very close to the harbour in Ceuta and was a bit surprised when she told me it was about 5 km away. Fifteen minutes later she texted me back to say she'd organised some local kayakers to pick me up and transport *Miss Grape* and me to the border. Everything was almost in order.

As I woke at dawn on Monday morning, thoughts and clichés, similar to many I'd had in similar circumstances over many years, came to mind. Triumph of hope against experience. No point spoiling the ship for a ha'p'orth of tar, and of course, as always, that line from The Clash: 'Should I stay or should I go?'

As the sky lightened, I could see the flag on the top of the Rock of Gibraltar flapping more than I wished to see. 'Ah that's just up high,' I reassured myself.

As I walked to meet Shane and Dan, a breeze was coming off the water and halliards were clanging on masts. 'Ah that's just funnelling between buildings.'

The forecast hadn't changed much. But what had I to lose? There was a big yellow boat coming with me, the *Dolphin Adventurer*; they were ready, I was ready. I grabbed a few bars and bananas, threw down a couple of coffees. 'You're the bloke on the front of the paper today,' said the guy in the cafe. 'Good luck with the rest of it.'

Just before 11 a.m. I paddled away from Gibraltar, from Europe. The next 30 km was neither Europe nor Africa; a sort of purgatory in between.

Heading towards Africa
in the Strait of Gibraltar

Miss Grape having fun on a wave in the Straits of Gibraltar

It was a bit lumpy at first but things eased as I headed toward Punta Carnero, heading south-west. It always feels strange to be heading away from where you're going, but I needed to bear away and use the current and changing tide to ferry-glide to Ceuta. As always it was tempting to turn too early toward my goal but I'm rather glad I didn't.

I'd never kayaked with a support boat before, and it was reassuring, when over 100 ships traverse the strait daily, to have this large yellow boat next to my tiny kayak. Shane was at the helm, Dan was keeping me posted on progress, Rosie was spotting dolphins and Louisa was crewing. Plenty of banter and conversation early on, but I realised I also had to buckle down. Off Punta Carnero I turned toward Jebel Musa, that mountain in Morocco. Now I was in the strait proper.

Conditions were pretty good; some small waves and a south-west wind slowed my progress a little. Plenty of big ships around. 'There's a big bow wave from a container ship on its way, Huw,' shouted Dan. 'Hey look at the dolphins playing in it,' said Rosie. It was all happening behind me. 'Probably about a minute away, Huw.' I glanced behind to see this big wave bearing towards us. *Miss Grape* was picked up as the wave hit but we pulled off the back.

'Eight miles to go. You'll be pleased to know a couple of big ships have just changed course to avoid us,' smiled Dan. I had learned that he was a businessman in his early 30s who had his fingers in a few pies. At that point he was manipulating a sandwich.

There was little doubt that the wind was getting up, a good 15 knots with some spray and waves broadsiding both our boats. Shane was doing a great job trying to hold

DECEMBER

123

the *Dolphin Adventurer* in position to offer me some shelter from the wind and waves. It didn't always work, and we had to be careful not to get too close to each other.

By 2 p.m. I started to see the outline of the buildings of Ceuta, a tiny part of Spain surrounded by sea and Morocco. But of more concern was Punta Almina, the easternmost point of Ceuta: would I make it inside the point before being swept past? Now it was getting harder. The sea was full of whitecaps and waves, the wind getting stronger all the time; much harder to paddle into.

'Wurble wurble, Huw.'

'I can't hear you, Dan.'

'TWO MILES, HUW!'

Now I was inside Punta Almina. That was a relief, but I was not there yet: the combined effect of salt-encrusted glasses and my heading, straight into the sun, meant it was hard for me to see where the harbour sanctuary was. A couple of decent sized waves broadsided me. *Miss Grape* was having fun. I thought how much of a difference it made psychologically being out in those sort of conditions with a powerful boat nearby.

Around 4 p.m. we came toward the high port walls of Ceuta. As we did so a large Spanish police RIB came charging out of the sun. I kept paddling, leaving Shane to drop the *Dolphin Adventurer* back and meet the welcoming party. A huge amount of politicking between the UK and Spain manifests itself in petty battles and point scoring.

In the sanctuary of the harbour I was stoked, absolutely stoked. It had been about five-and-a-half hours across. Only 24 hours earlier I'd given up hope of getting a suitable boat or suitable weather; I had been trying to resolve how I'd feel about having to take the ferry across the strait.

Then I realised something. I'd never gone back to walk across the neck of Gibraltar after Nigel had driven me across. A Brisbane River moment indeed.

Shane brought the boat into the harbour. I so wanted to buy the crew a drink to celebrate, but without going through all the paperwork they could not land in Ceuta. We shook hands through a drain hole on the side of the *Dolphin Adventurer*. Shane had done a brilliant job manoeuvring the boat, and Dan deserved a beer and a big hug for his generosity.

Having shouted my intentions to the police waiting for me ashore, I bobbed around in the calm of the harbour and rang Wendy. It was 3 a.m. in Australia but 5 p.m. in Ceuta; the time we had got married on that same day in 2001. She had mowed the lawn for our anniversary. I'd paddled to Africa.

As the sun went down over the Atlantic I hauled *Miss Grape* onto a marina pontoon, dealt with the Spanish police and spent an hour or so sorting gear and sending messages. In the following few hours I planned to leave Spain, enter Morocco, leave Morocco, leave Africa. That was the plan.

A message came in from Julio: 'Congratulations. A good news for everybody. A courageous and brave Aussi. Yes sir! A huge hug.'

★ ★ ★

Carlos and Juanfran turned up at dusk to transport me and *Miss Grape* to the Moroccan border. They told me that kayaking across the strait was now forbidden by the Spanish authorities. *Miss Grape* had a short trip on the roof rack of their van but was soon on her own wheels, weaving through the border chaos. For the first time I wheeled a kayak into a new country and we weaved across a no man's land that was full of men. Men shouting, waving, honking horns, walking. It was now 7.30 p.m.; my ferry left at 11 p.m.

'Where is your car?' asked the woman in the glass booth when it was my turn to roll past.

'I have no car,' I responded.

'Where have you come from with that ship?'

'From Gibraltera. Would you like my passport?'

'No I need the papers for your ship first,' she replied pointing at *Miss Grape*.

Here we go I thought; memories of Albania, Croatia and other crossings: 'I have no papers; it is a kayak.'

'No sir, it is a ship. You must have papers.'

By now other more senior officers were gathered around. I tried to explain but they would not listen. I tried to tell them that I was headed to Tanger-Med, 25km away and that in three hours I was leaving Morocco by catching the weekly ferry from there to Genoa in Italy. They would not listen.

'No ship's papers, no entry,' was the final call from the chief; an unbelievably officious gentleman nattily dressed in a fine wool overcoat with its collar turned up to his ears against the chill and complaining kayakers. Whenever his phone rang he would pull it out from an inside chest pocket, fully extend his arm to the side, flip his phone open and bring it sharply to his ear. This theatrical technique was repeated whenever I approached him, phone call or none.

I skulked away to one side with *Miss Grape* to consider my options. Beyond the frontier a man was waiting to transport *Miss Grape* and me to Tanger-Med. He had been organised by the Fédération Royale Marocaine de Canoë-Kayak. I rang my contact there. He told me to wait and he would make some calls. I waited, he called back to say that the president of the club was contacting the chief of police and others. I tried to get Mr FlipPhone to talk to Mr KayakFederation, but he waved me away with his phone.

I waited some more but the ferry was not going to wait for me. From my position in the shadows I thought it worth at least a try. The triumph of hope against experience… I casually grabbed *Miss Grape* by her bow and started wheeling her away toward the exit. But within seconds there was shouting, and I was surrounded by arm-waving and arm-pulling police. Mr FlipPhone glowered. By now it was 8.30 p.m.

Phone calls came and went. People elsewhere were doing their very best, telling me to wait for the next call, but the ferry was not going to wait for me.

Then I remembered. After fun and games on other frontiers earlier in the journey, albeit with less pressing deadlines, I'd asked Dave Felton, owner of Tiderace Sea Kayaks, the company that had given birth to *Miss Grape*, to email me a letter on their company letterhead saying I was the owner of the kayak. Dave had done so, and although I'd not asked him to, he had also included the serial number on the two-line letter. It was a long shot, but...

'I've found the ship papers. Look!' I said to the female officer in the booth.

She took the letter and stared a while. 'Go see the chief.'

Mr FlipPhone was 200 metres away. As I got within 50 metres, he did it once, did it twice with his phone.

'Sir.' It was time to be a bit more respectful. 'I have the papers. Look.'

He took the letter and looked; it was a start. He did the phone thing again, but this time made a real call. I understand no Arabic but there were enough common words – 'Australian', 'canoe' – for me to know he was talking about me.

'Follow me.' And obediently I did. Back at the booth he instructed the young officer to process a temporary import document. It was now 9 p.m.

The officer was obviously puzzled by the lack of information in the letter, but the long serial number seemed to impress her. 'Why there is not this number on your boat?'

'It is – but on kayak ships it is always printed on the inside,' I told her. Taking out my head torch I invited her to look deep down into the salty, rather smelly cockpit (there had been no opportunity to stop for a pee whilst paddling across the strait). She looked at the letter, looked at the number embossed under the deck. She read out four numbers/letters at a time, twice.

Back at the booth I was issued with the *Declaration d'Entree et de Sortie des Bateaux de Plaisance* (Declaration for Entry and Exit of a Boat of Pleasure).

I thanked her, respectfully thanked Mr FlipPhone and headed out of the border gate. There, waiting patiently was Mounir, the 10-time Moroccan kayak champion who had, unbelievably, driven 300 km from Rabat to drive me the 25 km to Tanger-Med. This was fine, as from now until my planned return to Ceuta on New Year's Eve, my travels were no longer part of my human-powered journey. But kayak champion he might be, his car had no roof rack. We made do, flipping *Miss Grape* upside down, and with some clothing, my sleeping mat, some foam and straps she was good to go. It was now 9.30 p.m. In an hour-and-a-half the weekly ferry to Genoa would leave.

Tanger-Med turned out to be a massive, sprawling new port. I laughed as we sped under a sign indicating directions to the Logistic Free Zone. There was no point going there with my *mediterr année* journey. We passed the turn-off to 'Ferry – Foot Passenger Entry' and continued to 'Ferry –Vehicle Entry' 4 km further on. We reasoned that whilst Mounir was not actually coming on the ferry with his car he would be allowed to drop me and *Miss Grape* somewhere near it.

I checked in while Mounir checked with the police to see if he could drive me to the ship. The answer was an emphatic no. They told him I was a foot passenger with luggage, so I needed to go to that terminal. It was now 10.20 p.m. I'd blown it for sure but perhaps the ferry would be late.

We went through the motions, driving the 4 km back to the foot passenger terminal. I thanked Mounir profusely but it was not enough; it could never be enough for what he had done for me that night.

I wheeled *Miss Grape* to the gleaming new terminal and up the first short set of stairs. I sort of knew what was coming.

Imagine now that you are late for an international flight at your international airport of choice or necessity. You are at the terminal door with your luggage. But your luggage includes a 5.3-metre hulk of fibreglass and Kevlar, and a big bag of soaking paddling gear.

There were no queues when I got there, but the metal maze signifying the queuing regime stood like barbed wire on a wartime beach as my next barrier. It was all too bizarre, far too bizarre. But I had to go through with it, to see that day to the end. With the assistance of some customs officers, I lifted and slid *Miss Grape* over and under barriers to passport control. I handed in my passport and my cherished Boat of Pleasure document.

A group of officers gathered around us. 'You cannot take this out of Morocco,' said one.

I didn't have the humour left in me to say that I was actually going nowhere, given the ferry left in 10 minutes. 'Why not?' I asked, explaining that Mr FlipPhone had said I could.

'Why you come into Morocco only one hour ago, and now you leave?' asked another officer, looking at the entry stamp in my passport.

I started to explain that I'd kayaked across from Gibraltar to Spanish Ceuta and walked into Morocco … It was too hard. I wanted to cry out in pure frustration. I was dog-tired, salt-encrusted and starving. But I held it together. My documents were taken away to a higher authority. As I waited I struck up a conversation with the one officer remaining.

'It is fine. If we let you go, you will catch the ferry.'

'But it is 11 p.m. now. Is the ferry late?' I asked.

'No it is not 11 p.m. It is 10 p.m.'

'Sorry?'

He repeated himself then showed me the time on his phone. 'Morocco is one hour behind Spain, one hour behind Ceuta. It is 10 p.m. here.'

I could not believe it. I just could not believe it. Despair to elation in 10 seconds.

'You can go with your ship to the ferry.' The other officers had returned.

They helped me load *Miss Grape* onto the conveyor belt of the X-Ray machine. I quickly took a photo of a 5.3-metre sea kayak sitting like an oversized hot dog in a far-too-small bread bun. An officer made me delete it.

'Now you go down the stairs and the bus will take you to the ferry. Thank you for visiting Morocco.'

Nothing now surprised me. Nothing. I took *Miss Grape* and my luggage, one bag still dripping, down an escalator; down a bloody escalator.

'We can do it, Mr Huw,' said Hussein, the bus driver. No way, I told him. No way can we shoehorn this boat onto your bus. 'It will be first time for me, but we can try.' He was so genuine. For *Miss Grape* too, it would be the first time. Somehow; somehow with millimetres to spare *Miss Grape* caught the bus. We were the only passengers.

Three kilometres later we got off the bus and I wheeled *Miss Grape* onto the vehicle deck of the good ship *Excelsior*. It was 10.40 p.m.

Three days earlier I hadn't felt I could fully celebrate arriving in Gibraltar, arriving at the end of Europe, until I had got across the strait to Africa. In the past 12 hours I had kayaked across the strait from Gibraltar to a tiny piece of Spain in Africa, entered Morocco then left Morocco. As I sank a celebration beer near midnight, the *Excelsior* steamed across the strait to take me away from Africa. I hoped to be back in Ceuta on the first day of 2015, and prayed that the Moroccans would let bikes in without papers.

I had 60 hours to rest and reflect. The shipping line, *Grandi Navi Veloci*, had kindly provided me with a complementary passage with a comfortable solo cabin where I finally got to dry my wet kayaking gear. I spent some time up on the bridge with Alessandro the captain whose cockpit was rather more extensive and rather less damp than mine on *Miss Grape*.

We docked in Barcelona for a few hours, where I caught up with Mark Turner and was attacked by the Butcher of Barcelona, the roughest barber of the trip so far; he was even worse than the Shearer of Supetar I'd managed to find in Croatia. Then we steamed on to Italy where, after a kilometre stroll with *Miss Grape* to get out of the port of Genova, I met Alberto who whisked us up to the snow-covered Italian Alps I'd walked through a few months before. Back at base with Marco and Elena and 10-day-old Giole. Their new adventure had begun.

5.3 metre long *Miss Grape* takes a bus to the ferry in Tanger-Med port, Morocco, at the end of the weirdest of days

Marin, celebrating his 27th birthday, arrived the following day, having driven 600 km from Slovenia so we could have a day discussing the million things for our row from Tunisia. *Mr Hops*, our home for up to 50 days, was hopping his way in a container from Cape Verde to Tunisia via Morocco, Algeria and Malta.

After we'd toasted his birthday at the airport in Milan, Marin took off with *Miss Grape* back to Slovenia for Christmas. I hoped I'd next see her somewhere in Turkey for our final weeks back to Gallipoli. I was headed for Christmas in England. Going through customs with only a daypack seemed rather strange: I felt rather naked. The officers confiscated an unopened present that Anna from Casa Dolce had given me that morning. They had opened it to reveal a jar of honey, and I was reminded of Necedet's gift after he had chased me down the beach in the first days of my journey back in Turkey. Continuing the theme, Marin had also told me on the drive to the airport that 'med' from his surname, Medak, meant honey in Slovenian.

★ ★ ★

'Welcome to Easyjet's flight to Gibraltar. Or maybe not,' was the pilot's welcome on New Year's Eve. 'Very strong winds in the strait mean we may not be able to land. Let's set off and see what happens.' It was a less than encouraging way to try and land at Gibraltar for my second time. When we did eventually get down onto the runway the steward asked us to take our hats off to the captain for bringing us in. 'I didn't think we would land in Gibraltar today,' she finished. I was looking forward to being under my own steam again.

JANUARY

You'd be so lean, that blasts of January would blow you through and through.

William Shakespeare

The break in the UK had been good but all too short. I was as well looked after by Mum and Dad as I had been 50 years ago: there is not a vegetable known to man that was not on our Christmas dinner table. Meats too, but I don't care for those. A pleasure too to spend a little time with my three nieces, who I saw all too rarely. But it was hard being there and not with my family back in Australia, not being with Wendy. I also felt out of place away from my incomplete journey. As snow fell in London I

witnessed possibly the most frightening thing I'd seen since that journey began; the Boxing Day sales on Oxford Street. Fortunately I had some protection behind the window of the no. 73 bus.

Now back in Gibraltar, I was met at the airport by Paul with my bike. The border was 100 metres away, and within a minute I was back in Spain and pedalling the 20 km to Algeciras to take the ferry to Ceuta. I dodged a double mattress that flew off the roof of a passing car and laughed at the potential headline: 'Man found under bed with bike'.

Julio, the Algeciras harbourmaster, who it turned out was responsible for every Spanish port between Tarifa and Estepona, found me in the ferry terminal cafe. He was weighed down with food he had brought for me from a local bakery and we hugged; the hug he had promised me in his first email. This fine man, perhaps in his mid-sixties, was as I expected, gentle and enquiring. It didn't surprise me when he told me he was also head of the local Red Cross branch. It did surprise me when, after I'd told him that the kayakers in Ceuta had informed me of the illegality of crossing the strait by kayak, he replied that indeed it was. 'You will see I never sent you a formal email; only from my personal account. I wanted to help you, to encourage you as best I could from the position I was in.' Julio had, more than anyone, maintained my belief in giving the crossing a go. Tears welled up in his eyes as we hugged goodbye and as he warned me to be safe in north Africa.

Julio, the Spanish harbourmaster for the Strait of Gibraltar, gave a lot of quiet encouragement for my paddle across the strait

In Ceuta I saw the New Year in; with a little more time to explore on this visit I found it to be a large, attractive and seemingly affluent city. Riding along the coast to the border with Morocco I wondered if Mr FlipPhone might be on duty and whether perhaps he'd got a smartphone for Christmas.

With a bike, entering Morocco was a breeze; no papers required. I was now finally heading east, facing Turkey, heading toward Turkey after so many months with my back or side to her.

It was good to be on the move again although I felt wrecked, utterly fatigued. Perhaps my body, after two weeks off, thought it could relax, thought perhaps the journey was over. My hamstrings felt like they could snap at any moment and my pedal strokes seemed lifeless. I was shivering even though it wasn't cold, and my head was pounding. A strong headwind didn't help much. But I pushed on along a beautiful coastline, thinking how good it would have been to kayak it.

I'd ditched the tent; I knew that in Algeria I'd be made to stay in hotels as a condition of my visa. At Oued Laou I found a cheap room on the beach and ate fish at a cafe where half a dozen cats drove me insane. It didn't matter how much I pushed them away, kicked them, threw knives at them; they were straight back on the table

Unloading the catch at
El Jebha, Morocco

Repairing the nets at
El Jebha, Morocco

Fruit Market, Rouadi,
Morocco

pawing at my plate. An old *Lonely Planet* guide I'd found, from 2005, described Oued Laou as: 'More of a fishing village than a resort town, it has the easy going charm of an undiscovered paradise.' Perhaps things were much changed in the past decade or the author had low standards for paradise. For breakfast the next morning I fancied the *pains au raisin* sitting in a bakery display. I ordered two and watched the flies I had thought were raisins take off as the shopkeeper lifted the pastries from the shelf.

The ride onto El Jebha was a rollercoaster along the Mediterranean shores as the road shot down to occasional black sand beaches then climbed away again. Given the beauty of the coast right on their doorstep I really was surprised that the kayakers of Gibraltar did not see this as their backyard playground, particularly with the ferry connections available at either end. The people of the Mediterranean coast and the Rif mountains that rose behind were Berbers. The women wore colourful capes with a small sombrero-style hat decorated with pom-poms whilst the men wore woollen capes with a pointed hood that reminded me of Gandalf.

At dusk I entered El Jebha, a fishing harbour tucked in behind Pointe des Pêcheurs, just as the muezzins were calling the faithful to prayer. Soon a glass of Moroccan mint tea was in front of me in a cafe pungent with the aroma of another leaf, a leaf the Rif mountains were famous for. If breakfast in Oued Laou had disappointed me, the Hotel El Mamoun in El Jebha made up for it with a huge spread that would see me right for the 900-metre climb up into the mountains. Before I started the ascent I witnessed a frenzy of activity after a couple of trawlers had entered the harbour. Dozens of people were involved as fish were unloaded, money counted, nets repaired. All seemed to leave with plastic bags full of fish whether as a payment or a purchase.

Back from the sea, my route cut across the grain of the land and as such climbed over ridges and plummeted down to valleys for the 80 km to

Looking out across the Mediterranean from Morocco

the village of Rouadi. No accommodation was available, but Faisol, the local fireman, invited me to use the storeroom beneath his family's apartment. As his mother brought food down to me, Faisol sat and watched, and as the night progressed got more and more stoned. I just hoped there would be no fires that night.

I was back on the coast near Al Hoceima, a coast not as spectacular as before but pleasant enough with low headlands and rocky bays. The gendarme at a checkpoint below Tzarghine told me there was nowhere to stay in the village, but I went looking anyway. At the large, modern Cafe Dola, an unctuous young man told me that of course they had rooms. He showed me to an apartment upstairs that was obviously where someone lived: the kitchen was filthy, and bedclothes and towels all well used. I moved on. Further up the road, Mustafa, a man in white sunglasses and berber cape, showed me a room where there was no issue with dirty towels or bedding. The room was completely empty, a true AirBnB. Beggars can't be choosers and I took it, but only after the local police came twice to check me out and twice to berate Mustafa for making a few dirhams on the side.

Just over 24 hours after waking in that bare room I was sat in a little bodega in a narrow alley in the Andalucian city of Almeria. I was eating my first Spanish paella, back in Spain in the company of Nico, a tug boat captain, and his wife. My return to Spain was all to do with neighbour disputes. Not the 'turn that bloody music down' variety but more 'you really shouldn't have invaded the Western Sahara'. For over 30 years the border between Morocco and Algeria has been closed as the two countries have continued to argue over the fate of the Western Sahara. Thus I had always known that it was going to be impossible for me to ride from Morocco into Algeria or take any form of human-powered transport. My only option was to take a 250-km ferry trip from Nador, 70 km from the border with Algeria, across the Mediterranean to Almeria. I did that overnight on the *Sherbatskiy*, a name better suited to a Russian icebreaker than a Mediterranean ferry. Then, after 20 hours in Spain, I took the weekly ferry from Almeria back across the Mediterranean to Ghazaouet in Algeria. Ghazaouet is 40 km from the Moroccan border. To cover that land distance of a little over 100 km I got to do two eight-hour ferry journeys, and covered over 500 km by sea.

I had planned lots of jobs for those 20 hours back in Spain. Sorting parts for my bike, a new phone to replace my broken one. Then I discovered that 6 January was of course the *Fiesta de los Reyes*, the Day of the Three Kings, the Epiphany, the day of giving presents in Spain. Everything was closed.

If 6 January was an ancient Christian festival, only hours after I arrived in Algeria on 7 January a terrible stain committed in the name of Islam occurred. In Paris, two French brothers of Algerian descent entered the offices of the satirical magazine *Charlie Hebdo* and shot dead 12 people.

I wheeled my bike off the ferry into Algeria, the largest country in Africa and the largest on the shores of the Mediterranean; my 15th country. Throughout Spain and Morocco people had warned me about Algeria, and certainly my concern had been heightened after the kidnapping and beheading of French trekker Hervé Gourdel four months earlier. A policeman came up to me as I alighted from the ship and fast-tracked me through the tin shed that was Algerian customs. I wondered why I was deserving of such treatment. Even though my concerns about Algeria were tempered by the reality that things are invariably better on the ground than in the media, I had surprised myself by taking some small precautions; for example, I'd ensured that Israel was no longer showing on the website of my journey as a country that I'd originally planned to travel through. Also I'd decided not to wear my *mediterr année* cycle jersey that, in the manner of a rock band tour T-shirt, listed the original 20 countries including Israel. Finally I registered my Algerian crossing plans on the Australian government travel portal. It was the first time in my travels I'd ever taken such steps.

I was at the front of the queue when the door of the shed was opened and we were allowed out into Ghazaouet.

'Mr Huw, Mr Huw. Welcome to Algeria,' said a man in black polo neck, black pants, black wool overcoat and black cap. 'I am Faisal. I will take you across Algeria.' Faisal worked for Cheche Tours, the agency I had worked with to get me into Algeria. We shared a coffee in the port cafe before Faisal stood and asked 'We go, Mr Huw? You are ready?'

Faisal climbed into his new Peugeot, ready to begin the slowest drive of his life. As he pulled out through the port gates, two police cars, lights flashing, took up position, one behind me, one in front. No one had told me that I was to have a police escort for 1,500 km and two weeks across Algeria. Nothing had been mentioned in the dozens of emails between Cheche Tours and me.

View from the bike of my ever-present police escort for 1500 km across Algeria

My ride across Algeria passed in a fog of police sirens, motorways, pollution and cities. It was all rather presidential at times. Whenever we entered a built-up area, came upon a roundabout, traffic light or traffic jam, the sirens would go on and vehicles directed to stop or pull over. We took the lights on red and the roundabouts were all ours. Police on the ground directed traffic, and the army manning the many roadblocks, knew what to do as we approached. The Algerian people stopped to stare, expecting something interesting or someone famous. All they got was a middle-aged bloke in a peloton of one, on a bike, smiling and waving regally.

This madness was not some hastily arranged escort after *Charlie Hebdo*. In fact we left Ghazaouet around the time that murderous act took place. No, my escort had been planned with military precision, as had my route. At pre-arranged locations, as we moved from one police district to another, my guard would wish me '*Bonne route*' and '*Bon courage*', and another would take their place. My hand felt presidential on some days when up to eight changeovers took place, necessitating 16 lots of hello and goodbye handshakes to four cars full of officers. The police were invariably friendly and good company when we pulled up for coffee or more. Most understood my pace. Whilst others …

'Please try to keep up.' We were on another foul motorway when a young police officer in the front car pulled over to wait for me up a hill. 'Please try to keep up. We finish our shift at noon and don't want to be late. Please try to keep up.' I explained the difference between an accelerator and a pedal, to which he responded 'Yes, yes, I know. Just try harder to help us.'

I was angry at times. Angry that although I'd been told before I arrived in Algeria that I could work out a route with Faisal across the country that would take me along quiet roads and through villages, the reality was that the police had approved a route, hotels had been booked and change was not possible. Faisal felt my wrath on a number of occasions when after another day of 150 km or more dodging trucks and sucking in carbon monoxide, we'd go out of our way to reach another half-built, nondescript city. Then strangely enough, once I was in the city and had checked in at the hotel, the police disappeared and I was free to wander at will.

I arrived in the city of Oran after 170 km on a day that was supposed to be 130 km, tired, hungry and very thirsty. I'd drunk less than a litre of water all day. Faisal asked in hushed tones in the street near the hotel and soon we were in a dark shop selling alcohol. It was illegal but it wasn't. Faisal had told me alcohol was officially banned in Algeria but you could get a licence to sell it. It all seemed contradictory. It seemed that provided you had a 'strong man' or someone high in the military as a sponsor, they could make it happen. The term 'strong man' was used often by people in my journey when describing how Algeria worked.

I bought two cans of Weidmann Ultra Strong Beer after the man in the shop had said 'Try this one; Oran juice!' Back in the hotel I lay on the bed, opened a can and started to drink. I'd had less than half and was feeling decidedly affected. I looked at the gold can and saw the words 14%. I kept sipping. Now I might love beer and I might love chocolate, but never the twain should meet in my book. But I was starving and all I had was a Mars Bar, which I washed down with slugs of Weidmann. I was sozzled. I wandered into the bathroom to take a shower in an effort to clean off the day's grime and sober up. Throwing open the curtain over the bath I was confronted by a woman. It shocked me first until I realised she was a full figure on the wall tiles, and I felt a little better after the shower. I lay on the bed to write some notes on the day in a new notebook I'd bought. I went to put a *mediterr année* sticker on the front. I was confused. Where was the front? The front was upside down, the back was where the front should be. I was momentarily lost. But less under the influence than a realisation of course that in the Arabic nations they write from back to front. I stuck the sticker on upside down and all was well.

By early evening I'd sobered further from my one-can experience and joined Faisal for dinner. He was praising my strength but knew what was coming. I had another go about the route; spread my map out on the table and showed him all the little side roads offering often shorter, more direct routes. 'It is impossible, Mr Huw. Our route is approved. The government will not allow change. We go to the cities.' I sensed I was fighting a losing battle on this one and was just going to have to deal with the nightmare until I could wake up in Tunisia.

If German style ultra-strong beers were my downfall at night in Oran, the next morning I found myself being escorted out of the city not just by two police patrol cars but now with three motorcycle outriders on BMW bikes. They would block off traffic coming into the main road or huge city roundabouts so that my route was clear. On these cold winter days a thick pall of pollution lay over much of Algeria. With diesel at 10 cents a litre and petrol below 20 cents, nobody bothered to turn off their engines. I'd often come out of a hotel in the morning to find Faisal had been 'warming up' his engine for nearly an hour.

Oil and gas is the mainstay of the Algerian economy. The population of 40 million seemed to accept a strong-arm government in return for free education (right through to university) and free healthcare. Most large businesses were government owned and any private business that gets pretty sizeable seems to have a military or government 'strong man' supporting them. The military were a visible presence everywhere, showing the people that dissent would not be tolerated. The authorities were keen to keep a lid on any Islamic State uprising. Faisal and others told me that the government did not care for tourism in any real sense, and wanted to avoid any bad news stories. Hence my escort across the country.

But 2015 in Algeria seemed so much better than what I heard about the 1990s. Then people were terrified to go out after dark, the secret police were utterly feared and up to 100,000 people had died in the civil war.

Once beyond the hell motorways of Oran the route to Relizane was bad, but less so. I could tell this as I even started to sing again on the bike, to relax a bit. Our convoy passed through a series of small towns and villages and, being Friday, tinny speakers in the mosques offered a sound that was some relief from the motors around me. The less bad didn't last long, though, and I was soon waving angrily and uselessly at trucks that came too close. The stops for coffee or food were the good parts. The Algerian men were invariably friendly and interested in my journey. Many times I would go to pay only to be told at the counter that someone, often someone I may not even have been directly speaking with, had picked up the tab. I'd thank them and the usual response was, 'It is for your journey.'

I say men because for the most part women were absent. Always in countries where this is so, I feel a big hole. Something is missing in the joyful company of men with women, women with women mixing with men with men. Cafes and shops filled with men are grey to me. In Algeria, women were for the most part absent or glided quickly by.

The weather was clear and cold, with snow on the mountains north of Khemis Miliana. I was feeling the drop in temperature after I had been shorn by a Berber barber in Chlef the night before. Either side of the roads the potato harvest was in full swing. On the roadside itself, mixed in with the fruit stalls, were a series of stalls offering both crockery and guns; an unusual mix. The meticulous planning had gone awry at Khemis Miliana when the hotel we were booked in appeared to not exist, and Faisal eventually found us a rough and very basic hotel in the centre of town. The call to prayer was drowned out by the cheers of nationalism as Algeria scored a goal against Tunisia in the African Cup of Nations. Like everywhere along the Mediterranean, soccer was the defining religion for many. This neighbourly battle ended in a draw.

As I was making my way across Algeria, Marin was making sure that a deluge of things were coming together for *Mr Hops* and the row. In the previous weeks I'd invited a third person to join our row. I had thought it might be good to have someone in reserve; someone who, if either Marin or I got sick or injured, could take over and keep the row going. There was now so much invested in this section of the journey – a section that was a huge undertaking on its own merits let alone as part of my bigger journey. I immediately thought of Dimitris Kokkoris back in Greece. In the short time I had known him in Athens he had struck me as a fit and pretty focused individual who might be up for the challenge if it fell his way. Then, soon after Dimitris confirmed he was keen to be in reserve, I realised that if Marin and I made it to Turkey after 40 days or more of rowing, I still had another 40 days or more of sea kayaking up the Turkish coast to my finish. I did wonder what state I might be in after the row. Perhaps having someone join us for the last weeks might take the pressure off me a bit. Three of us on the boat would mean that instead of a two hours on, two hours off rowing regime, it would become two hours on, four hours off. My body would have a bit more recovery time before the final push to Gallipoli, albeit in the confines of an ocean rowing boat built for one rather than two, and certainly not for three.

Marin agreed with my suggestion and Dimitris was keen to have a definite expedition to look forward to rather than one that might come about only by misfortune. The plan was to collect him in Crete if the winds would allow us to reach there. If not he might need to charter a fast boat to find us in the Mediterranean.

Anyone looking at a map of Algeria would see that to go from Khemis Miliana east to Bouïra there could be no reason to go north to Algiers, the capital of Algeria and a city of 4 million people. I didn't want to, knowing that cities and bikes are rarely good friends. But what I wanted didn't come into it, and I found myself riding through the homesickness-inducing suburb of Eucalyptus en route to a traffic-choked motorway that I was relieved to be spat off right by Algiers airport. Why in God's name had I ridden 140 km to stay in an airport hotel in a city I had no wish to visit or fly from? 'It is the permitted route, Mr Huw,' was all Faisal could say as I vented in the car park before he left to have dinner with his mother.

That same bastard of a motorway took me away from Algiers for the first 30 km before I climbed south into the hills. I reckoned there was a lot more chance of being swiped by a truck on those motorways than of being kidnapped on quiet roads in the Algerian countryside. We pulled up on the outskirts of Bouïra to wait for the city police to take me the final kilometres. While we waited, two of the current escort – two balding, rather rotund and smiling gentlemen – told Faisal and me that in our hotel that night we would find beer and women available.

A Nissan Patrol filled with police in flak jackets turned up and led me to the unprepossessing Royal Hotel. After checking in and dumping bags I wandered into the hotel cafe in search of that beer. The waiter looked at me with some disdain and told me there was no beer available. I had coffee.

A couple of hours later, after doing some work and cleaning up, I went back to the ground floor and followed some stairs down from there. In the basement I passed a door behind which I could hear music. The door was blank and offered no sign of what was beyond. I hesitated for a moment but decided to open it. In a country where alcohol is officially disallowed and where women are rarely seen I found myself in a dimly lit large bar full of men and women. The women were almost all heavily made up, wearing short skirts and high stiletto heels, and strangely the vast majority were overweight. I ordered a beer at the bar, fending off the advances of a young, drunk Algerian man. Then I sat and observed this surprising scene thinking how the women would have been well covered when entering or leaving the place.

Despite the constraints I was riding under and my frustrations, I liked Faisal. He wanted to be the man about town in his black polos and hats, but didn't quite pull it off. Of course whenever there was a section of road that was quieter, narrower and altogether more enjoyable to pedal along he would come to me for approbation. 'I see you are happy. You like the route I plan for you?' I certainly clung to those all-too-rare scraps of cycling enjoyment.

Since I'd begun my journey little world news had permeated my world and I did not seek it out. Occasionally someone would tell me about the spread of Islamic State or a tragedy in Gaza or Egypt. Occasionally in a cafe a TV would show me a foul madness in a Pakistani school. For an avid news fan it was somehow refreshing to take a year out. But in Algeria I saw more news. Perhaps because I was forced by security concerns to stay in hotels where often a television hung in my room. Perhaps I was more aware because I was being escorted across a Muslim country.

Faisal, my Algerian minder, who endured the slowest drive of his life for two weeks across the width of Algeria, Africa's largest country

The Syrian crisis was worsening by the month, and with it further discontent was spreading into neighbouring nations. Not just discontent, but a flood of humanity, of refugees. The money that I was raising for Save the Children was going directly to that snowballing crisis where over half a million defenceless children had been affected. Where in recent days snowfalls had made life even more miserable.

And like the sane world, I followed the aftermath of the *Charlie Hebdo* tragedy. A tragedy not just of life lost but that some feel that satire, criticism, alternative points of view and reporting should be murdered too. But of course where I was many disagreed with my thoughts so I kept them pretty much to myself. Cars passed me on the roads bearing stickers proclaiming '*Je suis Mohammed*'.

On my second Friday in Algeria large demonstrations took place in the cities against the *Charlie Hebdo* magazine. I picked up a copy of *Le Quotidien,* whose front page proclaimed '*Les Algerians dans la rue*'. Then above the masthead: '*Le corps d'Hervé Gourdel retrouve*': the beheaded body of Hervé Gourdel had just been found in the snow-covered mountains I'd ridden under a couple of days earlier.

My last few days in Algeria coincided with a wet cold front that swept across the country. I had all my warm and wet weather gear on as I outpedalled the snowfalls, descending from 1,200 metres toward the coast. The roads were closed behind me. I did manage a little victory in convincing Faisal and the police that it wasn't necessary to go through the port city of Annaba. My punishment was to ride in the rain through the rubbish tip of the town of Dréan, a foul-smelling steaming pile that spilled across the road. Cows grazed nonchalantly amongst the plastic and organic matter.

My final night in Algeria was in El Taref, at the very friendly but rather grandly named Hotel Paradise Palace some 50 km from Tunisia. In the African Cup of Nations Tunisia were playing the Cape Verde Islands; the place where my row boat had left from against the place where I hoped to soon meet her for the first time. At dinner I gave Faisal a *mediterr année* T-shirt and a card. He was overjoyed. I had spent more time with him than with anyone on my journey to date. Faisal was looking forward to a good hit out in the Peugeot on the way home after its 10–30 kph crawl of the past 1,500 km. That 1,500 km had daily scores to make an opening batsman happy: 170, 140, 115, 120, 95, 130...

It was the final 10 km winding through wooded hills on a narrow, quiet road up to the border that was the best of all. It seemed to taunt me, to show me what might have been in Algeria. Instead I'd had, for the most part, busy roads, motorways, pollution and large cities. I knew from the map and distant views from my saddle that there were other ways. But it had been a means to an end. I chuckled when I passed my final road sign: '*La Gendarmerie National à votre service*' (The police at your service). They gave me quite a send-off on the last day, with a couple of police motorcycles and a military police 4WD joining the patrol car.

At the border the police took me straight to the front of the queue at passport control. Here, as my departure from Algeria was processed, the police chief at the border took a keen interest in my journey. With passport stamped, I shook hands with my final escorts and gave Faisal a big hug. Then I loaded my panniers onto the bike for the first time in two weeks and rode through customs and into no man's land toward Tunisia.

'Kingston. Mr How.' I kept pedalling, ignoring the voice behind me. Sometimes it is better that way.

'Stop Mr How. Come back.' I glanced over my shoulder and the police chief was beckoning me. I turned around and rode back into Algeria.

'Kingston, Mr How, I want to have my photograph with you,' said the chief, handing his smartphone to a junior officer. I did likewise, seeing a golden opportunity, a quid pro quo; throughout my route my police escorts had tried to ensure I did not photograph them.

'No, no, no, Mr How. I can take photo of you, but you cannot take photo of me. It is forbidden,' he beamed.

With that, I rode into Tunisia and breathed a sigh of relief. I felt a sense of freedom, felt that the journey was mine again; an enjoyable nakedness. I sang my inane songs to the wind as I flew down the hill to the Mediterranean Sea and the laid-back coastal town of Tabarka.

In London just after Christmas I had spied a tiny book at the checkout of a large bookstore: *The Sea Close By*. I knew little about the author Albert Camus, but liked the title's link to my journey. Then on opening the book, I learned that Camus was from Algeria, from Algiers, so I bought it.

The sea was close by again now, and in three days' riding I planned to be at Hammamet, where Marin and I would prepare *Mr Hops* for our voyage.

After 2,000km of riding since New Year's Day, I thought I might take a day off in Tabarka, but wasn't sure whether to just push on toward Hammamet. In the end my body made the decision. Rejecting and projecting the remnants of Algeria and all that Tunisia had offered me on my first evening into a bucket, I lay wasted in bed for much of the day at the Novelty Hotel. I probably needed that day off. In Tabarka I enjoyed my first *hamman*, where a young man showed me the ropes; what to do and what not to do.

There are two things that can be found everywhere throughout the Mediterranean: football and rubbish. The former is harmless enough if a little noisy at times. The latter is an affront to anyone who cares at all about this beautiful but fragile planet. It is obviously not enough people. The majority component of the rubbish strewn on the roadside, on riverbanks, washed up on beaches is plastic; the number one item is plastic bottles and containers.

Shopkeepers usually look at you strangely when you refuse a plastic bag; some have even tried to force them on me. At least in France they banned them from 2016. We don't need them; the wildlife doesn't need them, fence-lines don't need them blowing in the wind. Don't kid yourself about these 'biodegradable' bags. Once in landfill, without oxygen, they don't.

Worse still are the plastic bottles of water. The stuff is everywhere, both in countries where the water from the tap is perfect, as it is across Europe and in places here in north Africa where it is a bit more uncertain. But here's the rub. The prevalence of bottled water gives government and municipalities the opportunity to say, 'We can get away with not providing healthy drinking water because the people can/do drink bottled water.' And indeed the people can; it is cheap in these countries. But it is the poorest of the poor who cannot afford even that. So they end up with poor quality drinking water and an expense they can ill afford. When told, 'The people, they have no water,' a modern-day Marie-Antoinette would no doubt respond, 'Let them buy bottled water.'

So what does a traveller do? We have the money to buy the stuff if we want, and sometimes it is the only option. But we need to be aware that many of those bottles we use will end up in the sea or strewn across the land. I am generally happy to drink water from most sources – streams, rivers, taps – and I have very, very rarely got sick. On occasions I use a silver chloride tablet that kills bacteria, viruses and giardia. A pack of 100 tiny tablets will treat 100 litres. There are also, of course, small water filters you can carry, but I never have.

And while on the issue of the environmental cost of plastic – the bar of soap was a fine invention hundreds of years ago. User-friendly with minimal packaging. So why in God's name has the past five years or so seen the prevalence of liquid soap in plastic bottles? Apart from a totally unnecessary bottle, half of the soap gets wasted as it slips off fingers and bodies straight down the drain.

I enjoyed a stunning ride in fresh air and fine scenery from Tabarka to Beja. The landscape reminded me of the Yorkshire Dales although whilst the comparison might be valid on a cold January day I'm sure in the midst of a north African summer such comparison would not hold. I had pedalled away from Tabarka after some fine conversations with Thouraya, a trained teacher unable to find a teaching job in five years. Thouraya, like so many Muslims I met, told me that Mohammed would have been appalled by the actions being committed under his name. She sent me off with good wishes and the hope I might find Islam in my travels.

It felt strangely unnerving to be alone. I was loving it but couldn't quite shake off the madness of my escorted Algerian traverse. But also people in Tunisia warned me of trouble and that there had been terrorist incidents in Tunisia in recent times.

As I rode south on a lonely road beyond Nefza, two motorcyclists came toward me in the opposite direction. They split in front of me, one crossing to my side to head me off. My hair stood on end, but all they wanted was to say hello. Mind, this was only some kilometres after I'd stopped for a piss 100 metres beyond a building, thinking I was out of sight. But when I was in the middle of relieving myself, there was lots of shouting and waving, and men started running from the building toward me. With business still unfinished I tried in vain to turn the tap off and quickly rode off wet-legged and looking behind. No one followed, but this incident didn't aid my nervousness.

From Beja I had two choices to Hammamet. The route I had originally planned cutting cross country on minor roads avoided Tunis, the dominant city of Tunisia. But people from Tabarka onward had separately told me: 'Take the route toward Tunis; it is better for you.' Ordinarily I would ignore such advice. It is often given by people who sit behind a steering wheel not handlebars; people cocooned behind glass and travelling at one with the speeding vehicles around them. Large cities spell traffic, motorways, pollution; all things a cycle tourer hates. But each of these people had also added 'Il est pour votre sécurité, it is for your own safety.

I was also a new arrival in this country, not knowing how it had reacted to the happenings in Paris two weeks before. I was also fresh from my cocoon in Algeria. Lots of things went through my mind. Taking the rural route would be a tiny risk, no more so than in any country, versus I was only two days from finishing this bike stage, from finishing my movement across north Africa. Going to Tunis would be horrible and potentially more risky with traffic, so take the tiny risk. Such thoughts as I'd never had before on this journey or indeed on others.

I always remember the line from Nicholas Crane's book on his walk across Europe: 'The wall between caution and paranoia is hard to hold up with one pair of hands.' I had first read it when I was solo kayaking on my first crocodile-inhabited river 15 years ago.

So I rode toward Tunis.

All was great for the first 90 km or so from Beja. In fact I planned to stop around that distance but there was nowhere to stay. So I rode on toward Tunis. A grey sky lay ahead; that pallid yellow-grey of pollution mixed with a likely storm that reminded me of an old smoker's face. After 100 km the traffic started to build but was not too bad. I rode on toward Tunis. Then I was on a motorway; there was no choice. I hugged the inside edge as Thursday evening traffic sped by, Thursday night being the start of the Moslem weekend. Trucks came too close and lightning started to fork horizontally across that yellow-grey sky. I decided to head for Hammam-Lif, east of Tunis. A junction was signposted, but the lane for Hammam-Lif was the far lane of the motorway. It was impossible for me to cross three lanes of non-stop speeding motorway traffic to reach it.

I came off at Ben Arous and, as I did, I narrowly missed being wiped out by a minivan. I breathed a sigh of relief as I rode down some suburban streets. I stopped first to ask if there was a hotel, but there were none and then to ask the way to Hammam-Lif. I followed two lots of instructions – and found myself back on the bloody motorway. Thunder accompanied the lightning and it started to rain a little. The Olympique de Radès, the national stadium, glowed in the eerie half-light. I took up my shoulder position for more motorway madness, put my head down and, despite 140 km in the legs, sprinted hard to get off the nightmare. I did just as the heavens opened and darkness fell. I found a cafe for temporary shelter then a hotel for something more permanent. I felt I'd made the wrong decision for sure. But six weeks later gunmen massacred 22 people, mostly tourists, at the Bardo National Museum in Tunis. It was followed two months later by a mass shooting of 40 European tourists in Sousse.

I arrived in the Tunisian coastal resort of Yasmine Hammamet on 23 January. En route I'd passed through the village of Turki. I figured that if something happened to stop us rowing from Tunisia I could claim I'd started in Turkey and finished in Turki. I was pleased to be in Hammamet, perhaps the end of any further biking on my journey. It was a blustery winter's day and the forecast was for heavy snow in the mountains. I looked out at the whitecaps whipped up by the wind and, in the dark, tried to imagine living life out there on a little rowing boat.

Yasmine Hammamet consisted of a long strip of hotels set back from the beach and a large marina with boats in it and restaurants around it. Most places were closed, although a smattering of European tourists wandered around in fleece and down jackets hoping the winter sun advertised in the brochure might eventuate. The vast majority of the yachts and motor cruisers in the marina were shut up for winter, although a few people, mostly French, were wintering over in the marina. It was far cheaper to do so in Tunisia than on the north side of the Mediterranean. Marin had booked an apartment for us that turned out to be owned by Zornati, the marina general manager. I settled in for a few days to wait for Marin as the only resident in the complex.

Marin had put the call out through his networks for anyone in Tunisia who might help us with arrangements there. Vili Gošnak answered the call, and on my first full day in Hammamet I had a delightful long lunch with Vili and his wife Raja, he a Slovenian businessman living in Tunisia, she a Tunisian professor living in Slovenia. Vili, the first European I'd seen since Ceuta, would turn out to be yet another legend of my journey, running us around to get supplies in Tunis, helping in our campaign to free *Mr Hops*.

Our row boat had originally been called *Paraguacu*, but I'd decided we'd rename it *Mr Hops*, a nice beer-flavoured counterpart to the wine-tasting *Miss Grape*. He would also allow me to hopefully hop past Libya. The day *Mr Hops* arrived in Tunisia, a hotel in the Libyan capital Tripoli was bombed, killing 10 westerners. A day later, 20 were killed in a demonstration in Cairo. I was increasingly seeing the row as a wise move. The day before, 26 January, was Australia Day, and marked exactly nine months since I'd left Gallipoli. I toasted both with Yann, a French yachtsman wintering over in the marina.

As Marin headed toward Tunisia on the weekly ferry from Genoa in Italy, I spent some time preparing for *Mr Hops* to arrive from Tunis, not realising quite how long Hammamet would be waiting for his arrival. Zornati at the marina wanted to help, and offered free berthing in the water but first we needed a week or so on the hardstand to work on the boat. For that we had to use Rodrigues, a private boatyard at the marina. Tafen, the assistant manager, who I took an immediate dislike to, gave me a price that was totally over the top; €800 for a week. It might be irrelevant, though, as the shipping agent then rang to say the bill of lading showed that there were zero items in a container that should contain one item: a row boat. I hoped they hadn't forgotten to put *Mr Hops* inside in Cape Verde.

Vili and I met Marin, weighed down by vast quantities of luggage, at Tunis port. The first thing I noticed when unpacking back at the apartment were endless pots of Sudocrem. The reality of the next stage was starting to sink in. Other gear was not so lucky. Our EPIRB, the emergency satellite beacon that boats and ships are required to carry, had been off on a merry journey from the UK to Slovenia, arriving too late for Marin to bring. Vili assured us that if it was sent on to Tunisia, customs would hold it for a month or more. The manufacturer suggested that they didn't have a dealer in Tunisia but that we might find one 'nearby.' Nearby? Where – Libya? Algeria? We had been told that all our dehydrated food and the parts needed to repair our desalinator had been sent to Slovenia, but it turned out to be a false promise. It looked like Malta might be Christmas for us, with any number of parcels being redirected there.

The desalinator was a worry. Water, water everywhere indeed. Without a working desalinator we couldn't make fresh water and it could mean we'd have to stock the boat full of bottled water, a complete anathema to me. Perhaps it was a conspiracy by the bottled water industry to trap me? We actually had to ensure we had enough water not only to get us to Malta, but also for the full 40 days we thought we might be at sea, given there was no guarantee the weather would allow us to reach Malta or indeed land anywhere.

FEBRUARY

Even though February was the shortest month of the year, sometimes it seemed like the longest.

J.D. Robb

O ur first challenge was to release *Mr Hops*. Day after day we took the 70-km journey to Tunis port. As we jumped through one hoop, the Tunisian customs would throw another high in front of us. Some were reasonable, others farcical. But we played the game and jumped hoops for *Mr Hops*. We visited office after office, but mostly we waited; then, after waiting, we waited some more. We drank bad coffee and spoke bad French.

Once the shipping company office in Cape Verde had assured us that there was actually a boat in the container it took some days to get the paperwork corrected. And, when it was, the Tunisian port authorities couldn't find the container. Back and forth we went, by train, bus and taxi. On social media we started a 'Free *Mr Hops*' campaign. Whatever we gave the customs, they asked for more, usually in triplicate and often witnessed by a public notary. We found one in the corner of a supermarket in Nabeul, 20 km from Yasmine Hammamet, and queued for his stamp. In the same supermarket I made my first ever purchase of underpants; having survived for nine months with two pairs I thought a third could be a nice treat, given we might be in Tunisia for some time. As I stood scratching my head wondering what size to buy, I realised that in over 50 years such things had only ever been bought for me. First by my mother, then girlfriends, and now wife.

Vili had put us onto his shipping agent, Monem, who arranged for Raouf to be 'our man in Tunis port'. Despite the cold, Raouf, a stocky man with a continually puzzled look on his face, turned up in a sweat each time we met him. The look and the sweat was no wonder really, given the running around he was doing on our behalf; the pleading too.

'You do not own this ship,' said the big cheese of the customs. 'You are Marin Medak, and you are Huw Kingston, but the registration papers of the ship say that the owner is Bernard Kingston.' We couldn't deny it. The row boat had originally been registered in the UK and it was simpler to keep it that way. But I couldn't register it, as I didn't live in the UK, nor of course did Marin. So we had registered the boat in my father's name. Legally he was the owner.

'You must receive the permission from Bernard Kingston to use the ship. Then we can release it.' I wrote a letter and sent it to Dad to sign, scan and return. The next day we took the letter back to customs.

'This is not allowed. We must have the original.' Bugger. It would take days to get a hard-copy letter couriered to us. Marin and I sat in the corridor and wondered what to do. What if we printed off the letter and I forged my dad's signature and brought it back to customs in the hope there might be a different office on duty? It was worth the risk – and hours later we'd successfully jumped through another hoop.

Some people, faced with life's frustrations, turn to shopping for solace. Shopping honestly scares me and it is beyond my understanding how people can see it as entertainment. Decades earlier I'd been the marketing manager for a chain of adventure stores, essentially with responsibility for getting people through the door and up to the cash register – seems strange, given whenever I walk into a shop I start to sweat. Departing Tunis port for yet another day, Vili dropped Marin and me at the biggest supermarket in Tunisia. To get to it we had to walk through the largest shopping centre in Tunisia, the first I'd been in since leaving Australia. Our spree, buying stock for 40 days, started with Marin buying a pillow and a frilly lace pillowcase. Now I didn't yet really know this man I was about to spend all this time on a small boat with. But, 'You will be grateful for this pillow. You will love this pillow,' was all he said. Marin also assured me he would spoon half a jar of peanut butter per day and didn't need any more than two-minute noodles for breakfast. We bought 35 jars of peanut butter and 250 packets of noodles. I told Marin that I'd be eating muesli and drinking coffee. We

Another wet night on the oars of *Mr Hops*

Cooking up in the sun from the cabin of *Mr Hops*. Ideally we needed to put in some 7,000 calories a day, three and a half times the usual requirement

Marin rowing into the sunrise

finished three hours later with 150 kg of stuff and a two-metre-long receipt which to me represented a serpent that had taken away hours of my life.

Conversations with Marin revealed that we had quite different philosophies to our adventures, our journeys. For Marin it was ultimately about the challenge. The other aspects of landscape and people were subservient to this. For me, I needed the emotional connection with the landscape and, as *mediterr année* had proved, would not shy away from human interaction and often embraced it. Marin described how, when he kayaked from Greece to Croatia some years earlier, he had tried to avoid people, tried to find empty beaches and just had a focus on the paddle. I had done many journeys in remote places where it was not a case of trying to avoid people; there were no people to avoid. I too loved the challenge of being alone and of not seeing people sometimes for weeks at a time. But I was rapt in the environment too. It was of course true that Marin was nearly half my age – indeed a few of the customs officers had asked if I was Marin's father – and I too probably had more drive in my mid-twenties. But it was Marin who was going to play the lead role in our row. He was the one with the experience from his Atlantic crossing in 2012, and was just so damn capable.

At Tunis port we were not alone in our frustrations, of course. We saw the same people, ate at the same kiosks, understood the same looks of hope then despair. Finally, 11 days after *Mr Hops* arrived in Tunis, everything changed once the customs had inspected her. Raouf turned up one afternoon absolutely dripping. He'd spent three hours in the container terminal looking for *Mr Hops* and now announced we had been granted visiting rights. After receiving more stamps than a philatelic collection, the rusty container door was swung back. There was *Mr Hops*, cowering in the back of his cell. We were allowed only 10 minutes with him, but it was good at last to meet him. For me it was the first time.

Despite us having told them, even having shown them pictures, the customs were, I'm sure, expecting to find a fancy speedboat owned by an ageing Australian playboy and his youthful Slovenian equivalent. What they found when they opened the container was a very dusty, rather worn-looking craft resting on a few old truck tyres. '*Il n'y a pas de moteur?* (There is no motor?)' they asked.

Previously we had been told we would pay a large bond, returnable when we rowed away from Tunisia. But when they saw *Mr Hops*, they took pity and reduced the bond to zero. They still put him against Marin's passport so he couldn't leave the country without *Mr Hops*. On his passport he was described as a '*Bateau (Kayak Rameau)*' (a 'Boat (Kayak Rowboat)').

Mr Hops, still in his container, arrived at Rodrigues' shipyard on the back of a truck. Tafen, despite a promise to me made earlier by Mohammed his boss, was insisting that the original price stood. A sizeable crowd had gathered to watch our rowing boat be craned out of the container and onto the hardstand. Work could finally begin. This delay had used up a chunk of our contingency days. My finish date at Gallipoli was finite, of course, but Marin just repeated the mantra 'We will just have to row harder'.

In bitterly cold conditions we made *Mr Hops* ready. We repainted the deck, fitted new hatches, new electrical equipment, put stickers on wonky, pulled them off, put them on again a bit straighter. On 6 February we had the first call with Jure, our meteorologist.

Mr Hops hadn't been near water for some three years, so we had plenty to do to make him ready for our voyage. Here Marin replaces the deck hatch covers

Jure Jerman worked for the Slovenian weather bureau, acted as the meteorologist for numerous ocean yacht races, and had worked with Marin on his Atlantic row. The fickle Mediterranean weather would challenge Jure's skills as much as it would ours. There was nothing positive in the forecast for the coming week, and anyway we still had much work to do to make ready.

As my 17th day in Hammamet passed, it marked the longest stint of not moving forward on my journey so far, longer than my knees-up on Brač in Croatia the previous July. I was itching to get going but was almost in a form of torpor from the lack of physical activity. Looking at *Mr Hops*, looking inside his tiny cabin, I so wanted to get back to living and sleeping in something small after nearly eight weeks of nights in houses, hotels and apartments. I did wonder, though, how much sleep I'd actually get in my two hour breaks from rowing.

We were keen to get *Mr Hops* off the hardstand and into the water, and by 10 February reckoned we'd done enough. I could see what was coming. Over the days Mohammed had made all sorts of verbal promises about making a fair price, usually conveying them to me via Yann or Claude, another French yachtsman. They all told me it was just a game, although most everyone I'd met around the marina said they tried their hardest to not use Rodrigues for any work.

I was in and out of the office door like a waiter in a busy restaurant. 'I'm just an employee. You must talk to Mohammed,' said Hafed, throwing up his arms in a pitch for innocence. But Mohammed was not answering his phone. I finally got hold of him and he said he would tell Hafed the new, special price. 'Yes, Mohammed rang me, but

After 10 days of *Mr Hops* being kidnapped by Tunisian Customs and my first fight in 30 years to prevent the same being done by the shipyard at Hammamet, it was a relief to see *Mr Hops* craned into the waters of the Mediterranean

How else would you launch *Mr Hops* other than with hops?

I carried my bike in the front cabin of *Mr Hops*. My wheel fitted in through the hatch with only millimetres to spare

the price is the same,' replied Hafed on my next visit. It was all rather maddening, and it seemed *Mr Hops* was hostage once again. Until we paid the ransom Hafed would not permit the crane to lift the boat into the water. It was mid-afternoon, it was raining, almost sleeting, and I was pissed off. I went into the office one more time and started to record a piece to video outside Hafed's office. I admit it was a little provocative but I didn't expect Hafed to exit his office and attack me. We tumbled down the corridor and smashed up against a door and onto the ground. By now some of the shipyard staff were in the building and pulling us apart. *Mr Hops* and now my camera were hostage.

With the workers around and Marin wondering what the hell had been going on, a friendly customs officer tried to broker peace. The police followed. Finally Hafed handed my camera over. We just wanted to get *Mr Hops* in the water and us out of that poisonous place, so I paid the extortionate amount. It was an unfortunate stain after all the goodness of my journey, and it had been my first fight in nearly 30 years, since tumbling to the snow with a ski instructor in 1986.

The crane started up, *Mr Hops* was put in the strop and moved slowly down into the Mediterranean Sea on 9 February. She floated: a good start. It was her first time in water for over three years. It was an exciting time as I thought back six months to the Dolomites and the original idea of rowing past Libya. Marin took up the oars and guided *Mr Hops* around to our berth in the marina. Here a small crowd was gathered for the launch ceremony, and a British sailor, Victoria, had a royal enough sounding name to do the honours. Whilst it is not considered good luck to change a boat's name, nor make it a male, our row boat was launched, with beer over the stern, as *Mr Hops*.

Somewhere, a long way over the horizon, was Malta, our first destination from Tunisia

We continued work on the boat, stuffing food and equipment into every nook and cranny. With wheels off, my bike just squeezed through the hatch into the front cabin. I did wonder how it would survive the inevitable saltwater ingress. Five kilograms of olives were divided up as Marin, along with the peanut butter, had said he was keen to eat 150 g of olives a day. I packed a few beers. Marin told me I wouldn't feel like drinking them. One hundred and fifty litres of bottled water were bought. I felt dirty, very dirty.

On 11 February Jure told us there might be a reasonable window in the weather from the following day, then the models were predicting a nasty storm around a week later. We knew we had to get moving; conditions would never be perfect in winter in the Mediterranean, and every day delayed was a day risking my scheduled return to Gallipoli. Malta was our first destination, some 350 km away. With reasonable conditions we might just make it before the storm.

In between hosting all the Tunisian TV stations and various other well-wishers, we worked long into the night before a final few hours' sleep in the apartment.

Finally, on 12 February, after clearing customs and border police and on a beautiful morning, Marin rowed us away from Yasmine Hammamet. Vili had come to see us off and there was much we had to thank that fine man for. The long oars dipped into the Mediterranean waters and we headed east, away from the Tunisian coast. When my first shift came around there was just one small thing. I'd never rowed before. I also realised that for the next 2,000 km I would be facing west again, facing away from Turkey.

After a couple of hour-long shifts to ease me in and some pointers from Marin, we soon dropped into the two hours on, two hours off rhythm that would to be strictly adhered to day and night. When my head lay on the frilly cased pillow for the first time I pondered how I'd cope, how my body would cope. But as we set off to row across the Mediterranean I also realised that any suffering was self-imposed; was nothing compared to that experienced by the tide of refugees flooding out of Syria right then, or the Anzac diggers trapped on the beaches of Gallipoli a hundred years before.

A headwind slowed our progress in the first 24 hours out of Tunisia, and I soon learned that these bathtubs of the ocean stall in any sort of headwind or sidewind. Pushing a tonne around the water with a couple of sticks is not conducive to speed. A few fishing trawlers came close during our first night, reminding us that throughout our voyage we needed to be alert for shipping.

It was hard to get into a pattern of living with never more than an hour of sleep. The blisters and sores came as expected; the Sudocrem was well used. I rowed whilst watching, for entertainment, Marin pierce the blisters on his hands one by one. Clear fluid flowed down to his wrists and dripped into the bilge. Any muscle that had hidden away in the past 10 months of walking, kayaking and riding now had its day. Too often I fell asleep at the

'NOT for pleasure use' said the build plate on our row boat. It was not wrong

oars in rain or sun and on a couple of occasions slipped off the seat. The build plate on *Mr Hops* ominously included the line: 'This boat is built for ocean rowing only and is NOT for pleasure use.' I could see that plate from the rowing position and those words shouted to me day and night.

I could add 'ocean rowing' to my CV now, but not yet with the prefix 'expert'. That remained the domain of Marin Medak, who outrowed me by a third as much on our two hour shifts. Then again his legs were a third longer and 50 per cent younger; poor excuses I know. But I was getting there. There was one shift, deep in the night with the sea and wind running onto our stern, when it all clicked; I felt the rhythm. Full compression of the legs each stroke, good catch in the water, late pull on the oars with legs fully extended. I didn't stop to eat or drink for 90 minutes lest it all fall apart. On the next shift it did.

'Ten minutes,' goes the call from the man on the oars ... You pull the sleeping bag a bit closer around your neck. 'Seven minutes,' you hear. You sit up, bang your head on the cabin roof which tends to wake you fully, and pull on jacket, pants. Don't forget to smear your butt with Sudocrem. Check your watch – five minutes to go. You pull on shoes and throw open the hatch door. 'Good morning/Good evening/How's the temperature?' says one. 'Did you sleep?' says the other. You reach for the cut-off plastic bottle and piss downwind. I've never known an activity where you pee so much. A final glance at your watch, pull on the gloves and at the allotted hour, to the minute, we swap places. You start rowing, he pees, climbs inside, eats, peels off clothing, closes the hatch, sleeps.

'Ten minutes' goes the call from the man on the oars ...

Marin called the shots and I was not about to rock the boat. There were three main reasons. Firstly he was way more competent than me; secondly he had done so much to make this leg of my journey a reality that I was happy, rarely for me, to put my fate in another's hands. Finally I just didn't have the energy beyond what I was doing now. There is a certain lethargy that gets you at sea.

We made good progress for five days, to within 60 km off Malta, before the sea and wind got up and we were forced onto the para anchor for a day and a half. Deploying this large cone of sailcloth into the water helped *Mr Hops* hold position as we sat out adverse wind and weather. Force 6 southerlies took us north before a sou'easter pushed us north-west. Finally the wind swung around to the north-east to push us back south-west. *Mr Hops* was doing circle work in the Mediterranean. Not rowing was worse than rowing. With the two of us crammed into a cabin made for one there was little comfort, and each wave that smashed into *Mr Hops* reverberated through our bodies and tossed us into each other. I couldn't face food, managing a couple of oranges and a slice of cake in the whole period. Worse was that, with two of us in the cabin only one got to rest his head on the frilly pillow. Marin claimed both purchaser's and skipper's rights.

Via a poorly functioning satellite phone, Jure told us that the big easterly storm was now due around the afternoon of 18 February. We were able to start rowing again on the morning of the 17th, and that night the wind swung in our favour, from the west. Behind our backs the lights of Malta showed and beckoned us on. Ships became more numerous, heading for the narrow channel between Malta, the main island, and Gozo. But by dawn on the 18th it seemed unlikely we would beat the storm, and when an easterly sprung up soon after, that seemed to seal it. It became a waste of time rowing into it so out went the para anchor again. The cliffs of Gozo were little more than 15 km away and whilst there was no chance of landing amongst them they represented something solid so close by. The Maltese authorities confirmed Jure's prediction; around noon the weather was going to get ugly.

Albert Gambina had already done legendary service for my journey. Nothing had been too much trouble for this son of Malta and keen sea kayaker, once he had heard of my journey and my plan to now include Malta as a *mediterr année* country. He had of-fered advice, was organising things for our arrival, and was also the post box that we were hoping would be full of all the things that had never made it to Tunisia – EPIRB, freeze-dried foods, desalinator spares and more. If he messed about in tiny kayaks for pleasure, it was big ships that provided his income: Albert was a ship's pilot on Malta.

Rocking and rolling on the para anchor off Gozo, Marin and I considered our options. They were few. Take the storm on the chin and endure three, four or more days being pushed back toward Tunisia,

Albert Gambina – Malta ship's pilot, sea kayaker; yet another legend of my journey

or call Albert to see if he could arrange a tow into Malta. I agonised on a decision that would deliberately break my human-powered rule, but so much time had been taken up in Tunisia that I was worried about my non-elastic Gallipoli deadline.

With mobile reception now available I rang Albert, as much for his thoughts as anything. 'I have been tracking you on the radar, Huw' he told me. 'The Rescue Coordination Centre in Malta are in touch with me too.' I mentioned the idea of a tow, but also my concern, knowing how these things can blow out of proportion, that the authorities might see this as a rescue of a vessel in distress, which was not the case. 'Huw, I will see if one of our pilot boats can come to you but we will keep this amongst ourselves.' A request for a tow to save time could so easily become 'Australian and Slovenian adventurers plucked from Mediterranean in wild weather' in the hands of headline-hungry media.

As Albert went about organising for one of the pilot cutters to leave Valletta and find us off Gozo, some 50 km away, Marin and I laughed until it hurt. As soon as I put the phone down to Albert the wind that had caused us to stop rowing and throw out the para anchor died to nothing and *Mr Hops* sat on an even carpet of green. Not a whisper, not a wave. We laughed at the absurdity of a vessel coming to tow us and finding us becalmed. We laughed because we felt like bloody idiots. Could the predictions be so far wrong?

But it was truly the calm before the storm, the Mediterranean toying with me again, much as she had so many times when I was kayaking her shores. Bang on noon the wind got up again, blowing from the east as promised. By half past the hour big waves were forming and we felt vindicated in our decision.

Bravo 1, skippered by Charlie Mula, called us for our position. It soon became apparent our on-board VHF radio was receiving but not transmitting and our handheld unit was fast running out of juice. We communicated with *Bravo 1* by phone. 'Are you near Gozo or Malta?' asked Charlie. We replied that we were close to Gozo. 'Well the position you gave us has you nearer Malta.' This was puzzling. We reconfirmed our position off the main GPS but Charlie told us this still showed us much closer to Malta, which was where they were now looking for us. Marin checked the position on his phone and discovered our main GPS had decided to give a wrong read. Dud GPS, broken VHF radio, no EPIRB, useless desalinator; the media could indeed have a field day. We relayed the new position and half an hour later could pick out the pilot boat heading our way amongst the whitecaps.

Getting a rope on board was problematical in the conditions and in part because *Bravo 1* didn't have one (we used ours from the para anchor), but after a few goes we had a line on board. As the tow began the heavens opened with torrential rain. We headed into the blackest of black skies with thunder and lightning applauding our decision. It was 12 nautical miles, some 20 km, to Mġarr, the only harbour on Gozo, and it was a long, slow, wet journey. Marin went into the cabin and I stayed on deck to steer and take the breaking waves full in the face. Charlie handled the tow expertly as we went into a second storm cell; force 8 winds with hail this time. I was freezing and soaked to the bone, but there was little point either me going inside and soaking everything or Marin coming out. The spectacular cliffs of Gozo were away to our left and for three hours we moved slowly toward Mġarr, *Mr Hops* shuddering his way through the maelstrom. Once we were in the limited sanctuary of Mġarr harbour, *Bravo 1* threw off our line, waved and motored off across the channel toward Malta. Marin jumped onto the oars to try and guide us to a pontoon without hitting other boats. One of many things ocean row boats are not designed for, unwieldy as they are, is to be manoeuvred close to land and other boats. Marin took us expertly to a pontoon where we tied off, glad to be secure.

I was glad too, to change into some warm and dry clothing and, after gathering documents, I jumped from the awkwardly positioned rear hatch to the jetty. My arrival on Malta, my 17th country, was less than elegant; a combination of precarious take-off point, elevated landing stage and sea legs saw me crashing badly onto the jetty and almost slipping backwards into the cold water.

Paul, the friendly Customs officer, seemed uncertain what to do about us and our craft and scrawled 'N/A' against most questions on his forms before sending me next door to the office of the small marina where Joe booked us in for as long as we needed without any charge. That man Albert had already ensured our welcome: 'Ah, Ian, here's an Aussie you should talk to,' said Joe to a man who came out of the weather into the office.

It was wind that had brought us under tow to Gozo, and it was that wild wind that had Ian Besson checking the mooring of his in-laws' yacht moored near *Mr Hops* in Mġarr marina. Another wild wind, Cyclone Marcia, at the other end of the earth then had Ian and his partner Leisa up all night scrambling for news as their own yacht, moored in Brisbane's Moreton Bay, was threatened. Fortunately both yachts survived.

That meeting with Ian led us to soon be ensconced in a house in Victoria, Gozo's main town, a house that only a madman could have conceived. Arches, alleys, stairs and terraces, some only accessible by ladder, all radiated off a courtyard with a small pool. It was perhaps the acts of a madman that had seen Ian and Leisa recently decamp from Brisbane, Australia, to Gozo. Australia, a country that should be a world leader in renewable energy, has by uncertainties and actions – at that particular time by Tony Abbott, the then prime minister of Australia – done its damnedest to decimate the industry. Ian, an expert on wind power, and boss of an international renewable energy business, described himself as an economic refugee from Australia. As business had died at home he had to look elsewhere to where coal is not king of all. A king that the Australian government of the day seemed subservient to.

For five days we stayed with Ian and Leisa and her sons Jack and Max. Five days of rain, gales and cold that gave us plenty of justification for our tow in. We learned from Albert that Marsaxlokk, the main port on Malta, was closed to all ships in the conditions. In our Game of Thrones house, Faith, an American resident of Malta a dozen years, fed us as if we were rowing, trying to maintain the 7,000 calories per day regime. They were good days with great people; interesting conversation on environmental matters and matters of finding a place to call home, a community in which to belong.

Gozo is part of Malta but you wouldn't think so. Across the water is the main island of Malta and people on Gozo spoke of a different world – all hustle and bustle. Four hundred thousand people live there, just 30,000 on Gozo. It seemed likely that I would never visit Malta itself; when that rotten, cold storm blew out we were hopeful we could leave Gozo direct for our next hop to Crete.

But Malta came to us in the form of Albert Gambina: the sea kayaker, ships' pilot, founder of Kayak for Charity-Malta came twice on the ferry to Gozo to meet us. He was weighed down with the flotsam and jetsam that had chased us around the Mediterranean and finally washed up in Malta: desalinator parts, EPIRB, freeze-dried food and more.

The kitchen bench in Victoria was soon awash with parts from our desalinator. Surgeon Ian, head torch on, picked and pulled at O-rings, and registrar Marin nodded approvingly. Sadly all surgery failed and it was deemed inoperable. On one night we had dinner with Chris, a former South African and Dutch world championship rower. I gleaned some more tips from this giant of a man and laughed when he could not fit through the hatch of *Mr Hops* to climb aboard for a look.

Our row from Tunisia had certainly taught us what foods we relished and what we couldn't stomach on *Mr Hops*. Muesli with milk was a winner night and day, but the 35 jars of peanut butter and 5 kg of olives were distributed to the good people of Gozo, as were kilos of coffee. I, a coffee addict, had my first coffee since leaving Tunisia in Victoria. Our next stop would see us jettison hundreds of packets of noodles, Marin deciding muesli trumped them every time. We felt like a supply ship, dispensing food across the Mediterranean and receiving hospitality in return. Not that payment was ever required.

Sunday 21 February passed, my 300th day since leaving Gallipoli. Time was ticking away faster than I wanted, and I dared not look at the schedule – a schedule that became ever tighter with each day lost. We were comfortable on Gozo, but our plan wasn't comfort but progress. Via Jure and the local forecasters things didn't look good for some days but, as happens in those situations, we started to make bad look better in our minds. With winds in the westerly quadrant, albeit up to 45 knots, they were at least due to blow in our favour. A frittata illustrated with a Maltese Cross was served for our farewell dinner, then late on a freezing cold and damp Monday afternoon, a small group gathered at Mġarr marina to toast our departure. We half-completed formalities: 'The police aren't here so don't worry about them,' said the customs officer as he wrote 'pleasure craft' down on his sheet against 'Name of Vessel'. We rowed away with a plan of making our next landfall on Crete, 800 km east.

Once out of the channel separating Gozo from Malta the wind and sea built from the west. This was it: my first time on the oars in a big following sea. Under darkening skies of cloud and dusk we flew through and past half a dozen ships straining on their anchors and felt so utterly insignificant in our little seven-metre row boat. Beyond the ships a big wave knocked us broadside. *Mr Hops* heeled right over and I was flung off the row seat and into the rope that served as handrail and safety barrier. As the water drained away and I scrambled back to my seat I saw the EPIRB was flashing. The EPIRB that was on its first outing, having finally reached us in Gozo. Minutes later there was a call on the radio from the Rescue Coordination Centre in Malta: 'We have received a distress call from your vessel. Do you require a rescue?' We explained not, explained it seemed we had a faulty EPIRB and agreed to keep in touch. After it went off a second

Mr Hops

time and with a long way to go to Crete, Marin and I decided we should try to land in Malta after all to have it checked out.

Surfing down to three four-metre waves we flew along the north coast of Malta in the dark in 35 knot winds. Marin's shift came around at 7 p.m. and I guided him using the GPS toward Valletta, where Albert had arranged a berth for us at Manoel Island marina. Reaching a spot where I thought we should turn in the pitch black, Marin believed it to be the shoreline with dumping waves so we continued a little further west. A long breakwater loomed off our starboard side and the rebound buffeted *Mr Hops*. Marin used all his strength, grunting and squealing like tennis star Sharapova with each pull on the oars, to get us inside the breakwater. Behind the wall, the wind was still screaming but the sea much less choppy. Valletta Port Authority was trying to reach us on the VHF but couldn't get our response. The challenge now was to not get swept into the far breakwater.

'Row, Row, ROW, keep ROWING. Row HARDER!!' came the shout from behind. I looked out from the cabin and was almost knocked over by a thick rope that simultaneously landed on *Mr Hops* and me. I followed the line of the rope and there was *Bravo 1*, the pilot boat that had towed us into Gozo five days earlier. I looked beyond Marin's head to see a large ferry steaming down on us, heading out from Valletta Grand Harbour. In the nick of time *Bravo 1* pulled us out of its path. The ferry had nowhere else to go in the narrow channel and had only seen us at the last minute. A close shave indeed. *Bravo 1* towed us to a berth beneath two towering ships, beneath the fortifications of the medieval city of Valletta, the capital of Malta. Bravo, Bravo.

Who had been monitoring all this? Who was there to meet us? Albert Gambina of course. We had indeed missed the entry to the channel that would have seen us reach Manoel Island. Understandably, the port authority were not best pleased with the fact that we'd entered the port without informing them and for the very, very near miss that ensued. They were right to be angry; it was poor navigation by us on a stormy night and not only did we need to fix the EPIRB, but our radio too.

Albert was keen to take us for dinner, but both Marin and I were tired and keener to stay with *Mr Hops* and cook up instead the first of our freeze-dried meals that Albert had delivered to Gozo some days before. Marin knocked over his, spilling pasta and gravy across the deck. It had been a frustrating few hours.

The following morning we found a marine electronics shop. A new aerial fixed our VHF radio problem but it turned out there was nothing wrong with our EPIRB. In the farce that had seen this device journey from the UK to Slovenia to Malta, that had seen it programmed wrongly, it turned out that, despite our instructions to the contrary, we had been supplied with a version that was set off when in contact with water. Given water was everywhere on and around *Mr Hops* an accidental deployment was inevitable. From then on, the EPIRB lived in a dry bag.

Our position, rubbing against the high stone wall in Valletta Grand Harbour, was less than ideal, and early afternoon we decided to row out of the harbour around to Manoel Island, this time alerting the port authority to our intentions. As we turned into the deep inlet leading to Manoel, the blackest of skies appeared in front of us. I sensed, and we soon felt, the nastiest of storm cells. Within minutes the sea was white and it became impossible to row against it. All we could do was run with it and turn back into the Grand Harbour to sneak along its edge until we found some buoys we could moor to. We sat there for some hours as squall after squall came past, until finally in the late afternoon we judged it safe enough to return to where we had started.

We were just readying ourselves to take up an invite from the ship next door to go on board for dinner when Albert rang to say *Bravo 1* would tow us around to Manoel. Copping another soaking, the skipper once again expertly pulled out around toward Manoel in a confused sea just on dark. *Bravo 1* was tight for time, needing to pick up a pilot off a ship, so we cast off the tow rope, perhaps a little earlier than we should have. We couldn't expect any more, given this was the third time she had come to our rescue. Bravo, Bravo, Bravo. As *Bravo 1* sped away we were left to battle a fierce wind to get up to Manoel. This was becoming a comedy of errors as Marin once again used all his strength to manoeuvre us away from the rocks of Valletta and inch our way to a mooring at the marina. Albert, of course, was there to meet us and on this occasion, after changing once again into dry clothing, we headed off for a cold beer and a hot Indian. I liked Albert a lot; his personality, his understanding and his sense of humour. He needed all of these with us.

We slept on *Mr Hops* that night, but the following day decamped to a nearby hotel where, with a cold brewing, I lay for much of the day. Everyone from Algeria to Malta had been telling me this was the coldest, stormiest winter in the southern Mediterranean for many years. Others on Malta had been following our journey, and that evening, as the very least we could do, Marin and I gave a presentation to the sea kayak club on Malta.

We left Malta on the morning of 26 February; now into my final two months. It was wet and cold for the first 36 hours and with a southerly wind we headed toward Sicily. Nearly a year before when I'd looked down on this part of the Mediterranean from high, standing on Mount Etna, the volcano that dominates Sicily, I'd had no plans whatsoever to be in a small boat rowing across that sea.

MARCH

*Only those with tenacity can
march forward in March.*

Ernest Agyemang Yeboah

oth Marin and I felt decidedly unwell – he used the bucket and I wasn't far from it. It is the lethargy that gets you. Everything is a chore; nothing to eat appeals, and you become aware of burning up but not replacing energy. Lots of ships were around in our first days from Malta. As we paid out the line for the para anchor on one occasion, a small coaster, the aptly named *Ozgun*, came nearby to see if all was well.

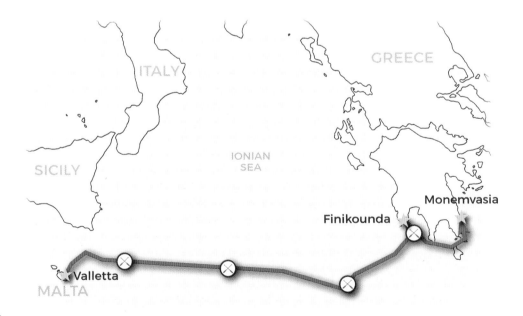

'Is all OK or are you just putting out your net for the fish?' they asked on the radio. The Italian coastguard came to spotlight us one night by ship, and buzzed us one day by plane. The Italian government were engaged in admirable humanitarian work via their Operation Mare Nostrum and the follow up Operation Triton, proactive policies that saw refugees pulled from smugglers' boats, mostly originating from Libya, and taken to Europe. We were not desperate refugees trying to escape troubled zones in north Africa but doing this for a challenge of choice.

Then finally came some warmth. The wind came with us too, and sickness was blown away. *mediterr année* had been full of milestones of both time and place, and so it was again as we passed through the area on the Mediterranean Sea furthest from any land; Italy far to our north and Libya far to our south. In celebration I pulled out a freeze-dried Mediterranean Fish Stew. Much like the Mediterranean itself, there wasn't much fish in it. A pod of dolphins travelled with us for hours one night: a sparkling, mesmerising show of phosphorescence as they swam around and under *Mr Hops*.

Strangely I was now finding that the maximum of an hour and a quarter sleep at any one time felt long and comfortable. I'd open my eyes from what seemed a long, deep sleep on the frilly pillow, certain the 10-minute call was about to come. But my watch would tell me there was half an hour or more to go. I'd drop once again into deep, energising sleep. On more than one occasion I lay listening to voices coming from under the boat through the hull; deep, echoing voices, conversations about what I didn't know or understand.

Two hours on, two hours off. Grabbing some sleep in *Mr Hops*

The westerlies pushed us toward Crete; we were averaging some 90–100km per day and night combined. Three-metre waves picked up *Mr Hops* and pushed him where we wanted to go, although it was often quite a fight to keep him in line. It was a week from Malta when we had our first calm, and despite it slowing progress I think both Marin and I were glad of the break from wrestling the oars. At night a full moon lit things up and *Mr Hops* glided on a roadway of silver. It was tempting to take a rest from staring at the compass and believe that just staying on the roadway would lead to our destination. Initially I thought March would be a month for the blue moon, but it was not quite. That said, sitting on and shitting in the bucket that served as our toilet one night ensured two full moons blazed brightly in the throne room of the ocean gods. Even less edifying was when, on one occasion as I rose from the bucket, an oar handle rose to meet me full on in an attempted indecent act.

We saw few fish jumping or wildlife of any description; just us, the sea and occasional passing ships. A tiny bird rested briefly on an oar, and I wondered where

Conditions we liked but rarely got – a tailwind and a following sea

he had begun his journey and where he would be going to next. The open sea does not offer enough to nourish me, much less so than a desert. In the desert you can at least move all around. This row across the Mediterranean was a very special solution for the continuation of my journey but overall the monotony and continual motion ensured that it was primarily a physical and mental challenge rather than offering the satisfaction I derive from changing landscapes.

Then Jure warned of a change afoot. Of a very strong easterly wind change that would reach us before we reached Crete. A wind that would stop us dead in our tracks and send us scuttling, helpless, backwards, for three or four days at least. Jure, with the computer models and weather maps of all Europe at his disposal, had been wrong before and we hoped he would be this time. Wrong not through any fault of his own but through the sheer unpredictability of Mediterranean weather in winter. But if he was right there was no way we could reach Crete before the storm hit. Initially it was a throwaway line I used, like tossing a baitless hook into the sea: 'Perhaps we should go north to the Peloponnese in Greece?'

Then on Thursday 5th, bad wind hit us and we paid out the para anchor again. For another 24 hours we were jolted left, right, left, right by waves. Every organ in my body was smashed against its neighbour in a cabin just too small for two. The wind was bad outside and in. I slept not a wink, everything ached. Then Marin announced a plan. This young man, possessed of fierce intellect and determination, had sketched out a 'give it our all' option to reach the Peloponnese. If Jure was right we might, just might, make it in time. But it was all or nothing, never mind the bollocks, every second counts rowing for 36 hours or so.

The wind swung in our favour so we hauled in the para anchor and began. But I had become lazy, my strokes insincere. With less than a half century of days to the end of my year-long journey I was thinking too much of that end. I was thinking of time back home with the family, of seeing a house that I had left as a half-renovated building site, now complete. Of the smells and sounds of the Australian bush.

Marin was not blind to my tardiness and announced part-way through my dusk shift that once my shift was done he would row the next 24 hours alone to improve our chances of success. He then shut the hatch door to sleep. I was pissed off; angry that he had announced his intentions without any discussion, disbelieving that on his own he could do better than the two of us.

But I was indeed letting the team down and had no excuse. Marin had kicked me in the arse and I woke up to myself and our position. I rowed as hard as I could for the rest of that shift and, when Marin appeared again, told him that sure he could row alone but only if I could not match his speed or at least come close. He checked the distance covered that past hour, smiled and simply said, 'Good job.'

We began to scrawl the distance covered per shift in red pen onto the inside of the cabin wall. H 4.3 miles, M 4.3 miles, H 4.6 miles, M 4.7 miles, H 5.1 miles, M 5.5 miles. We pulled on those oars like there was no tomorrow; we stuffed food into ourselves, we grabbed sleep ... We pulled on those oars like there was no tomorrow; we stuffed food into ourselves, we grabbed sleep ... We pulled ...

Ten days out from Malta and land appeared, hung over by grey. Rain squalls began to hit us. We pulled ... We planned one landing place then another as time and weather changed. The middle finger of the Peloponnese? No, not possible; it'll be the most westerly one, Methoni, perhaps. Finally we took aim for tiny Finikounda and told Dimitris. He was just about to take the ferry from Athens to Crete to meet us with some of his supporters. Indeed some had already left for Crete to put the finishing touches to a meticulously planned welcome party; a party we were not going to show up at.

Marin's cogs and wheels whirred and ground, calculating drift, wind, what time that fucking easterly would hit that could mean all was in vain. He feverishly plugged new waypoints into the GPS, and as if to challenge him further our electronic compass said thanks and goodnight. Bastard! We pulled ...

Darkness fell and the light show began. Clouds, blacker than the night, issued sea-shaking claps of thunderous applause first, before then opening their bladders to piss on us. Bastards! Hail, rain, cold. We pulled ...

As we came toward small Venetiko island it was Marin's shift. I peeled off soaked gear in the cabin and tried to warm up. Then I heard it amongst our tiny radio masts: I heard the whistle of a new wind. The wicked witch of the east had arrived. Bastard, bastard, bastard!! Soon the sea was up, and Marin, already 24 hours into this marathon, pulled ever harder toward the island. I shouted instructions: 2 miles, 1.7 miles, 1 mile ... Another cloud dropped its load and waves broke on rocks nearby, unmarked on our chart: 0.4 miles ... 0.3 miles ... 0.2 miles ... *Mr Hops* came around to turn up the lee of the island as the moon shed some light through a gap in the clouds. It was 8 p.m. and we were some 7 nautical miles from Finikounda.

The respite was temporary as we again felt the full force of the wind through the gap between island and headland. The moonlight went out, again. It was my turn, again. I squeezed Marin's shoulder hard as we swapped places and he collapsed into the cabin. Still-tired arms pulled on the oars, wasted legs sprung lifelessly against the

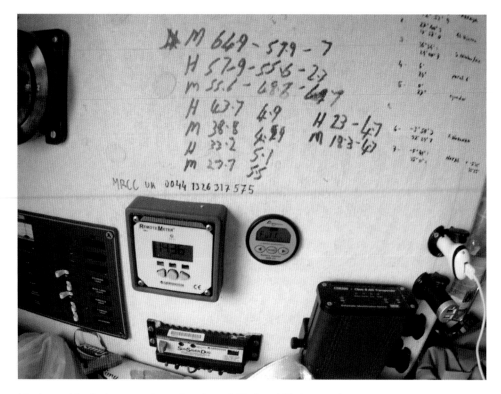

Marin and I tried to match each other shift for shift in our desperate attempt to outrun the approaching storm and reach the Peloponnese

footplate. The wind blew us sidewards, but *Mr Hops* inched his way across the gap. I was certain that, once in the lee of the headland, all would be calm. But we were pushed further out from it. Progress was painfully slow: less than a mile in two hours. I tried to pull back toward the land but my resolve began to weaken. It was pouring rain again. It was Marin's turn again. Better he sleep and stay dry than cop another soaking. I didn't wake him and buckled down and rowed as hard as I had rowed before. Finally, finally, I found myself in water that was calm aside from the raindrops on its surface. I rowed another hour, before the realisation that all I was doing was dropping a blade in the water and pulling it straight out again made me call '10 minutes'. After four hours on the oars and with two miles to go, I climbed into the sleeping bag, wet clothing and all.

As torches and headlights flashed from the wall of the tiny harbour of Finikounda, I exited my damp cocoon into a handshake offered by Marin: 'It's unbelievable what we have done, Huw.' An hour later, or even less, we would not have been there, could not have beaten the storm. Many months later Marin told me that there was no way he could have rowed solidly to get us to the Peloponnese. That his words to me were meant to motivate me to pull my finger out. They had indeed.

There, at 4 a.m. on Sunday 8 March, on the harbour wall was a small gathering of people. Amongst them, here in a place we never intended to be, arriving by a mode of transport I never intended to use, was Stavros Georgarakis, the Greek kayaker through whom Marin had first learned of my journey.

MEDITERRANEAN

164

Stavros Georgarakis, the glue that holds Greek kayaking together, was there at 4 a.m. on a Sunday morning when Marin and I landed from Malta onto the Peloponnese

We tied *Mr Hops* to the wall of the tiny harbour and climbed off to handshakes and hugs. Last time I had seen Stavros was when I had paddled away from Athens in early June the previous year. Then I was headed for the Corinth Canal, to bypass, via the canal, the only section of the Greek mainland I had planned not to visit on my journey; the Peloponnese.

Vassilis, a local, led us to his bar, which he had opened for our arrival. Here hot tea, toast and Metaxa brandy waited in celebration. Two friendly coastguard officers had driven to Finikounda to complete entry formalities. I asked Vassilis how he had known about our journey, our arrival. 'Dimitris Kokkoris has been holidaying in Finikounda for 35 years since he was a small boy with his family. He called me.' So – bizarrely and purely by chance – at the only land we could actually reach, the man who was to have joined us in Crete would now join us here instead, in this tiny village, which he knows and is known in, as if it is his second home. Events had, as my long journey had proven time and again, shown that connections meant that Finikounda was the right place to have come to. Vassilis guided us to some rooms where, after a hot, hot shower we collapsed into bed at 6 a.m.

I woke at 9 a.m., unable to sleep further despite the fatigue. I drank coffee and cleaned the boat with Stavros and another Dimitris – Dimitris Terzis, who had been part of our welcome group. Marin woke at 2 p.m.

We all lunched at the restaurant Vassilis owns, next door to Votsalo café, the bar Vassilis owns. At lunch Vassilis told us of the olive oil he produces from the 1,500 trees he owns, and the wine he produces from his vineyards. The man is everywhere. In the late afternoon Dimitris Kokkoris arrived from Athens, complete, in celebration of International Women's Day, with three of Greece's finest. Eva, Eirini and Dimitra, all here to help with the next leg to Turkey, who had all thought they would be in Crete to meet us. We ate again until overflowing. But before I could sleep we were required to visit another restaurant where 100 women were dancing the Greek dance in celebration of their day. The owner, a friend of course of Dimitris, had insisted we visit to take a drink even though the following night, Monday, they would prepare a dinner in our honour. We entered through the kitchen door and within minutes the quick drink became more platters of more food. Marin and I were announced to the 100 women and were asked to appear, Punch and Judy-like, with our heads in the servery hatch. A nice cheer and no tomatoes thrown from the Greek salads. But 8 March also belonged to a very special woman. It may have been the day we rowed into Greece. It may have been International Women's Day. But above all it was my mum's birthday.

Finikounda had one other surprise. On the narrow main street a mannequin stood forlornly in a doorway seemingly attached to no shop; belonging to no one. It wore a faded navy sweatshirt emblazoned with 'Rowing League' and 'Heritage Rowing Club.'

So I was in Greece again, in one of the most hospitable nations on earth. A crisis might have engulfed its people but generosity forever abounds. In the same way that I had never planned to travel in a row boat, I had also never planned for my *mediterr année* route to almost converge on its outward and homeward legs. But the wind dictated what we did and to a very large extent where we went. As Marin said, 'This is so, so much harder than rowing across the Atlantic with its consistent swell, its predictable wind.' It is why these unwieldy craft, these bathtubs, have rarely traversed Mediterranean waters. For those that like firsts, our row so far from Tunisia to Malta to Greece would most likely be the longest attempted in modern times in such a craft on this sea. It is of course, an esoteric claim.

If the weather had been cold and grey, the warmth of Finikounda was anything but. Whilst Sonia and Vassilis looked after us by day in Votsalo café, in what became our de facto office, brothers Nico and Ilias not once but twice put a feast in front of us. Restaurant Elena, which they have run together for over 30 years, was closed except at weekends at that time of year, but they lit the fire and warmed the building, and we feasted royally until the early hours. It was impossible for money to change hands.

If we had assumed that formalities with the Greek authorities were complete in the pre-dawn of our arrival day, we assumed wrongly. A couple of days into our stay the Greek coastguard sent a car to Finikounda to take us to Pilos, a larger town to the north. They were struggling to know what to do with our boat; how to classify it, wondering how we had come so far 'without a support boat' and whether such a boat should go on with us. It was reminiscent of the Greek coastguard in Nea Michaniona the previous May when I had stopped to ask for their advice whilst kayaking near Thessaloniki. Phone calls were made to ministries in Athens, advice given by those not qualified to give advice. I didn't want a bar of it and left Dimitris and Marin to that particular battle. Eventually they sent another car to Finikounda to have us sign triplicate letters saying we did not want a support boat: Xerox, the Greek god of paper, was back watching over us. Interestingly for the time we were in Finikounda, so were two plain-clothes policeman who were known to the locals. They generally sat in the cafes we sat in and seemed to be keeping an eye on us. The locals could offer no other explanation.

Dimitris, 38, invited along for this last hop to Turkey, had embraced the task well beyond expectations. With a full team – 90 per cent female, each allotted roles from Social Media Coordinator to Fitness Coach – plus a website, sponsors and half the Greek media on board, we hoped we could deliver the 'non-stop and unsupported' adventure he had promised. Our forthcoming journey together was certainly an opportunity to do something different in Greece, and it was good he was so inspired by both my whole journey and this segment. Born in London, educated in the US, Dimitris was about as sociable a person as you could imagine. Within minutes of entering a cafe he was a friend to most within it. But his was not a surface, bar room joviality. Dimitris had an intense side, a deep thinking side, and certainly a softness that was probably in part why women were drawn to join his team. It was rare that he was not on the phone or updating his status amongst a legion of social media friends. As with most Greeks, the economic crisis had taken its toll, his family printing business deep in debt with Dimitris' name on the papers.

Dimitris had brought along Dimitra, a young Greek film-maker who hoped to make a documentary of our row. Like any good film-maker she was engaged with her subject matter and along with all the outward signs of the archetypal young hipster she had much warmth. Having interviewed Marin at length she moved to me: 'I am inspired by you, your romanticism and your passion. What is it that drives you on this or any such journey?' I told her at length as best I could. She explained to me how Marin had told her that for him it was about the technical aspects of the journey: the planning, the equipment, the weather forecasting, the navigation. She had pressed him more on the environment and the people, but he kept returning to these aspects. I knew much of this of course and had discussed it with Marin but I had also sensed some change as we journeyed across the Mediterranean.

We repacked *Mr Hops*; tried to make a boat designed for one person now fit three. I offloaded my bike to go to Athens, the bike I had kept on board as insurance should I have needed it in Turkey to pick up time. The reality was that with three of us on board *Mr Hops* would actually be slower; the additional 150 kg of Dimitris, his equipment and the extra supplies for him would slow us down. When the storm did finally pass, our plan was to strike below the Peloponnese and out across the Aegean Sea to Turkey. From where we were Cyprus was not now an option; it was too far south, too far away. Delays as we campaigned for the release of *Mr Hops* in Tunisia, delays as we waited out bad weather in Malta, and now our position on the Peloponnese had made it thus. Our new plan was to head toward Rhodos and then make for Fethiye in Turkey, we hoped a journey of perhaps two weeks.

Talking of Rhodos, for some weeks *Miss Grape* had sat on that Greek island, not far off Turkey, sent there by that legend of legends, Stavros, after he had received her from Italy. Turkish kayaker Tolga Yücel had kindly gone to collect her and take her back with him to Turkey to wait my arrival. But nothing, as you know by now, is easy when taking kayaks across borders by land or sea: Turkish customs had kidnapped *Miss Grape* and were apparently now holding her to ransom in Marmaris. 'Free *Miss Grape!*'

Late afternoon on our fourth day in Finikounda, *Mr Hops* was cast off from the jetty. Team members old and new piled onto Nico and Elias's fishing boat to follow us out. Before we left, Vassilis attempted to load us down with endless bottles of his wine and his olive oil, but we had to strongly resist, partly for lack of room and partly to stop us once again becoming a food bank across the Aegean.

After a final toot from the horn, our escort waved farewell and we were left, three men in a boat. Within minutes the most spectacular of double rainbows arched crisply from the land into the calm sea, a sea turned turquoise by sunlight but pricked by a thousand drops as heavy rain began to fall. My rainbow of experiences around the shores of the Mediterranean pushed ever closer to the end, but it was proving a war of attrition, a series of hops in *Mr Hops*, to reach that end.

In the 48 hours from Finikounda we flew along the Peloponnese coast covering some 170 km with wind and waves in our favour. And a spectacular coast it was too. On

A war of attrition to the end of the rainbow. A spectacular double rainbow off the Peloponnese in Greece entices us onwards

the second night some entertaining storms hit, shook and soaked us as we passed close, perhaps too close, to Kythira, an island off the easternmost finger of the Peloponnese. It was a baptism of fire for Dimitris, who also felt the sickness that *Mr Hops* offered each new recruit. Armed with a list of shot angles and interviews to do for Dimitra, it was all he could do to retch into a bucket, row and lie down. Marin too was under the weather but resolutely plotted our course, doing an astounding job once again. *Mr Hops* had become a two-bedroom apartment now, with the skipper in the master suite at the stern and the crew crammed, where my bike and other supplies had been, up in the tiny bow cabin.

But then, before we struck across the Aegean, the latest forecast from Jure showed a coming period of very strong northerlies from a high pressure system stuck north over Europe. Fine if we wanted to head to Crete and Egypt, but useless for our track east now to Turkey. In the rain, we landed at Monemvasia, a village dominated by a rocky island just offshore. It was so frustrating, but we could only go when and where the gods of the sea dictated.

By the time we landed, the team had already been at work. Katerina, the attractive deputy mayor of Monemvasia, was on hand to meet and greet us and drive us to a hotel, the Flower of Monemvasia, that had offered to put us up. So much for non-stop and unsupported. On his Facebook page, before we left Finikounda, Dimitris had written how he had turned up as an Athens adventurer wannabe with his fancy gear and too much of it, to meet the two Spartans. Whilst I would never describe myself as such, it was fitting that above us, inland from Monemvasia, were the ruins of that famed warrior state of ancient Greece.

We settled into the hotel, none of us realising quite how long our stay was going to be.

Throughout the journey, my fundraising and profile-raising for Save the Children was an ever-present aspect. The charity had proven an excellent choice to work with, and in Fiona McAdam I could not have asked for a better or more enthusiastic liaison. Whilst the media coverage had been substantial, and was seen as equally important in the competitive world of charitable giving, the fundraising was never easy. I had done plenty before, but not for this length of time or on this scale. It surprised me that I had become the largest ever individual fundraiser for Save the Children Australia with a total that would approach AU$100,000. Perhaps my expectations were too high, but I felt a little disappointed. Then again I had only to think of the dozens of requests I received for fundraising from friends and contacts to realise how many I ignored, often without even reading them. I was not really able to fundraise in the places I was travelling through because I was unable to guarantee where and when I would be in locations to forward plan functions and the like. On the flip side, of course, so many people had been so generous and continued to be so. On the day I arrived in Monemvasia I heard that Neil Prosser, a friend in Australia, had bought three of the last four remaining countries for Save the Children. Only Turkey was left without an owner.

Neil was now the proud owner of Croatia, Algeria and Tunisia. This was on top of purchasing Albania previously, the first country to have been sold. On making the purchases, Neil sent a message:

> After following the challenges you faced getting across the first part of the Mediterranean trip I felt I should give you some inspiration and support to finish it off. You have faced so many trials and tribulations on your journey: natural and artificial, expected and unexpected, that it seemed only right to move towards completing the set of countries. Those of us who can should be donating more during these times to people, to children, much less fortunate than we are. I hope the donations to Save the Children continue to flow and you find a benefactor to pick up the big prize of Turkey, before, or as, you complete your journey.

It was a fit of megalomania that, in the right hands, was a very good thing.

We waited. Waited for the angry sea to stop smashing into the Peloponnese, for the wind to turn around and to drop. It was frustrating, and now every day bothered me. In the ten days I was in Turkey at the start of my journey I felt the warmth of the people there and was looking forward to returning to enjoy more of it. But as each day passed it was increasing the speed at which and the hours I had to keep moving in order to get back to Gallipoli on time.

We waited. But Monemvasia treated us well. Katerina had taken us out for lunch and more. On Monday she organised for George, the municipality plumber, to take a day off from crawling around underground pipes and cisterns, to instead crawl around underground. He drove us an hour or more the length of the easternmost Peloponnese peninsula, along winding mountain roads, through tiny villages to visit the magnificent cave of Kastania which was opened specially for our visit. It was one of the most impressive caves I have seen. We were presented to the great and the good of Monemvasia, and stories of our journey became hours focused on the madness of bottled water, a scourge of Greece as throughout the Mediterranean.

We waited. The cliffs of the island of Monemvasia, linked to the mainland village by 200 metres of causeway, hid a beautiful ancient village, the original Monemvasia, of tiny streets, tiny churches, tiny bars. The walk around the island is a classic; I did it numerous times to watch the Aegean waves foam against the cliffs and to look east in the direction of Turkey. I was somehow hoping that the longer I stared the closer it would come.

We waited. But it was a comfortable wait in the Flower of Monemvasia: three men from a boat, three men in a room. One day it was the turn of Stelios, the local barber, for our company. We had time for such idle styling.

We waited. Apparently, with our cuts and shaves, we all looked younger. But I was feeling older. Every time I stopped on this long journey I started to stiffen up; aches ached and pains pained me more. I wanted to stop waiting and start rowing again.

For two weeks we stared at and explored the Rock of Monemvasia as we waited, waited and waited for a break in the weather

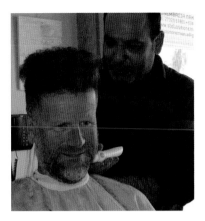

Marin, Dimitris and I all had plenty of time for such idle styling in Monemvasia

We waited in Monemvasia for ten days as the winds blew every way except our way. Actually it would be lying to say we were there all that time. Marin took off for a couple of days to visit Sparta aboard a dodgy old mountain bike two sizes too small for him, whilst Dimitris and I enjoyed an excellent overnight hike down the peninsula. In some ways the walk frustrated me more, as we'd gone somewhere but I hadn't actually gone anywhere. Following and feeling the connection between sea and shore also just made me want to get back to *Miss Grape* in Turkey. I felt as sorry for Dimitris as for myself. After all the build-up, he'd been with us for over two weeks and rowed for just two days.

I returned from our walk on 21 March, a month and two days before my planned finish date. The forecasts showed nothing helpful for at least another six days. I'd played a lot of cards on this journey, pulled rabbits out of hats to keep that arrival date in reach. And now, with access to Turkey blocked by the Aegean Sea, my pack was near dealt, the hat empty.

As I saw it I had few options. I could push out my arrival date but *mediterr année* was one year in the Mediterranean and I so wanted to keep it thus. I could perhaps abandon my plans of kayaking the final 1,000 km and use a bike instead, something that would allow me to cover ground much quicker across Turkey whatever the weather. Finally I could cut my losses and increase my chances by abandoning ship and using non-human power to get me to Turkey to start kayaking.

I counted days, scribbled options, measured distances. Even if *Mr Hops* did start moving again in a week or so, allowing time to row across the Aegean plus some bad weather time. I would have perhaps two weeks to kayak 1,000 km; at 70 km a day that was not possible, even with good conditions all the way, conditions I knew I wouldn't get. And what if *Mr Hops* managed just another small hop before being weatherbound again for a long period? The row–bike scenario was an option, but I was realising how strong the impulse to be on the sea, the body of water that defined my journey, was for the last stages of my journey. The idea of riding sealed roads, busy roads perhaps, just to eat up miles in a dash to the end was not what I wanted. It seemed too certain, too fast and in some ways an abandoning of the Mediterranean Sea that I wanted to be on and with to the end. Now it seemed the style of my final leg was as important as my human-power rule.

On Sunday 22 March I made what was without doubt the most difficult decision of my year. I made the decision to go to Athens, fly from there to Rhodos and from there take the ferry across to Marmaris and the captive *Miss Grape*. I told Marin and Dimitris of my decision.

The following day the three of us were in a car to Athens. We passed over and high above the Corinth Canal, now a place where my outward and inward journeys crossed for the first time. I felt rotten. Rotten to be travelling by burning oil, rotten to be not completing the row and rotten to be leaving the other two. In the car to Athens Dimitris received a call from the coastguard in Monemvasia suggesting *Mr Hops* be moved, due to big swells smashing into the harbour. Marin and Dimitris would wait it out some more and attempt to finally reach Turkey. It was important for Marin who had come so far, and of course for Dimitris, who needed to go further. I would get over my decision; I knew that. My journey had been filled with so many aspects, overwhelmingly positive, and this was just a part of my story, of my year. The circumference of my circumnavigation of the Mediterranean had become somewhat lessened in my missing of much of north Africa and the Middle East. But *Mr Hops* had made up for that in giving me a new and superb adventure. I'd been forced to take non-human power in the case of the ferry from Morocco to Spain and back across to Algeria, and had chosen to take it by means of a tow from *Bravo 1* into Gozo. This was but one further decision.

After a great dinner with the team, Marin, Dimitris and I yelled one more call of '10 minutes' in unison under the huge clock in Dimitris' apartment. Then I quickly crossed the Aegean, courtesy of Aegean Airlines, to make land on the island of Rhodos.

On the flight I watched some video footage shot in recent weeks on my camera. Amongst the clips I was surprised to find a piece to camera by Marin, shot by himself whilst lying in the cabin of *Mr Hops* on the night we had left Finikounda. On the video he talked about feeling scared and vulnerable, and questioning whether he wanted still to do long journeys, to take up difficult challenges. His piece was based on the generosity he had seen and the friendship he had experienced, particularly in Finikounda, but also in Malta. How this was the first time for him and how it had affected him so. It was a very touching and very human tale and showed, as I had seen with others before, that even the strongest need succour from others. Given he had filmed this on my camera, it seemed Marin had wanted me to see it.

I had been with Marin just shy of two months, by far the longest with anyone on my journey. From the moment I had read that email from him on the summit of Mont Blanc back in October, he delivered everything he promised as an organiser, as a rower, as an expeditioner. He had been wrong a few times, just enough so that I knew he was human. I owed Marin Medak a lot.

2+2+2+2+2 ... the row across the Mediterranean from Tunisia had promised to provide the ultimate rhythm of my journey, the rhythm that I so often craved and felt on previous long, more remote journeys. In the end my row had been a stop–start stuttering progress that had featured long periods of waiting, waiting, waiting.

Two hours on a tiny ferry took me from Rhodos to Marmaris. Back to Turkey. Coming into Marmaris we motored past a very rocky, indented coast that had me excited for the paddle and, as always, a little nervous in expectation. Excited too to be travelling along on my own and to be living in a tent again. I realised the last time I'd spent a night under canvas had been at Buenos Noches in southern Spain. Three months had passed since then.

As I followed the line of people to passport control, someone had left a large, very long package on the covered footway. I almost tripped over it. The package was in fact *Miss Grape*. She'd been sat there on that path, waiting for over two weeks. I'd imagined I was going to find her in a shed somewhere. An hour spent sweet-talking Turkish customs, and she was free to leave, free of charge; the €300 import tax waived. As though we were a married couple, *Miss Grape* was added to my passport so that I couldn't leave Turkey without her.

Craving chocolate, I wandered into a small general store in Marmaris.

Shopkeeper: Where are you from?

Me: Australia.

Shopkeeper: You speak very good English.

Me: Well, yes, but English is the language in Australia.

Shopkeeper: Don't you have your own language?

Me: Yes, English.

Shopkeeper: Hmmm. I speak better Arabic than Turkish.

Me: Where are you from, then?

Shopkeeper: Turkey.

Me: Why do you speak better Arabic?

Shopkeeper: I'm from Syrian part of Turkey. Where is your father from?

Me: Wales.

Shopkeeper: Aha, I speak Welsh: *Nostar*. ['goodnight' in Welsh]

Me: Very good.

Shopkeeper: I know that the Welsh are sheep shaggers. Up in the hills.

Me: Well that may be what the English say. Australians have been heard to call New Zealanders sheep shaggers too.

Shopkeeper: I see. Sometimes, when Turkish people from small villages in the mountains come here, I think they also ... well it is very quiet in our hills ... they also are sheep shaggers.

Me: What's your name?

Shopkeeper: Jimmy.

Me: (handshake) I'm Huw. Jimmy isn't a very Turkish name.

Shopkeeper: No; my real name is Gokhan but many tourist people pronounce it Gothan. Gok means 'sky' but Goth mean 'ass', so Turkish people laugh at me. One day I was telling a Scottish man this and he said, 'Easy, just call yourself Jimmy.' So I am Jimmy.

It was the best value chocolate bar of the trip.

I found a grim but cheap hotel in Marmaris and began preparations for my final leg. My first day back in Turkey, 25 March, was Greek Independence Day, commemorating the start of the War of Independence in 1821 that finally saw Greece shake off 400 years of Turkish rule. It was also one month to Anzac Day, when another battle had begun on Turkish soil.

Tolga, the Turkish sea kayaker who had kindly helped move *Miss Grape* to Marmaris, called with some news. Each year on 18 March, Turkey commemorates its victory in the Dardanelles and at Gallipoli. Tolga told me that the Turkish president, Recep Erdoğan, had recently announced that for 2015 he was moving the commemoration from 18 March to 24 April. Ostensibly this was to put the Turkish commemoration within a day of the Anzac Centenary so that both events were joined up. However, many in Turkey and most of the world's media saw it as a cynical attempt to try to deflect interest in another commemoration: on 24 April 2015 Armenians across the world would commemorate the centenary of the Day of the Armenian Genocide. It is widely accepted, but never admitted by Turkey, that the Ottoman Empire was responsible for the genocide of over one million Armenians, a massacre that began on 24 April 1915 with the arrest of Armenian intellectuals in Istanbul.

Erdoğan had invited 100 world leaders to join the 24 April activities. My planned arrival date of 23 April was going to come hard up against some major events and the attendant massive security. I hoped I could slip through and finish my journey as planned.

I climbed into *Miss Grape* for the first time since kayaking from Gibraltar across to Africa, and pushed off the beach at Marmaris on a wet and grey 27 March. 'Have a good trip. Be careful; there is bad weather for next three days,' hailed one passer-by. As the rain sheeted down I paddled past some dramatic mountain and coastal scenery, feeling typically nervous back in the kayak again as rebound off the cliffs pushed me this way and that. The sea, in fact any large body of water, looks immediately unfriendly when the sun goes away. What was blue or green and sparkling looks threatening in monochrome.

Late afternoon I landed in a dumping shore break at Ciflik, a collection of buildings. It didn't take long for my Mediterranean welcomes to kick in again. Cousins Yasar and Engin were preparing their bar for the coming season and said I was welcome to camp there, under cover, out of the rain. For 20 years Yasar had run a clothes shop in Marmaris but hated it: 'I tell them the price but they say it is too much. We have to play the game every day on the price.'

So two years earlier they had rented this land and built, completely unapproved, their bar and restaurant. 'We paid the council officials to leave us alone; this is how we do it here,' Engin told me. They had to make their money quickly in case things changed, also given the fact they could never sell an illegal business.

While I was reacquainting myself with the process of packing the kayak, the cousins came down to see me off the beach on a sunny morning. I didn't get far. Once I was out of the shelter afforded by an island, offshore both wind and sea were very much against me. I bounced around for a while before turning round and heading back to Ciflik. Killing time, I wandered down the beach and explored a derelict luxury hotel. I had seen this so often along the shores of the Mediterranean: half-built, or completed but later abandoned tourist developments. It wasn't just a waste of resources but more so it represented a permanent degradation of the land, a degradation that would take decades if not centuries to rehabilitate. I walked past swimming pools green with growth and filled with brown water. I entered a restaurant where the ceiling had fallen in onto tables still laid

The shores of the Mediterranean are littered with abandoned or half-built tourist developments

with cutlery and stained serviettes. Rooms led to balconies with broken handrails. Engin told me that it had only been three years since the hotel had been abandoned, but it looked to me an impossible task to bring it back to life.

I sat on a crumbling stairway and switched on my phone. Two things stood out from the emails that arrived. Firstly the great news that five days after I'd left them Marin and Dimitris had just set off again in *Mr Hops*. Despite the warnings of local fishermen and other naysayers, all of whom had moved their boats in the most recent storm, Marin had backed their own and *Mr Hops'* ability to get out of Monemvasia into open water. I still of course felt pangs of regret at my decision, at my abandoning of the row.

The second email of note was from Fi, back in the Save the Children Australia office. Before I read the email I opened the photograph attached to it. I was surprised to find it was a black and white school photograph from Radyr Primary School. It had been taken in 1971 when I was seven years old.

I then read the email:

> Huw, I am writing with some incredible and very exciting news. Your old primary school teacher in South Wales, Mary Butlin, has been following your journey. Today she sent the attached picture of you from the last time she saw you, 45 years ago. She felt so moved after watching your video clip posted to Facebook explaining your decision to take non-human power to Turkey that she has bought Turkey, the last remaining country, for $11,000 for Save the Children. I'm sure you will agree that this is truly astonishing, and I imagine that you might have tears of joy in your eyes all the way back to Gallipoli. Not sure what else there is to say after that, so I shall just say bye for now.

The tears indeed flowed as I read this. In an abandoned hotel in Turkey, my abandoned journey was somehow much more than worthwhile. The work that could be done with this money for children abandoned, orphaned or maimed by the Syrian conflict was worth so much more than my selfish journey and my own disappointments. I didn't recall being a teacher's pet, but I would take this willingly. In her teaching career Mary Butlin had helped hundreds of fortunate children like me. Now, long retired, she continued to help children; those unfortunate ones whose lives had been devastated by war and conflict.

I paddled off the beach again with some vigour, strengthened by this news and shouting songs to the wind as I went. I stayed well offshore to avoid the worst of the rebound off a coastline that offered little opportunity to land. Ahead of me the small island of Kizil was engulfed by an approaching squall that soon hit *Miss Grape*. Absolutely torrential rain came down; I just sang louder above the noise and paddled harder into it. Toward the end of previous long journeys I had usually felt powerful, both physically and mentally; felt as if I could deal with anything the outdoors might throw at me. I didn't really have that feeling on *mediterr année*. Perhaps it was an age thing; I didn't trust my body as much as before. But more, I think it was the endless human interaction on this journey. A lack of time spent alone in wild places during the past year, the endless assistance had, perhaps, not developed the inner resolve I was used to.

The squall passed and the sun came out to dry me. In the relative shelter of Kizil, I bobbed around and pulled out the map to see where I might reach to camp. I had a marine chart of the section of coast from Marmaris which turned out to be the last decent map I would find all the way to Gallipoli. The rest of the coast I did essentially blind.

Just before 6 p.m. I finally landed on a small rocky beach in a deep inlet. I thought to camp but noticed that my water bag had leaked most of its contents into the cockpit and I had only a litre or so left. The map showed another cove with some buildings 3 km further on. Buildings might equal water, so I got ready to paddle again, knowing it would be touch and go to reach there before dark. As I pushed off a wave dumped straight into the cockpit before I'd had chance to put my spraydeck on. More minutes were spent emptying the water and in the end I decided I'd blown it; it was too late to leave.

I pulled *Miss Grape* above the beach and discovered a small stony field beneath the cliffs. Some judicious moving of rocks would allow enough space to camp. With the tent up I went to explore and wandered toward a dry gully that fed into the field. Less than 50 metres from the tent I almost tripped over on some short timber planks. I looked down to see they covered a perfectly round stone well. Some 2 metres down was water which I assumed would be brackish. But it had been a lucky day so far. I rigged up a length of cord onto my water bottle and dropped it into the well. Fine fresh water filled it to complete a perfect camp.

★ ★ ★

'You must be Huw?' said a man on the beach as I landed at dusk on the Datca peninsula soon after I'd passed a boat laden with beehives. It was the first village I'd seen all day, the first time I'd got out of the kayak in nine hours. I'd left that morning from camping in a parking lot for *gulets*, classic Turkish 20–35 metre bulky timber sailing boats. The day previous to that I'd come around a rocky headland in a thunderstorm and, when the sky cleared, spied across the bay, some 7 km away, a load of masts. I assumed it must have been a marina. By then I had no map to guide me. I was a bit annoyed with myself for not having filled up with water at the well that morning. How many times, how many dozens of times, had I rued such a thing over the years? On this journey, how many times had I told myself to always carry a minimum of a day and a night of water? Not only for potentially dry camps but also to save detours to find water. I headed across the bay toward the masts. Less than a kilometre away I could see that the masts were not moving. Five hundred metres away and I could see the masts belonged to hulls that were not in water. I landed to find over 100 gulets, all beached on a muddy parking lot reached only by a steep dirt track from land. A couple of Husseins and one Ahmed working on the boats served me cay (tea), and told me it was their home for winter; each craft was taken out of the water in October and parked there until May. Each one had to be put back in order, a gulet at the back needing to wait until the dozens in front of it were moved.

'Emma told me about you,' said the man on the beach at Hayitbükü. Emma Dunnage, a friend of mine in Bundanoon, my hometown back in Australia, had worked on charter yachts in Turkey more than 20 years ago. She'd told some of her old contacts of my voyage, and Ogun was one such. It was unbelievable that of all the beaches I might have landed on, this was where he lived. And not only that, but that Ogun happened to be on the beach when I landed. In reality of course, nothing about my journey was unbelievable any more. Soon I was in a comfortable room above Ogun's restaurant/bar which, like most, was not yet open for summer. That night there was a superb dinner at his brother's house in my honour. Kadir's wife, Zehra, had prepared a vegetarian feast in the two hours between my landing on the beach and my landing at her dining table. Vegetarians are uncommon in Turkey, but this country was delivering as fine a finale as I could have hoped, with an endlessly stunning, indented coastline and warm welcomes.

APRIL

April hath put a spirit of youth in everything.

William Shakespeare

L ate the following morning I was avoiding the rain by working away on my laptop and charging batteries, when the power went off. Ogun told me the power had gone off all over the peninsula. Then as time passed he told me it was off in Marmaris,

in Istanbul, Izmir, Ankara. Somehow in a country of some 80 million people, power had failed to nearly all of them, and was to be off for much of the day. I had no excuse not to paddle on. Anyway I really needed to reach Knidos, at the end of the Datca peninsula.

But when I reached Knidos I had a problem I needed to solve. Most of the large islands just off Turkey are actually Greek. One such, Kos, lay directly between two Turkish peninsulas; it was 15 km off Knidos, and a further 10 km straight on would take me back into Turkey, west of Bodrum. If I cut across that way it could save me a fair bit of paddling around Kos into the gulf of Gökova. But via Kos there was the issue of me leaving Turkey, entering Greece, leaving Greece and entering Turkey again all in one day: the usual issues of kayaks and paperwork.

There was also the major problem of people being smuggled from Turkey into the EU – the rapidly increasing tide of refugees from Syria, Iraq and other places trying for a better life. Many of these people were attempting to reach the Greek islands close to Turkey, meaning that both sets of coastguards were on the alert. I had already been sprung and questioned by the local police as I had landed at Knidos, having been spotted from a lookout earlier on the coast. I didn't tell them of my plan.

If I cut close to Kos but didn't actually land, could I claim I hadn't landed in Greece, so hadn't left Turkey at all? Worth a try. I left early on a calm, sunny day and paddled beneath a lookout high above the cliffs. I made good progress under cover of daylight to Agios Fokas, the easternmost tip of Kos, all the while expecting a visit from a coastguard boat, I saw nothing save a small cargo ship. Nothing except a number of lifejackets and bits of clothing floating in the water.

At Agios Fokas, I could see men inside a lookout. I waved, stayed a few hundred metres offshore and continued along the coast of Kos. Perhaps they were satisfied that a bloke in a single kayak flying an Australian flag was of no concern. The wind and sea picked up as I left Greek waters and headed back across to Turkey, the call to prayer from a mosque at Kemer carrying across the waters as a welcome back. No one had bothered me thus far, and so it was once I was across in Turkey.

Now, on the end of the Bodrum peninsula, I hit my first real section of holiday apartments. They were numerous but whilst ruining a fine landscape they at least had a certain style compared to the total ugliness of Spain's Costa del Sol that I'd kayaked in December. I paddled to the tiny village of Gümüşlük, tucked away in a deep bay. Here, on the site of the ancient city of Myndos, boats were tied off on fallen blocks and columns two thousand or more years old. Here too I met the Hawkins family. Philip, a retired forensic psychologist from Oxford who had worked with some of the worst and best known criminals, serial killers and murderers in the UK; Tulin, his delightful Turkish wife, and the equally delightful Isik, their daughter, over from London for Easter. Tulin and Philip had bought a lovely little cottage right on the water at Gümüşlük and now spend their summers there. It was a slightly shabby but obviously chic place, with a collection of renowned fish restaurants. The owner of the most famous restaurant claimed that meeting *Miss Grape* was the best thing he'd seen in some years. This was not bad given Gümüşlük in summer was, apparently, the haunt of the A-list and their superyachts: Roman Abramovich, Kate Moss, Naomi Campbell, *Miss Grape*. She fitted in well; had that effect on people.

After a fine send-off the following morning, strong headwinds soon blew me back to Gümüşlük for a second night of great hospitality with the Hawkins family. The next morning, despite my sore head, I left early while Tulin, Philip and Isik slept, to save a second goodbye and to take advantage of calm seas.

Whilst I had been living it up in Gümüşlük, the most excellent of news reached me. Marin, Dimitris and *Mr Hops* had reached Turkey, travelling far, far farther north than we ever would have imagined possible in our original planning. They had arrived in Çeşme, near Izmir, on a journey from Monemvasia that had taken them six days. Finally the weather gods had smiled: 50 days since we had left Tunisia, Marin deserved nothing less. Dimitris too could be proud of his own achievement in rowing across the Aegean.

But Çeşme was over 250 km north of my location. I secretly wondered whether *Miss Grape* might actually get to meet *Mr Hops*. But it was not to be. Much that *Mr Hops* had done had been unplanned. He thought – we thought – his journey on Mediterranean waters was over at Çeşme. Dimitris left to go home to Athens, whilst for a week Marin did battle with Turkish bureaucracy to arrange to ship *Mr Hops* to the UK where I hoped he would be sold. 'It's worse than Tunisia,' Marin told me as he shuffled between customs, translators, notaries and others all wanting their cut. Some crazy, crazy quotes to truck *Mr Hops* to Izmir were the last straw. Sod 'em, we decided, and *Mr Hops* took to the sea again. On his own, Marin rowed the 15 km from Çeşme across to the Greek island of Chios. In the EU and with numerous legendary Greeks who would make sure *Mr Hops* at least got to Athens, it was a better bet.

For two weeks I stuttered up the Turkish coast. On even days I got to paddle and on odd days the wind and seas kept me on the land. Winter was not yet done. The days I paddled were long, to compensate for the frustrating days – and 23 April, my

Waiting for the wind to drop on a Turkish beach near Gümüşlük

planned finish day, loomed ever closer. The act of finishing on time, and the juggle and struggle to do so, were preoccupying me, but now too were thoughts on my feelings about finishing the journey. I think I was ready for the end. It had to come some time, as every journey must finish. I had been so lucky so many times with so many people and places that I could not expect that luck to be endless. I was full to bursting with all the generosity and hospitality that I needed time to digest it all. I was of course also keen to be home with Wendy and a part of me was keen to be in one place for a while; at home. Basically, though, given I was so close to finishing, I was ready to finish.

After four days of go a day/stop a day, I knew that another day or more of very strong wind was coming. I left Zeytinli Kuyu early on Easter Sunday, my PFD pockets stuffed with chocolate in celebration. I stayed out well offshore, heading in the direction of Didim, as three dolphins came to play off the stern of *Miss Grape*.

After three hours I was by a small island off Didim. I was keen to get around the corner, to start heading north, before the forecast sou'easter hit. Five hours of paddling saw me there, passing a light and turning north. But the land was dead flat here, as flat as any I'd seen in Turkey. Mid-afternoon I pulled up on a small beach for a late lunch, pleased with progress.

Continuing north past a couple of small towns and beaches I reached a large harbour empty but for a couple of trawlers. Then soon after the harbour, continuing north, my paddle hit a sandy bottom. Weird. Then I saw only shallows in front of me. Heading away from shore; what I first took to be a series of fish farms was in fact a long, low sandbank. How could this be? How could a sandbank jut kilometres out into the sea in the Mediterranean? I wondered about landing and pulling over it. It was a good job I didn't. Mapless, what I'd hit was a major river delta, that of the Büyük Menderes. I followed the sand westwards and finally turned a corner to the north-west. It was then the delta became apparent to me, the turbid water giving it away. Pelicans flew above me, curlews darted on the sand. The day was pushing on, the sky already dark from black clouds. When early evening came I could see beyond the delta to cliffs and high mountains beyond.

My eyes knew they were further than they looked – but fools who think wishfully never learn, and my mind made them nearer. I paddled on and a fireball of a sun dropped out from behind a black curtain and fell into the sea, its north pole still hidden in cloud as its south pole hit the water. Then as I looked into the gloom ahead I saw a light amongst the distant cliffs. Something there perhaps, a beach to land on? As darkness fell, more lights; cars coming and going in what I hoped might be some form of cove. Then I wondered.

Not far from these cliffs, perhaps 15 km away, was the Greek island of Samos. Eleven months earlier, in northern Greece, I'd sheltered from an electrical storm in a small *limani* (harbour). Shelter was in the form of the coastguard office, and there Constantinos had told me many things, one of which was that he was posted regularly to Samos to patrol for illegal immigrants crossing the narrow strait to it from Turkey. I had heard much more of this since being back in Turkey.

I suddenly wondered if I was about to stumble on a night-time people smuggling operation. A spotlight showed from the cliff, I heard a gunshot, and my imagination went into overdrive. But I was committed; it was now dark and I needed to land somewhere very soon. I glided past some cliffs, under some lights, into more lights and past small boats. The water quickly shallowed and *Miss Grape* was grounded. Ahead was a small sandy beach, a couple of buildings and the Karina Balik Restaurant. No people smuggling here; just people having a good time. Soon I was being offered food and a place to camp by the beach.

The following day was forecast for south-east winds of force 6 or 7 but I woke to just small waves on Karina's little beach. The sea beyond looked OK, and I thought wishfully again: perhaps the forecast for this fickle sea would be wrong again, might be delayed. It would be some 15 km to get along the cliffs and around the headland out of any wind; two to three hours' paddling. I had delayed too long. I didn't know if there was anywhere to land en route if things blew up. I'll stay. I'll go. I'll stay. I'll go. I went. Out through the small waves and out of the small cove to start down past the cliffs. It was windy then; uncomfortable paddling. What if it worsened? Was it self-preservation, fear or a second sense that made me turn around? Soon after I was back at Karina. Very, very soon after that the wind was howling and the shore awash with waves.

It had been a good call, and the following day I got to enjoy the coastline of the Dilek Peninsula National Park. On one small beach I was cooking up some lunch on the stove when a police car pulled up on a track high up above me. Three officers scrambled down to the beach and approached me very cautiously. Phones were pulled out by two, and a gun by a third. I offered a handshake but it was ignored. Then I was beckoned to speak to someone on the phone. He had good English and I explained what I was up to. All was well. Still, one of the police officers asked for my passport but I waved the request away and he did not pursue it. I wasn't being difficult, just not keen to have to unpack drybags to find it.

Turkish hospitality was immense, from my landing in the dark at tiny, tiny Karina cove to surfing onto a long beach near Kuşadasi when the wind got to be too much. There Adil greeted me in an Irish accent; he was a Turk who had spent seven years in Dublin. I camped in his not yet open (but with beer in the fridge) beach bar. It was going to be strange to be home; to know where I was going to sleep each night. I could see myself wandering around Bundanoon, asking people if I could camp in their garden. Although perhaps with a two-person tent and in the company of Wendy.

On 8 April I kayaked nearly 12 hours, from soon after first light until dark, in the knowledge that another spell of wild wind was on its way. The day had alternated between cliffs, quiet beaches and some more developed, whether large hotels primarily for foreigners or summer houses for the Turks from Izmir and elsewhere. As usual I had no idea where I would stay. Decades of enjoying wild places as a solitary animal should aim me toward the quiet beaches, but often I found myself drawn, like a moth, to the light. There were practical reasons. If I was to be stuck for a day or so then it offered an opportunity to plan, to work, to charge batteries, to seek out that holy grail of modern travel: 'Do you have wi-fi?'

I nudged *Miss Grape* onto a beach near a mosque and some scruffy buildings. Three children, matching the buildings, ran down to see what had arrived from outer sea. But the place didn't feel right. After five minutes I pushed off into the gathering dark, the kids running and shouting after me in words I sadly did not understand. Less than a kilometre along the beach I saw the light. Even from the sea, 100 metres away, I could pick out the telltale neon of a Coca-Cola fridge through the windows of a barn of a building that looked partly derelict.

I pulled *Miss Grape* out of the water and, tired, wet and salty, wandered up to knock on the door. Pictures on a ubiquitous widescreen TV indicated someone might be around. A middle-aged woman came to the door from the kitchen. What do you say when a middle-aged man in a neoprene skirt, white lipstick and a padded sleeveless jacket appears in the dark and asks, whilst making triangle shapes with his hands, in a language you don't understand, if he can camp? You of course reply, in a language he doesn't understand, but with a nod that he does, that of course he could.

I dragged *Miss Grape* up the beach and started getting organised to camp, changing first into some dry, warm clothes. Within ten minutes, the woman, Murvet, appeared with a tray of food. A bowl of hot soup, bread and a plate filled with pasta and bolognese. So I don't eat meat. But on this occasion, faced with such kindness and after a long day on the water, I didn't have the empty heart or the full stomach to refuse. Anyway the stray cats, everywhere in Turkey, were already prowling and would be on it within seconds. I am not a lover of cats.

That night the wind blew hard and by dawn the sea was white. I crawled out of my tent to face a man carrying a tray holding two cups of boiling water, a jar of Nescafé and a bowl of sugar cubes: Halil Ibrahim, a Turk from Bulgaria, was the caretaker of this complex of Turkish holiday homes for which the building was apparently the social centre in summer. This was all explained to me by a man who soon after turned up on an ancient racing bicycle. Rauf was a retired English teacher in his late fifties who told me he was now a writer and that he was 'half famous'. 'I want to travel by bicycle,' he told me. And went on to explain that his monthly pension of some 1,600 Turkish lira (AU$900/600 euro) meant he would have to go to cheap countries. 'I will ride the Silk Road with another Turkish man who is a cyclist in America. But first I must make my legs strong. I started riding 5 km but now I can ride 40 km in a day. My friend tells me I must be able to ride 150–200 km each day. But anyway perhaps I am too old to travel; I do not know what will happen.'

I welcomed Rauf to the expedition fold by applying a *mediterr ann*ée sticker to the pitted and rusted top tube on his bike and told him to just start his travel, his ride, his dream; everything else would flow from there.

By now Ahmed had turned up who, I learned later, was Murvet's husband. 'You cannot leave today in this wind. You can stay in the building,' Rauf translated. I started to pack up to move inside but not before Halil Ibrahim had brought another tray stacked with meat and bread. A bolognese when starving is one thing, large hunks of meat another. Rauf translated that I did not eat meat and then happily tucked into my portion. I felt embarrassed. 'Also I have checked; they have wi-fi in the building.' That sealed my stay.

So I was there for two days. The place was closed but open. Murvet prepared me breakfast, lunch and dinner. In truth she prepared this food for four builders who arrived for each meal then disappeared. But when they were gone she baked me cake too; served with endless cups of sweet Turkish tea. It was a weird place, but sometimes it is hard to picture these places cleaned up for summer, full of sun and people. Murvet and Ahmed left at night for their house in the complex leaving the only other occupants, 30 or 40 caged birds, to sleep with me. As everywhere in Turkey pictures and posters of Atatürk peeled off the windows and walls. A few days earlier a young man – 'My name is Mustafa but my name is Elvis' – showed me his tattoo of Atatürk. Does anyone in Australia have a tattoo of a former prime minister? Or of the Queen perhaps?

Halil Ibrahim simply interlocks his fingers to tell me how strong the friendship between Turks and Australians is

There are two things that most Turkish people seem to know about Australia. Firstly, Harry Kewell played football for Galatasaray in Istanbul from 2008 to 2011. Secondly, the speech that Atatürk made about Gallipoli, a speech he made some years after leading the Turkish troops to victory in that terrible battle 100 years ago. He made the speech in 1934 as the first president of modern Turkey. It is easy to be magnanimous in victory, but they are very powerful words in a 'victory' that saw tens of thousands of Turks killed. Halil Ibrahim, who spoke no English, locked his fingers together in a sign of friendship and said simply, 'Australia, Turkey.'

Rauf returned with a copy of his book of short stories for me: *Yol Hikayeleri* (*Stories from the Road*). Prominent on the cover was a rather incongruous silhouette of a mountain biker. It was just another example of the welcome I received from strangers whose lives I'd dropped in on. Whilst my journey had been human-powered and physically demanding, it had been the power of human kindness that nourished me at every turn, in every country.

Murvet, here baking fresh bureks, and her husband Ahmed fed and sheltered me for some days as a storm blew through in Turkey. Just another example of the welcome I received from strangers whose lives I dropped in on

Despite no real improvement in the forecast I took a calm dawn as a signal to move on. Every day delayed meant I was just getting fatter, would need to travel faster to reach Gallipoli. Murvet, whose grandfather it turned out had fought at Gallipoli, sent me off with a packed lunch of still warm *bureks*, cake and a large jar of preserved fruits. I'd gone less than an hour before I found myself battling into the wind and having those short, steep, cold Mediterranean waves soak me. A tiny gap, no more than 2 metres wide, allowed me to avoid the worst of it around an island headland but once through I hit the north-west wind full in the face. I pushed hard into it but it was useless, going half a boat forward, half a boat backward with the wind trying to wrench the paddle from my hands. I pulled up onto a tiny beach: 12 km I'd gone, 12 miserly kilometres advanced in three days. In the past ten days I'd paddled on five and gone nowhere on five. I sat, salt encrusted, on the beach. I sat there for six hours just looking out to sea, letting frustration mount. Frustration at the lack of progress and the possibility of missing my arrival date. At 5 p.m. I convinced myself that the wind and sea had dropped but of course they hadn't, and I wasted half an hour battling them again before admitting defeat and returning to the beach to camp.

That evening I climbed onto the top of the cliffs above me and got a bit of a phone signal. The forecast told me nothing I wanted to hear to help me head west across a wide, deep bay and continue around to Çeşme. Back at camp I switched my laptop on and discovered that without internet I could still get some basic views on Google Earth. Looking at the fuzzy satellite picture I saw that if I headed north to Siğacik near the head of the bay, I might then be able to walk across the narrowest part of the 100 km-long peninsula that starts at Izmir and ends at Çeşme. My original plan would have entailed some 200 km to Phocaea, maybe four to five days. But the kayak–walk option looked about 70 km of paddling and 15 km of walking: two or three days in all, perhaps? There was no pressing need to call in at Çeşme; *Mr Hops* had left, Marin had left. All I needed to do was find someone in Siğacik to transport *Miss Grape* while I walked. It was a plan worth pursuing.

The next morning it took me nearly five hours of headwind paddling to cover the 25 km to Siğacik. After a five-day test that had notched up innings of 55, 0, 0, 12, 25 km it was time to execute the second part of my combined tactics approach; time to walk.

In Siğacik I went into the cafe nearest to where I'd landed. The owner was soon on the phone and then told me in an hour a *camionette* would arrive to transport *Miss Grape*. I took this to be a small truck. Ufuk and Attila subsequently turned up with a maroon-coloured ute (a small pickup truck) with no roof rack. We tried different approaches to tying *Miss Grape* on. She started in the missile launcher position – stern in the tray, bow pointing 45 degrees up. We turned her upside down and back to front, until eventually we alighted upon a precarious strapping regime that entailed arms out of windows to keep her stable.

It was a slow 35 km drive across to Torasan on the north side of the peninsula. So much for the 15 km walk distance I'd calculated. Next up was to find somewhere to store *Miss Grape* overnight, as it was obvious I had run out of time to do the walk that day. We drove straight into a major four-day dinghy sailing regatta finishing that afternoon. Ufuk went in search of the organisers to ask about storage and returned with a friendly young man in a blazer who promptly had me on the presentation stage for an interview and gifts of caps and pendants followed by a lunch. *Miss Grape* was soon sorted and Attila and Ufuk, both from Izmir and both obviously enjoying their unexpected day out, drove straight back to and through Siğacik and up to their mate's house. More a humpy than a house there was an array of caravans, dogs, old cars all set amongst the much older ruins of the ancient city of Teos and the Temple of Dionysus, the Greek god of wine.

Birol did the right thing by opening a bottle and serving dinner, yet insisting on calling me 'Peach' and unnervingly doing the 'finger through the hole' sign whenever I mentioned my wife, my kayak or just about anything. I made my excuses when the raki came out, knowing I had a big day coming, and returned to Siğacik, to a cheap hotel.

After a six-hour walk on a warm morning, I was back to the Torasan sailing club and preparing to set off in *Miss Grape*, getting away about 3.30 p.m., satisfied my plan had worked out. About 6.30 p.m., with the sun going down, I hopped across to Uzun Ada. On the east side of the island I passed a couple of spots that looked ideal for a camp but decided to push on until dark. A little further on I came into a decent-sized bay with a largish concrete jetty jutting out from a beach. I glided in semi-darkness past a boat moored to the jetty: 'MTB No. 7' it said – an ancient motor torpedo boat of the sort I'd fantasised about captaining as a young kid. A light was on in the boat and I called out. There was no answer, so I landed on the beach beyond. Then a teenage recruit came out of the boat and walked toward me, stopping some 10 metres away. He looked hesitant and scared. Within seconds I was surrounded by a dozen or so young Turkish naval recruits, all waving hands and babbling at me. Even though there was no English amongst it, it was clear I'd landed on a Turkish military island.

'I want to hug you and I want to give you my bed,' were the words of Lieutenant Commander Engun after I'd told him my story. The duty commander of the island had driven over from the main base on the other side, to see what was going on, who this captive was. He was sympathetic to my cause but unfortunately that sympathy was not translating to his superiors in offices far away from the island. Military regulations forbade me to stay on the island. From the comfort of the recruits' mess, calls went back and forth. I put Engun onto Bulent, a man I'd never met but who had been so helpful to me in Turkey. Bulent further explained my purpose. As he moved ever further up the chain of command of the Turkish Navy, Engun's apologies became more and more profuse, apologies for the rules he had to enforce.

Playing for time, I made it clear I was not going to paddle off in the dark. As a dinner was served to me about 9 p.m. I asked Engun if he could put me under house arrest until the morning, but he wouldn't do so. Then Baris, an English teacher from Mersin doing his military service, explained to me that a coastguard boat would come out from Mordoğan, on the peninsula to the west of the island, to pick up *Miss Grape* and me, and take us back there. I told him there was no way I would do that. Not only would it put me a lot further from my goal after the gains of my hard won 35-km stroll that day, it would also see me then needing to do not one but two open crossings. I hammed up the fact that bad weather was coming and such a plan would put me so far behind schedule. An hour later a fast coastguard RIB arrived. By now I was planning to keep eking out time, keep everyone talking and offering ideas until dawn approached when I could just set off again.

I reiterated, now also to Ali from Sahil Güvenlik, the Turkish coastguard, that I could not go on the boat with them as it would obliterate my human-powered journey, telling the small white lie that such a lift would be the first of my journey. I agreed to walk back to the jetty to look at their boat. When I saw it was about the same length as *Miss Grape*, I made it totally clear that there was no way I would put her on the RIB. Engun suggested towing her, a suggestion I also rejected. We trooped back into the mess and drank more tea. I called their bluff by suggesting the coastguard send a bigger boat. They called mine by agreeing and calling for it. Baris whispered to me that he understood what I was doing and encouraged me to keep talking, keep refusing to leave. I spuriously suggested that perhaps I should speak to an admiral or similar, or that I should speak to the Australian ambassador. My bluff was called again when Engun agreed. 'Perhaps that is the right thing to do for protocol, then your ambassador can talk to the admiral.'

Ali was a bit of a comedian and laughed at the developments and toasted the situation with more tea. Then, as midnight approached, Ali went all serious: 'Why don't you come back with us to Mordoğan, we leave your kayak here, and then in the morning we bring you back?' Another toast with tea to a brilliant idea. Engun received permission to do this and by the time he had done so, a coastguard ship had docked on the jetty. Everyone trooped back down to *Miss Grape* on the beach for photos; allowed but not allowed. I grabbed some gear and then we all continued to the ship where Engun, putting protocol aside, gave me a big hug and offered yet another unnecessary apology.

At 2 a.m., after a day that had included a 35 km walk, a 25 km paddle, six hours of negotiations and a slow trip in a big boat, I fell asleep in a bed at the Mordoğan coastguard base under a Sahil Güvenlik-embossed bedspread.

Before dawn, after I'd had no more than three hours' sleep, a fast RIB sped me back to the military island to find *Miss Grape* had been lovingly placed on a bed of coiled ropes for the night. Breakfast was laid on for me before another send-off and an escort out from the bay on a beautiful calm and warm morning. It was about 10 km across to the mainland before a run up through some small islands. I passed what appeared to be a recently wrecked ship, the MV *Bodyer*, Istanbul, pushed up onto a beach. It was a sign of things to come as, with a strong wind now blowing, I surfed between ships at anchor and sunken ships in what seemed a very exposed port with no real form, jetties appearing at all angles from the land. Twelve hours after leaving the military island I landed, again just before dark, on a beach before a headland. It was obviously the site of another derelict tourist facility: rusting umbrella frames, collapsing jetties.

No sooner had I put the tent up when the first fluoro-vested security guard arrived. He indicated I could not camp there. I couldn't believe it: two nights running. Was my luck running out, my welcomes not assured in this last 10 days of the journey? Phone calls were made and soon the Turkish equivalent of Mr FlipPhone (remember him from Morocco?) appeared. Mehmet was all swagger, with Güvenlik embroidered on shirt, jacket and pants. He brandished any number of phones and two-way radios, and gave off an air of unrequited military authority and precise theatrical movement. He paced around photographing everything: me, *Miss Grape*, the tent, my kayak clothing drying on a beach umbrella pole. More fluoro vests arrived, and I sensed this one was not going to go in my favour. I was too tired to argue much.

It seemed I'd stumbled this time onto some sort of industrial site. One guy, Ahmet, who worked there and was not part of the security cordon, spoke good English but would only say: 'The problem is this is a security zone; it is a very important place for Turkey.' Next up, three *jandarma* (police officers) came onto the beach. I tried to get

After being apprehended landing to camp on what turned out to be a Turkish military island, I was taken off the island. When I was returned next morning Miss Grape had been lovingly placed on a bed of coiled ropes overnight

across what my project was, and the police were happy to listen, unlike Mehmet earlier. They checked and photographed my passport. Mehmet was desperate to do likewise but I bullshitted that international law forbade anyone other than customs or police doing so and he slunk away, visibly disappointed.

Finally, at 10 p.m., two hours after I had landed, it was agreed I could stay provided I did not stray away from the beach. I was tired, dog-tired. It had been a long 24 hours.

The Güvenlik were around early to ensure I would be, too. On the headland I passed another rusting ship on the rocks before striking out across Çandarli Körfezi (Candarli Gulf). A small island, after about 5 km, broke the crossing; off it, with the cormorants diving and seagulls wheeling, I shed a few tears, something that was to occur a few times over the coming days – the mixed emotions of finishing, of saying goodbye to all of that, of everything that the journey had delivered.

Equilibrium was restored that evening. When I landed at the two-mosque village of Denizköy, a much more welcoming Mehmet came onto the beach to invite me to drink tea with him and two of his daughters. Soon I was ensconced in the family hotel that was being prepared for summer, and enjoying a feast with all of Mehmet's family and at least 30 stray cats.

The next couple of days saw good progress, 100 km or so, as I threaded a route beyond Ayvalik. The Greek island of Lesvos loomed away to the west, an island that more than any was at the forefront of receiving refugees and migrants fleeing the worsening Syrian crisis. In the last months of my journey and in the year following, the numbers of men, women and children who were looking for refuge from the madness in their home country escalated to such an extent that over 11 million people – half the population of Syria – were displaced from their homes. Half of these, over 5 million, had left the country, many trying desperately to reach the EU or more specifically the EU countries of northern Europe. Greece was but a hoped-for staging post for this worst human refugee crisis to hit Europe since World War II.

It was fitting that my fundraising was going doubly well those last weeks – a drop in the sea, but still a very worthwhile drop to assist the children of that crisis.

On 17 April I set off on my last major open water crossing, 20 km or so across Edremit Körfezi . As a reward the wind and waves were on my back. I blasted out time and again as much as I could remember of 'And the Band Played Waltzing Matilda' as shearwaters skimmed the waves in front of me.

I say 'major crossing' because still to come, 30 km from the finish, was a minor crossing that was rather major; the Dardanelles, where I would cross from Asia Minor, the Asian continent, back to the European continent.

The Dardanelles, the long channel down which the waters of the Black Sea and the Sea of Marmara flow into the Mediterranean is, at its mouth, only 4 km wide, and currents of up to 4 knots bring those waters rushing out. It is also one of the busiest shipping lanes in the world, giving access to Istanbul and the Black Sea ports of the Crimea and other areas. The Dardanelles were the whole reason for the disastrous 1915 Gallipoli campaign. The Allied fleet, having failed to take control of the Dardanelles by force, was mined by the Turks. Churchill then decided to attempt to take the Dardanelles from the landward side, across the Gallipoli peninsula. I had no wish to conquer the Dardanelles – just to paddle across the strait safely.

Landing *Miss Grape* on a pebbly beach on the northern shore of Edremit Körfezi, I jumped out to pull her out of the dumping shore break and promptly pulled the bow of the kayak hard into my ankle. Immediately the ankle began to swell and remained painful for some days; a warning that whilst the Fat Lady might be slapping on some mascara she was a long, long way from taking the stage.

Paddling directly into a low sun I started looking for a suitable beach camp, but everything was rocky, with sizeable waves breaking. I didn't want to hurt *Miss Grape* either at this late stage, so carried on, unable to see anything beyond a few hundred metres into the sun. The sun said goodnight and dipped behind a hill, and ahead I saw a scattering of buildings. This turned into the beautiful little harbour and village of Assos. Like many such places in the world it was given over more to tourism than hard labour now, but it was nice all the same. I landed at the back of the harbour and took tea with some fishermen repairing their boats. I then joined Cassandra and Gareth, a New Zealand couple over for the Anzac Centenary, for a beer that turned into a dinner, before retiring to the Yildiz Hotel. The owner had seen me paddle into the little harbour, and shouted me a fine room. Having no map and not being a GPS user assured me a surprise around every corner. I was now little more than 120 km from the end with six days to reach it.

With more unhelpful wind, Assos held me for another day and the six became five. The forecast held mostly northerlies, the direction I was headed. The Mediterranean was playing with my mind and my muscles one last time, and bureaucracy just with my mind. In Assos I received a call from Esad, a contact I had in the Turkish government; he was ringing to tell me that the government had decided to extend the Military Exclusion Zone on the Gallipoli peninsula to now include 23 April, my planned finish day.

I had always known that landing back at Anzac Cove on the 24th or 25th would be out of the question, but until then had believed the 23rd would be fine; such indications had been given to me by the Australian government before my journey had begun. But now my good friends the Turkish coastguard and Turkish navy had been instructed to keep all craft out of the zone on 23rd as well. Esad suggested I land on the 22nd. This was easy enough to suggest – but Wendy was not arriving in Turkey until that night, and I'd be buggered if I was going to finish without seeing her on the beach after she had flown all the way from Australia. Esad's next suggestion was that I get the Australian government to write to the governor of Çanakkale Province requesting permission for me to pass through the security zone.

The Australian government officials organising the Anzac Centenary commemorations needed my problem like they needed a hole in the head, only days away from the Centenary, days away from probably the largest ceremony ever held outside of Australia, and involving more than 10,000 visitors to Turkey. But I had to have somewhere to land; I couldn't believe my journey could peter out just short of my finish point.

The Australian embassy in Ankara gave me a phone number for one of the on-ground organisers of the Centenary. I rang Devrim Eskiyerli to plead my case. That same night I received an SMS from her telling me there was nothing she could do. I fired back a reply, another pleading. The following day Matt McKeon from the Australian Department of Veterans Affairs called me to explain the difficult situation they were in, but offering to do their best.

While I waited out the wind in Assos, I also received an email from Serdar Vatansever. A couple of days before I'd set off the previous year I'd met this Turkish musician on a beach in Gallipoli. Marco and I had brewed him up an Italian coffee, and Serdar provided some cake made by his wife. A few months earlier Serdar had contacted me to say that he wanted to commemorate the Anzac and Çanakkale Centenary in music and song, but equally importantly wanted it to celebrate the great friendship that now existed between Turkey and Australia. I suggested he play and sing 'And The Band Played Waltzing Matilda'. While I waited out that wind, and the day after I'd blasted out that song to the shearwaters, I watched a wonderfully produced music video by Serdar in which *Miss Grape* and I had bit parts. I took this as a good sign for my hoped-for landing back at Gallipoli.

On Sunday 19 April I left from Assos early, before sunrise. Soon a coastguard ship was shadowing me, so I radioed across to them. Once they were happy I was not involved in any people smuggling or was a refugee myself, they wished me well. At Babakale I made my last big turn, to the north, and finding no wind pushed on hard; every kilometre gained could be important for the days to come. But 10km further up the coast the wind hit me again with a vengeance and I took shelter. It was only 1p.m. but I'd covered another 35km toward my goal. Monday 20 April offered little to please me but on a grey and blowy morning I buckled down for a solid 10 hours of headwind grinding. This day was key; I had to get to within a spit of the Dardanelles given the forecast was telling me that Mr North was in control, apparently also bringing in Mrs Rain for some extra fun. Just before I left camp I received an email from Matt with a letter attached that had been written to the governor. I forwarded it to Esad and crossed my fingers.

At 3 p.m., out of food and starving, I pulled in by a small harbour. As I ate, I saw there were four missed calls from Esad. I returned the call and Esad told me that the Australian government letter had gone to the wrong person: it was not actually the governor who should have received it, as he had told me, but the Turkish Minister of Foreign Affairs. I was pissed off. Pissed off with the wind, pissed off that I had nowhere to finish, nowhere to land with three days to the end of my journey. I asked Esad to contact Devrim or Matt to give them the news. It seemed to be as hard to land in Anzac Cove in 2015 as it had been in 1915.

I pushed on for another five hours as the wind finally relented, giving me time to enjoy a beautiful sunset. Up ahead I started to see ships disappearing eastwards as they moved from the open sea in the west. It was the Dardanelles. After dark I landed on a beach by a harbour below the village of Yakiloy. That beach, 50km from Assos and perhaps only 7 km from the entry to the Dardanelles, was to be my final camp of the journey. I rang Tolga to confirm that he could arrange a local fisherman he knew to spot me across the Dardanelles, to give the endless shipping a bigger target to see. He did and I arranged to meet the fisherman at Kumkale, the southern headland, at 7.30 a.m. I needed to get across early, needed to get across before the wind got up again. A friend of Bulent's, Gurav, rang me too. He was a Dardanelles pilot and told me he was on duty in the morning at Sedd el Behr, on the north side of the passage, and would keep an eye out for me.

I left Yakiloy before dawn on the 21st and turned around Kumkale at exactly 7.30 a.m. on a mirror-calm sea. Ercan was waiting for me in a tiny open boat, shorter than *Miss Grape*. I followed him into the Dardanelles for a kilometre or so before he signalled to me to start across the channel. Ships went in and out including a couple of big cruise liners, no doubt packed with people attending the Anzac Centenary commemorations. A pod of dolphins swam through the heads too in front of me. Conditions were perfect, with the current pushing me north-west toward the northern headland, the Gallipoli peninsula. I crossed to below the 30-metre-high obelisk of the Helles Memorial, in memory of the Commonwealth casualties of the Gallipoli campaign.

There can't be many kayaks or kayakers who could say they had crossed from Europe to Africa across the Strait of Gibraltar and from Asia back to Europe across the Dardanelles. It felt good, good to be beyond the last barrier of my journey in conditions that were both welcome and unexpected. After all the will I?/won't I? of the past weeks, I now had, with little more than 20 km to go, all the time in the world to finish, if not a place to finish. For Wendy, and for the media, we'd agreed an 11 a.m. arrival time on 23 April; National Children's Day in Turkey. But where would I land? Would I be permitted to land?

I shook Ercan's hand and set off north along the Gallipoli peninsula. It was a beautiful but tragic length of coastline: shallow waters of earth and rock cliffs, and later some of the best beaches I'd seen in Turkey. Here and there were reminders of the campaign; concrete pillboxes now half-collapsed into the water. I wondered how it must have felt then, 100 years ago. The fear mixed with adrenaline. Landing in the dark, craft hitting unseen rocks, an enemy sitting on the clifftops, cold water. I shivered again, much as I'd shivered a year earlier when I had left Gallipoli.

The Mediterranean had one final performance for me. Less than an hour after I crossed the Dardanelles a vicious squall hit. The sea threw everything at me: rain, hail and a wild wind that I battled into for close to an hour. I laughed and called out to this companion of mine, 'You bastard; you beautiful bastard!' Eventually the sun came out and the sea turned from black to a vivid jade green. It remained rough – but strangely, very strangely, a trail of calm water snaked amongst the rough water in front of *Miss Grape's* bow. It was like a surreal roadway on the sea, leading me through and reminding me perhaps of my long journey, the challenges that I'd met and a safe arrival soon at hand.

In that 20 km run up the peninsula I saw no one. The green water, the clean beaches, the waves, the quietness reminded me of the south coast of NSW; reminded me of home.

In the distance I could see the coast running away to the headland on the north side of Suvla Bay, the coast I'd paddled a year before. Then I saw the Sphinx in the cliffs above Anzac Cove. I briefly toyed with the idea of keeping going and finishing back at Ari Burnu while I still could, before the blockade was set up. Of perhaps not telling anyone until after, not even Wendy. But no, the urge to arrive at the finish point with her there as well was too strong, too important. Around a stubby headland, a small harbour and scattering of buildings came into view: Kabatepe, the ferry port for the Turkish island of Gökceada. I had two nights to wait, and less than five kilometres to finish. Some Turkish fishermen encouraged me to land on a large concrete slipway by their boats, but the sea was too rough. They told me there was no accommodation in Kabatepe. In the harbour I saw a yacht flying the Australian flag and called out, but there was no one on board.

Eventually I landed on a beach south of the harbour and started pulling *Miss Grape* up, thinking I might be able to camp but also wondering how I'd manage to go wild camping with all the security for the commemorations. My plans were soon dashed by a man with a large dog; it was clear that camping was not allowed. I left *Miss Grape* and climbed a fence back to the harbour. A man was sitting on a mooring bollard by the yacht. We got talking, and Tony told me how he'd read about my journey on the plane over from Australia. He and his business partner Al were from Orange in western NSW and had chartered the yacht from Greece. 'Why don't you stay on the yacht with us?' Tony asked. So in the final act of kindness, the final nights of my journey would be spent with thanks to Australians. It seemed fitting too that my last nights would be spent actually on the sea, not next to it. As I climbed aboard with my gear I saw the yacht's name: *Carpe Diem* – Seize the Day.

I had the following day free to think, to write, to talk. Tony and Al were good company and looked after me well. Tony was a keen military historian and had been to Gallipoli on a number of occasions. For Al it was the first time there.

Twenty-four hours before my planned finish time I rang Esad. He didn't answer, but responded to my missed call with an SMS to say I should ring Devrim for an update. I did so and she informed me that the Australian government had sent another letter, this time to the Ministry of Foreign Affairs, the previous day. She promised to follow up.

I'd have probably preferred an adrenaline-charged rush to the finish rather than this waiting, but I was happy to be so close, to be on time. At 6 p.m. that final night Esad rang me; I had been granted permission to enter the exclusion zone and land at Mimosa beach, some 3 km away from Ari Burnu, the place I had begun my journey. This was obviously disappointing but there were positives. I could ditch *Miss Grape* and walk the final short stretch of my journey with Wendy. It actually seemed somehow a very, very good thing.

I had gulped down a mouthful of the salty Mediterranean waters just before finishing, but the first kiss with Wendy was the sweetest of all things

On a cool but sunny and calm morning, *Miss Grape* and I left Kabatepe. I was soon at the headland with a view to Mimosa beach, Anzac Cove and beyond to Ari Burnu. When I was 500 metres off the beach I could see a small, familiar figure walking back and forth. Perhaps 200 metres offshore I stopped paddling. I looked ahead to the beach, then leaned forward and rested my chin on my right hand. I dropped my left hand into the clear, shallow water and snaked it around as I had done so many times before. Snaking around in a sea that was the glue that had held my year together. And I sobbed; sobbed big salty tears that ran off my hand into the sea. They were tears of happiness for the end, for being with Wendy at last, for sadness that this was the end, for the carnage that had occurred here 100 years ago, and for everything that had gone before for me during that last one year. I cupped my left hand in the water and brought up a mouthful of the Mediterranean Sea and drank it as the tears flowed. I thanked that sea for everything on that journey.

Miss Grape nudged onto the beach. I threw my paddle into the water and, in my rush to get into the arms of one very special person, ripped my foot open on a branch sticking out from the sand.

EPILOGUE

DAYS

Landing with *Miss Grape* on the beach at Mimosa seemed like the end. I had transitioned for the final time from the Mediterranean Sea to the Mediterranean shore, and I was with Wendy again. After a long time hugging, the two of us walked along the length of Anzac Cove to Ari Burnu Cemetery. Here, in contrast to the day I left, were hundreds of people, and I was just another in the crowd. The shell that Elena picked up and gave to me just before I departed did not go back onto the beach as she had instructed. Instead I carried it back to Italy and gave it to four-month-old Giole, Elena and Marco's first child. I hoped it would inspire him to adventures around this rather beautiful but damaged planet.

Soon, *ménage à trois*-like, Wendy, *Miss Grape* and I left Turkey by ferry to the Greek island of Lesvos. As we docked, hundreds of desperate people, children included, were sat on the concrete apron of the port; they had been caught and rescued from small boats that had set off from Turkey the previous night.

In Athens Wendy and I left *Miss Grape* to be shipped home and continued to Italy and a wonderful week with family, including grandkids,

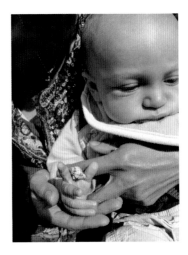

The tiny shell from the beach at Gallipoli that Elena had given me at the start of my journey was not returned to the beach as she had instructed. Instead I pressed it into the tiny hands of Giole, her and Marco's son born eight months into that journey

who had flown in from Australia to meet me. Then it was to the UK for more time with family and friends. They were good days but also rotten days. News came in that one of my dearest friends had been killed in a tragic accident back in Australia. Jenny Caldwell – crazy, gentle, hardcore, loveable Jen – had been en route to race in a cycle event run by my business.

WEEKS

After more than 14 months away, it was finally time for me to fly home. In 24 hours in the air I covered the same distance as I had in 12 months on the ground and across the water. As we drove into Bundanoon a crowd, the whole of the local school included, was there to greet me under a great big Welcome Home banner. The following day Wendy and I flew again to celebrate Jen's wonderful life of generosity, friendship and adventure. After that celebration I dived into the Pacific Ocean surf as dolphins played in the waves around me.

A week later, after days of walking on eggs and weeks of expecting it, I put my back out and found myself on the horizontal. Another journey done, it was always thus.

MONTHS

A couple of months after I had returned home I was in my local cafe when I opened the newspaper to see the body of three-year-old Aylan Kurdi lain face down on a Turkish beach opposite the Greek island of Kos. My youngest grandson was staying with us that week. Jack was three years old. We had watched the news together the previous night, and he had asked 'Why are children walking on the railway tracks Papa?' How do you explain?

Only a few months before, I had sat next to *Miss Grape* on a Turkish beach opposite the Greek island of Kos. My journey around the Mediterranean from Gallipoli back to Gallipoli was only weeks from finishing. I then kayaked the 15 km of open water from Turkey across to Kos. The previous days I'd witnessed the saddest kinds of flotsam and jetsam in the sea and on the beaches. Ripped, deflated tubes and broken plywood from home-made inflatable boats. Boats made to last just one journey – to a Greek island. Still-inflated car inner tubes bobbed around me – the 'survival equipment' if the boats went down – clothing and more.

Human kindness had nourished me in each of the 17 countries I traversed. With my two passports and a flag flying I was beyond lucky to travel freely, to be free, to be welcome.

The Mediterranean has no real tide, but all that year and the year following a human tide flowed across it; a tide in search of a better life, or any life at all. For thousands of those people, taken by the waters of the Mediterranean, there was life no more.

I returned to Australia a little unnerved by the self-interest and what to my mind seemed unnecessary fear-mongering there: within days I was listening to warnings of 'threats to national security' and to politicians wrapped up in the 'successful' offshore processing of men, women and children. But these were tiny, tiny numbers of people compared to the millions Turkey, Jordan, Lebanon and various European nations were dealing with.

Some months after Wendy and I returned home, her father passed away. It also transpired her parents had actually been following my journey around the Mediterranean. Soon after I reconnected with her mother; it being the least I could do for Wendy and a small gesture in a world that I knew needed much more forgiveness on all sides.

Whilst *Miss Grape* eventually found her way back to Australia to be with me, what of *Mr Hops*? I've said before that ocean rowing is an esoteric sport, so there are limited options for selling such a craft. Marin listed *Mr Hops* on a couple of websites and the day after I arrived home in Australia I received an email enquiring if my sailing boat was still for sale. I responded that yes it was but that it was a rowing boat not a sailing boat. Those emails, at the end of May 2015, began a chain of over 350 emails. The original writer, based in the US, was enquiring on behalf of his friend, Ruihan, a Chinese man. Back and forth the correspondence went: Shuping in the US, Marin in Slovenia, Dimitris in Greece, my father in the UK, me in Australia.

At the end of June 2015, during the worst week of the Greek economic crisis that saw all banks closed, Ruihan arrived in Athens. We tried to ascertain his plans and it seemed he wanted to row the Atlantic. But to get to the Atlantic he would need to go west and row across the Mediterranean first, something we told Shuping was a near-impossibility. We had little information on Ruihan's plans, and he seemed disinclined to take advice.

After nearly two months of on again/off again negotiation, way more complicated than it needed to be, Ruihan finally bought *Mr Hops*. He then set about preparing for a voyage that we were not convinced he knew where it would lead. Finally in late September he left Athens. Only a few days later, less than 50 km into his voyage, he shipwrecked on rocks near the Greek island of Poros. A flare he set off set fire to the vegetation on a small offshore island which alerted authorities. A local boatman rescued both him and *Mr Hops*, and Ruihan then spent another month on Poros repairing the damage.

In early November he set off again, we understood for Italy. To get there, he needed to travel south and then west. But in mid-December we heard from Shuping that Ruihan had travelled south-east, to arrive in Port Said in Egypt, at the mouth of the Suez Canal. Apparently he was taken with the idea of going through Suez but the Egyptian authorities would not allow him and gave him 48 hours to leave Egypt.

In January 2016 Shuping told us that Ruihan was back in China, and that we should Google 'Chinese man arrives in Israel by boat – without meaning to'. This we did, to find reports and photos in the Israeli media of a Chinese man found unconscious on a beach near Haifa with a shipwrecked boat. Ruihan was arrested and some days later deported to China.

A damaged and stripped *Mr Hops* now languishes in a police compound in northern Israel.

A YEAR

A year after my journey was complete, I revisited the Greek Island of Lesvos; this time I was there with Save the Children to see first-hand the work they were doing.

In the two refugee camps on Lesvos on a near 40-degree day, I spent a very informative day with some very special people. Everything was very complex: all the Greek government departments involved, the EU, UNHCR, NGOs. Nothing can move quickly and whilst some aspects absolutely challenged and saddened me I could not judge things on such a flying visit in such a complex situation. I was also hugely uplifted both by the refugees I spent time with and theSave the Childrenstaff I met.

During my Mediterranean journey I spoke often of the welcome I received everywhere I went, and the freedom I had to receive those welcomes when, coming from the sea, I just turned up on a beach somewhere.

The two camps on Lesvos, Moria and Kara Tepe, together then housed about 3,000 people. The word I heard so often, from both refugees and workers, was 'stranded'. Up until the end of 2015 people were arriving on boats from Turkey – over a million Syrians, Afghans, Iraqis, Pakistanis and others – and after registration they moved on within a day or two. But now, with the borders across Europe closed and a deal between the EU and Turkey in place, people arriving in Lesvos stay on Lesvos.

How long for? How long is a piece of string?

The beautiful people I met – adults and children – were so grateful for the welcome they had been given: the place to stay, the food to eat, the people that help them. 'It is not right that poor people should impose upon poor people' was a refrain I heard a number of times from the refugees. Greece is not of course poor by world standards but it is a country in economic crisis that, purely by geography, was and is at the frontline to receive people fleeing from desperate times in their own countries.

When I was on Lesvos, the flow of people arriving by boat had slowed to a comparative trickle but now those 'stranded' had to wait. Wait to have their cases for asylum heard as to whether they could stay, where they could go and whether, in many cases they could be reunited with other family members who they had become separated from.

Save the Children offer Child Friendly Spaces in the camps, secure places where children and mothers can go to play, eat, learn, breastfeed or whatever. They are very popular. At Kara Tepe I met a lady, Noor, who had left the north west of Pakistan. Through tears this highly educated woman told me that after a long time of being persecuted, and two days after the Taliban had beheaded her husband and brother in the local market, she had fled with her three-year-old daughter, and had arrived eventually on the coast of Turkey. Then she paid a smuggler to take her on an inflatable with 20 others by night to Lesvos. She was so grateful for the safety and peace she had. 'If I lose hope I lose everything,' she told me. Her daughter asked for her father every night. 'This place saves me,' Noor told me, referring to the Child Friendly Space. 'I come here every day' she said as her daughter ran rings around us. The woman's brother, who was also on Lesvos, had said he would give up and go back to Pakistan; he did not want an endless wait. Noor implored him not to. She had already lost too much.

A year after my journey finished I returned to the Greek island of
Lesvos to visit some of the refugee camps to see the work being
done by Save the Children with the monies I had raised

I spent nearly two hours with Sera, a Syrian woman, and her family of seven
girls and one boy (lucky boy? unlucky boy?), aged 18 months to 13 years. She and
her husband were from a Syrian town close to the border with Turkey. A city that had
been destroyed by the so-called Islamic State (IS). Sera and her family were Kurds, an
ethnic group that has long been persecuted in Syria and elsewhere. After nearly five
years of dislocation, moving away from and back to their town but always within Syria,
the murder by IS of their close relations made them flee. Fleeing with eight children.
Imagine. Eight children.

The eight children were all beautiful. Of course children are the world over.
Beautiful with their smiles, their impishness and their inquisitiveness. Their innocence.
They were there in a refugee camp, living in one small, unbearably hot 4 metre x 3
metre hut in a camp where the water was turned off for six hours each day. They were
there only because of an accident of birth. My grandchildren are living free in Sydney,
Australia, a place that is their home. They are there only because of an accident of birth.

One of Noor's eldest daughters showed me a photograph. The photograph shows
her and some of her sisters holding a painting they had done. On it there is a boat full
of people surrounded by a sea full of people. On it there are girls in a cell crying for
help with a guard outside. In the foreground children are running. Running away.

The kindness and involvement of people was uplifting. People who months ago
probably thought they would never use a skill they had and now do so in the camps.
Like Ioanna, the young part-Greek, part-Egyptian lady who translated Sera's Arabic for
me. Or Costas, who for 25 years had lived on Lesvos. Lived there since he had left Libya
and met a Greek girl whom he married. Lived there with a Libyan passport even though
he feared ever travelling to Libya again. Now Costas worked to entertain the children,
entertaining them in Arabic, a language he thought he'd never use again. His original
Libyan name, Adel, means 'justice' in Arabic. Justice indeed.

There are sadder sides to the camps of course. The self-harm, the endless high
barbed-wire fences, the infiltration of smugglers, boredom, the loss of dignity, the
conditions – for many people, tiny tents on angled stony ground are their only shelter
– and much more.

At the time of my visit there were some 2,000 unaccompanied minors in Greece; children under 18 who left, lost or became separated from their parents. On Lesvos these children were kept, detained in one area of the Moria camp, unable to move even within the camp itself. Detention of children is never in the best interests of the child. Indeed forced detention of asylum seekers of all ages is against international law. Locking children behind high, barbed-wire fences can and does lead to long-term psychological damage. They were there only because of an accident of birth.

'*Inshallah*' (God willing). I am not a believer in any god but I heard many people clinging to a hope that God would see them through. This despite the fact you could argue that religion is bound up in the current madness. I cannot deny that clinging to a hope in God may see them through. It may be the only way to retain hope. I don't know; I've never had to cling to a future.

I waited many times on my Mediterranean journey. At one point I waited for two weeks on the Greek Peloponnese to cross to Turkey in a rowing boat. But at any point I could choose to stop my waiting and take another path. The people in Moria and in Kara Tepe cannot choose to stop their waiting.

Part of me felt guilty for the pleasures I had taken from the Mediterranean at a time of such conflict. It is of course a sea given to offering pleasure to millions of people year after year. Most take this pleasure and leave little in return as a gift to their host. Most head home at the end of the party, leaving the Mediterranean to deal with the plastic, the rubbish, the derelict and abandoned developments. I can only hope that more people will start to consider the environment of the Mediterranean as something to be cherished, and that many more will consider helping those whose lives have been shattered on it or near it. A charmed and troubled sea indeed.

A YEAR IN NUMBERS

Apart from when I placed myself in the capable hands of Marin Medak and *Mr Hops*, I used no GPS to measure accurately how far I was travelling. These days of course many people seem to calculate everything to the nearest few metres; trusting to the array of devices that beep, burp and flash. Right is an estimate of how long my journey was. I did use a bike computer most of the time when cycling but the kayaking and walking distances are merely guesstimates as I travelled; calculated off maps of varied scales, some no better than road or tourist maps.

Obviously the dates and days given below include periods when I might have been stuck because of weather, injury or hospitality that was impossible to wrench myself away from. Any periods of non-movement longer than a week are noted.

In the end I travelled some 13,000 km across and along 17 countries over 363 days.

A sticker on the bow of *Mr Hops* indicates a change of plan

Days	Total Days	Dates	Country	Distance	Mode of Travel	Notes
		2014				
1-6	6	26 April to 1 May	Turkey	100km	Sea Kayak	
6-54	48	2 May to 18 June	Greece	2150km	Sea Kayak	
54-63	10	18 June to 27 June	Albania	360km	Sea Kayak	
64-68	5	28 June to 2 July	Montenegro	120km	Sea Kayak	
68-97	29	2 July to 31 July	Croatia/Bosnia & Hercegovina	640km	Sea Kayak	Included two weeks on Brac island with knee injury
98	1	1 August	Croatia/Slovenia/Italy	90km	Bike	
99-184	86	1 August to 26 October	Italy/Switzerland/France/Monaco	2250km	Trek	
185-193	9	27 October to 4 November	Italy	-	-	Resting and planning ahead
194-204	11	5 November to 15 November	France	840km	Bike	
204-222	20	15 November to 3 December	Spain	1370km	Bike	
223-233	10	4 December to 14 December	Spain/Gibraltar	320km	Sea Kayak	
234	1	15 December	Gibraltar/Morocco	30km	Sea Kayak	
235-250	15	16 December to 31 December	Italy/UK	-	-	Ferry from Morocco to Italy then Christmas break in UK
		2015				
250-256	7	31 December to 6 January	Morocco	420km	Bike	
257-269	13	7 January to 19 January	Algeria	1470km	Bike	
269-273	5	19 January to 23 January	Tunisia	300km	Bike	
274-291	17	24 January to 11 February	Tunisia	-	-	Freeing and preparing *Mr Hops*
292-305	13	12 February to 25 February	Tunisia/Malta	400km	Ocean Rowing Boat	
306-316	11	26 February to 8 March	Malta to Greece	800km	Ocean Rowing Boat	
317-331	15	9 March to 23 March	Greece	170km	Ocean Rowing Boat	Includes two weeks waiting for weather in Peloponnese
332-363	31	24 March to 23 April	Turkey	1000km	Sea Kayak	

A YEAR IN NUMBERS

Early morning paddling along the Turkish coast

Monument at Gallipoli inscribed with the words of Kemal Ataturk, the first President of modern day Turkey

Undercut triangular rock formation
in the Ionian Sea, Greece

These boots were made for walking and that's just what they did. Italian Alps

EQUIPMENT

My journey by kayak, foot, bike and rowboat across four seasons from sea level to nearly 5000 metres above it required a fair variety of equipment. I was lucky to have support from some of the world's leading outdoor equipment brands both through my major sponsor; Australian adventure and travel retail group Paddy Pallin, as well as individual brands.

So a big thanks goes to Paddy Pallin, Osprey packs, Ex Officio clothing, Princeton Tec lights, Scarpa footwear, The North Face clothing, Nemo tents and sleeping mats, Wilderness Equipment tents, Marmot clothing, Wigwam socks, Optimus stoves, Western Mountaineering sleeping bags, Expedition Kayaks, Tiderace kayaks, Peak UK kayak clothing, Sandiline marine clothing, Eckla kayak trolleys, Ground Effect cycle clothing, Limar helmets, Nikon cameras, Tabacco maps, Teva footwear, Certton clothing, Alcom prescription sports eyewear, Bolle sportsglasses, Sea to Summit equipment.

By far and away the most important piece of kit I ever carry is of course my faithful orange plastic mug. In 1979 I was given a second hand plastic mug which has been my constant companion ever since. It's dirty, worn, cracked and taped. It's even been under the knife for a spot of plastic surgery but The Mug is ever reliable.

SEA KAYAKING

Miss Grape was the perfect craft for the job with plenty of storage room and, despite being dragged up and down beaches and rocks, finished up still looking pretty good at the end. My go to kayak clothing were the neoprene shorts and Pallin *mediterr année* Tech T-shirt. The Nemo Obi 2P tent had a mesh inner so it was cool and insect free on the warm nights and had plenty of space despite weighing less than 2kg. The Nikon 1-AW1 camera was slung around my neck nearly all year and didn't miss a beat.

- *Miss Grape* - Tiderace Pace 17 tour sea kayak – 5.3 metres, Hardcore XCT layup with keel strip, SmartTrack rudder system, Silva deck mount compass, electric pump
- Tiderace neoprene spraydeck
- Skee Carbon split paddle
- Skee Razz split paddle as spare

- Peak UK Explorer PFD
- Standard Horizon HX851 VHF handheld radio
- ACR Personal Locator Beacon
- Marine flares
- Paddle float
- Handpump
- Eckla kayak trolley
- Pacific Outdoor dry bags (10 litre, 15 litre)
- Sea to Summit dry bags (various 1 litre to 13 litre)
- Osprey Airporter gear bag
- Osprey Rev 24 daypack
- Nemo Obi 2P tent
- Nemo Zor Standard sleeping mat
- Nemo Fillo pillow
- Western Mountaineering Highlite sleeping bag
- Sea to Summit silk sleeping bag liner
- MSR Dromedary waterbag (10 litre)
- Osprey hydration bladder (2 litre)
- CamelBak Podium Chill water bottle
- Optimus Nova+ multifuel stove (first 3 months), Optimus Crux gas stove (Spain and final month in Turkey)
- Optimus Terra Weekend cookset
- Small chopping board
- Plate
- Spoon
- The Mug
- Teva Toachi sandals
- Scarpa Aria shoes
- Watership sunhat
- Ex Officio cap
- 'no name' neck tube

- Icebreaker Pocket 200 merino hat
- Ex Officio briefs (2 pairs)
- Wigwam socks (1 pair)
- Ex Officio Airstrip travel shirt
- Pallin *mediterr année* Tech T-shirt
- Certton *mediterr année* organic cotton T-shirt
- The North Face Paramount shorts
- The North Face Paramount travel pants
- The North Face TKA100 fleece top
- Marmot Approach windproof fleece vest
- Marmot Hyper waterproof jacket
- Peak UK Explorer kayak sprayjacket
- Peak UK Thermal Rashie kayak shirt (Spain and last month in Turkey)
- Solution neoprene kayak shorts
- Sea to Summit microfibre towel
- Kayak repair kit
- First aid kit
- Miscellaneous repair kit
- Matches/lighters
- Toothbrush and paste
- Suncream and Lip Balm
- Princeton Tec Vizz headtorch
- Suunto Vector watch (with altimeter)
- Spot gen3 tracker
- Nikon 1-AW1 waterproof camera
- GoPro Hero3 video camera
- Sony Xperia Z phone
- Toshiba Laptop
- Leatherman Skeletool multitool
- Spyderco folding knife
- Diary and pens
- Maps
- Sunglasses

TREKKING

I carried around 15kg through the Alps in the Osprey Aether pack that took the punishment very well. As autumn approached I swapped tents to the Wilderness Equipment Space 2W as it had a full fabric inner for additional warmth. This helped as I decided to continue using the very compact Highlite sleeping bag that was really designed for summer conditions. Despite the comfort of the Scarpa Delta boots, I needed something that would take a crampon for the ascent of Mont Blanc so changed to the Scarpa Rebel Pro's that were comfortable enough to stay on my feet all the way from the summit to the sea at Monaco. The Ex Officio Nio Amphi shorts were worn on every day of the trek.

- Osprey Aether 60 litre pack
- Osprey Packcover
- Nemo Obi 2P tent (first half of Alps traverse)
- Wilderness Equipment Space 2W tent (second half of Alps traverse)

- Nemo Zor Standard sleeping mat
- Western Mountaineering Highlite sleeping bag
- Sea to Summit Reactor sleeping bag liner
- Nalgene Lexan water bottle (1 litre)
- Optimus Crux gas stove
- Optimus Terra Weekend cookset
- Spoon
- The Mug
- Thongs/Flip Flops
- Scarpa Delta trekking boots (first 50 days of Alps Traverse)
- Scarpa Rebel Pro (Mont Blanc ascent and last month of Alps Traverse)
- Ex Officio cap
- Icebreaker Pocket 200 merino hat
- 'no name' neck tube
- Ex Officio briefs (2 pairs)
- Wigwam Merino Hiking Outdoor Pro socks (1 pair)
- Wigwam Comfort Hiker socks (1 pair)
- Manzella Ultra Max Liner gloves
- Manzella Trekker Windstopper gloves
- Ground Effect armwarmers
- Ex Officio Airstrip travel shirt
- Pallin *mediterr année* Tech T-shirt
- Icebreaker Apex merino lonjons
- Ex Officio Nio Amphi Convertible shorts
- The North Face travel pants
- The North Face TKA100 fleece top
- The North Face Thunderdown jacket
- Ground Effect Vespa windproof vest
- Marmot Hyper waterproof jacket
- Rab Bergen waterproof pants
- Komperdell Expedition Vario trekking poles
- Sea to Summit dry bags (various 1 litre to 13 litre)
- Osprey Digistow pouches
- First aid kit
- Miscellaneous repair kit
- Matches/lighters
- Toothbrush and paste
- Suncream and Lip Balm
- Princeton Tec Vizz headtorch
- Suunto Vector watch (with altimeter)
- Baseplate compass
- Spot gen3 tracker
- Nikon 1-AW1 waterproof camera
- GoPro Hero3 video camera
- Sony Xperia Z phone
- Toshiba Laptop
- Leatherman Skeletool multitool
- Diary and pens
- Maps
- Sunglasses

BIKING

I took my trusty Rolloff equipped steel hardtail mountain bike that has seen good service for 15 years around the world. I try to keep it light on the bike and used my Ortleib Front Roller panniers slung on the rear rack with a dry bag on top. Other equipment was stored in my hydration pack or handlebar bag. I ditched all the camping gear for Morocco and Algeria knowing I was to be forced to stay in hotels during my traverse of the latter.

- Custom made (in 2001) steel hardtail 26 inch mountain bike with 14 speed Rolloff Speedhub, Shimano XT hydraulic brakes, Fox front suspension, Time ATAC pedals (replaced in France with Crank Brothers Candy)
- Limar Ultralight helmet
- Old Man Mountain pannier rack
- Ortleib Front Roller panniers
- Dry bag (15 litre)
- VauDe handlebar bag
- Osprey Manta 20 hydration pack with 2 litre bladder
- Wilderness Equipment Space 2W tent (France and Spain)
- Nemo Zor Short sleeping mat
- Western Mountaineering Highlite sleeping bag
- Sea to Summit Silk sleeping bag liner
- CamelBak Podium Chill water bottle
- Optimus Crux gas stove
- Optimus Terra Weekend cookset
- Spoon
- The Mug
- Thongs/Flip Flops
- Specialized Rime bike shoes

- Ex Officio cap
- Icebreaker Pocket 200 merino hat
- 'no name' neck tube
- Ex Officio briefs (2 pairs)
- Wigwam socks (2 pairs)
- Ground Effect High Five gloves
- Ground Effect Chipolata windproof fleece gloves
- Ground Effect armwarmers
- Ground Effect legwarmers
- Vaude waterproof helmet cover
- Vaude neoprene shoe covers
- Pallin *mediterr année* Tech T-shirt
- Froggy Line *mediterr année* cycling jersey
- Ground Effect Exocet cycling knicks (2 pairs)
- Ex Officio Nio Amphi Convertible pants
- The North Face TKA100 fleece top
- The North Face Thunderdown jacket
- Ground Effect Vespa windproof vest
- Marmot Hyper waterproof jacket
- Marmot Paclite waterproof pants
- Sea to Summit dry bags (various 1 litre to 13 litre)
- Osprey Digistow pouch
- First aid kit
- Misc repair kit
- Tools and bike spares
- Matches/lighters
- Toothbrush and paste
- Suncream and Lip Balm
- Princeton Tec Vizz headtorch
- Suunto Vector watch (with altimeter)
- Spot gen3 tracker
- Nikon 1-AW1 waterproof camera
- GoPro Hero3 video camera
- Sony Xperia Z phone
- Toshiba Laptop
- Leatherman Skeletool multitool
- Diary and pens
- Maps
- Sunglasses

ROWING

On *Mr Hops* we were both able and needed to carry a lot of equipment. This list is not comprehensive. For example we carried my bike to Greece from Tunisia and all my cycling gear but that was obviously not necessary for the row. And of course when we picked up Dimitris he came with his own baggage.

- *Mr Hops* – Woodvale Solo Class, 7 metres, glass fibre
- Garmin 550S fixed GPS
- Magellan Explorist 610 handheld GPS
- Navionics App (on Marin's iphone)
- Spot gen3 tracker
- Nasa Marine electronic compass
- Comar CSB200 AIS system
- Fixed VHF radio
- Standard Horizon HX851 handheld VHF radio
- Globalstar GSP-1700 satellite phone
- Solar Panels – 3 x 55W
- Batteries – 2 x 75Ah
- Katadyn Powersurvivor 40E watermaker (never worked)
- Katadyn Survivor 35 Manual watermaker
- ACR Personal Locator Beacon
- McMurdo Fastfind EPIRB (picked up in Malta)
- Throwline
- Marine flares
- Fire Extinguisher
- Xcell Ocean oars (2 pairs)
- Para anchor
- Rope (70 metres)
- Large buckets (2)
- Life jackets with harness (2)
- Pacific Outdoor dry bags (10 litre, 15 litre)
- Sea to Summit dry bags (various 1 litre to 13 litre)
- Osprey Airporter gear bags
- Pillow with lacy pillowcase
- Paddy Pallin Synthetic sleeping bag
- Waterbags and jerry cans for water
- Jetboil gas stove and gas cylinders
- Plates
- Miscellaneous utensils and knives
- First aid kit
- Comprehensive toolbox and repair kit
- Matches/lighters
- Sudocrem
- Charts

A frilly edged pillow was possibly the most loved piece of equipment on *Mr Hops*

HUW – PERSONAL EQUIPMENT FOR ROW

- The Mug
- Teva Rifugio water shoes
- Scarpa Aria shoes
- Ex Officio cap
- Icebreaker Pocket 200 merino hat
- Ex Officio briefs (2 pairs)
- Wigwam socks (1 pair)
- Sea to Summit fingerless kayaking gloves
- Ex Officio Airstrip travel shirt
- Pallin *mediterr année* Tech T-shirt (2)
- Certton *mediterr année* organic cotton T-shirt
- Icebreaker Tech T Lite long sleeve shirt
- Ex Officio Nio Amphi Convertible pants
- The North Face TKA100 fleece top
- Marmot Approach windproof fleece vest
- The North Face Thunderdown jacket
- Marmot Hyper waterproof jacket
- Sandiline marine waterproof jacket
- Sandiline marine waterproof pants
- Peak UK Thermal Rashie kayak shirt
- Froggy Line lycra shorts (2 pairs)
- Sea to Summit microfibre towel
- Toothbrush and paste
- Suncream and Lip balm
- Princeton Tec Vizz headtorch
- Suunto Vector watch (with altimeter)
- Nikon 1-AW1 waterproof camera
- GoPro Hero3 video camera
- Sony Xperia Z phone
- Toshiba Laptop
- Leatherman Skeletool multitool
- Diary and pens
- Sunglasses

A herd of Chamois skip across the hillside in the evening light, Mercantour NP, French Alps

On the flanks of Mont Blanc near the Tête Rousse Hut

Putting thoughts down in a small bivi
hut in the Valpelline, Italian Alps